sixth edition

Writing
Clear Paragraphs

Robert B. Donald
James D. Moore
Betty Richmond Morrow
Lillian Griffith Wargetz
Kathleen Werner

Prentice Hall, Upper Saddle River, New Jersey 07458

Library of Congress Cataloging-in-Publication Data

Writing clear paragraphs / Robert B. Donald . . . [et al.]. — 6th ed.
    p.   cm.
  Includes index.
  ISBN 0-13-646571-4 (pbk.)
  1. English language—Paragraphs.   2. English language—Rhetoric.
3. Report writing.   I. Donald, Robert B.
PE1439.W7 1998
808'.042—dc21   98-13747
                                                              CIP

Editorial Director: Charlyce Jones Owen
Senior Acquisitions Editor: Maggie Barbieri
Director of Production and Manufacturing: Barbara Kittle
Senior Managing Editor: Bonnie Biller
Production Editor: Joan E. Foley
Copyeditor: Mary Louise Byrd
Editorial Assistant: Joan Polk
Manufacturing Manager: Nick Sklitsis
Prepress and Manufacturing Buyer: Mary Ann Gloriande
Marketing Manager: Robert Mejia
Art Director: Jayne Conte
Cover Designer: Joe Sengotta
Text Illustrator: Jonathan D. Bagamery

This book was set in 11/12.5 Usherwood by The Clarinda Company
and was printed and bound by RR Donnelley & Sons Company.
The cover was printed by Phoenix Color Company.

©1999, 1995, 1991, 1987, 1983, 1978 by Prentice-Hall Inc.
Simon & Schuster/A Viacom Company
Upper Saddle River, New Jersey 07458

Printed in the United States of America

10 9 8 7 6 5 4 3 2 1

ISBN 0-13-646571-4

Prentice-Hall International (UK) Limited, *London*
Prentice-Hall of Australia Pty. Limited, *Sydney*
Prentice-Hall Canada Inc., *Toronto*
Prentice-Hall Hispanoamerica, S.A., *Mexico*
Prentice-Hall of India Private Limited, *New Delhi*
Prentice-Hall of Japan, Inc., *Tokyo*
Simon & Schuster Asia Pte. Ltd., *Singapore*
Editora Prentice-Hall do Brasil, Ltda., *Rio de Janeiro*

Contents

PREFACE   v

chapter 1   **THE PARAGRAPH**   **1**

Organization of a Paragraph   1
Topic Sentence   4
Body   11
Conclusion   14
Sentences   16
Words   20

chapter 2   **NARRATING**   **25**

What Is a Narrative?   25
Organization of a Narrative Paragraph   27
Topic Sentence   35
Body   36
Conclusion   37
Sentences   40
Words   53

chapter 3   **DESCRIBING**   **61**

The Uses of Description   61
Objective vs. Subjective Description   62
Organization   67
Sentences   79
Words   93

chapter 4 **EXPLAINING A PROCESS**   **100**

Organization   100
Sentences   117
Words   125

chapter 5 **EXPLAINING WITH EXAMPLES**   **132**

Organization   132
Conclusion   151
Sentences   154
Words   165

chapter 6 **COMPARING OR CONTRASTING**   **177**

Organization   177
Body   184
Sentences   197
Words   209

chapter 7 **CLASSIFYING**   **217**

Organization   217
Sentences   232
Words   246

chapter 8 **DEFINING**   **257**

Organization   257
Structure   269
Sentences   278
Words   286

chapter 9 **FROM PARAGRAPH TO ESSAY**   **292**

Introduction   292
Body   293

chapter 10 **PERSUADING**   **309**

Purpose of Persuasion   309
Types of Persuasion   309
Organization   310
Assignment   315
The Persuasive Essay   326
Words   346

SOURCES   354

INDEX OF EXERCISES   355

INDEX   356

Preface

FOR THE STUDENTS

This book explains itself in its title. It aims to teach you how to communicate with all the people who share your personal world . . . a large aim with a very simple tool, the paragraph. Once you have mastered the paragraph, you will be familiar with a basic tool for writing.

The paragraph is built with three parts:

1. the topic sentence, which tells what you are going to talk about (your subject) and how you are going to treat it (your attitude).
2. the body, which gives the details explaining and supporting your topic sentence and reveals how you feel about your subject.
3. the conclusion, which sums up your subject and confirms your attitude.

Because competent writing improves everything you do, you need to organize your paragraph effectively, to write understandable and convincing sentences, and to choose precise and pleasing words. This is all . . . and everything . . . you need to communicate well.

FOR THE INSTRUCTORS

We certainly have no advice for you, only gratitude. We are pleased that you have found our book a help in our mutual task of sharing the problems and joys of teaching. We are especially grateful to those of you who have pointed out areas where your experience can improve our efforts.

Some of the changes we have made to accommodate your suggestions are as follows:

> We have put the assignment early in the chapter so that the students know what is expected of them and will respond to the rest of the chapter with a purpose.
>
> We have rewritten—and improved, we hope—all of the exercises except those that you, the instructors, asked us to retain.
>
> We have improved the format, adding more headings and breaking up long paragraphs. We have also added more cartoons.
>
> We have added more examples of documentation using student essays.

We would like to thank the reviewers of the sixth edition: Kate Gleason, Berkeley College; Carin Halper, Fresno City College; and Judity O. Scott, Sandhills Community College.

We hope you like the changes, and, as always, we are open to any further suggestions you may have to improve the book.

The Authors

chapter 1

The Paragraph

ORGANIZATION OF A PARAGRAPH

✓ Prewriting

Before writing a paragraph, there are certain activities, called *prewriting*, that can help you to find a topic:

Keep a journal. Carry a notebook with you to record any happenings that seem significant. These notes might later suggest topics for your paragraphs. Don't worry about "mistakes." The important thing is to turn your ideas or feelings into words as quickly as possible. You can write about almost anything in your daily life:

a personal experience
something that amused or interested you
a gesture or comment you found significant
a problem to resolve
likes or dislikes
feelings about school, home, work, friends
someone you love

Brainstorm. Another way some people find successful in arriving at a topic is to "brainstorm." Choose a likely subject and as quickly as possible—ten minutes, perhaps—scribble down anything that may pertain to your idea. Eliminate the less appropriate items and try again on those you have left.

Cull your memories. Think over your experiences and your feelings. Recall those of this morning, of yesterday, of your childhood. Recollect an adventure your father told you about, or a love affair you read about in an old letter of your great-grandmother's you found in the attic.

Use this textbook. Ideas for topics are given in the Suggested Activities and Assignments sections in each chapter. Also, the sample paragraphs in the text may suggest topics.

Read, read, read. The world is filled with libraries; the libraries are filled with books; the books are filled with ideas.

✓ Definition of a Paragraph

A *paragraph* is a brief unit of communication in a relatively fixed form. It is usually made up of several sentences that discuss a single idea. A paragraph can stand alone, or it can be part of a longer piece of writing. Just as words are the building blocks of a sentence, and sentences are the building blocks for a paragraph, so the paragraph is the building block for longer forms of writing. The paragraph may also stand alone as a single unit of writing.

✓ Functions of a Paragraph

Expository paragraphs are primarily used to explain ideas. *Exposition*—the explaining of ideas—is the writing that you will be doing in this course and in most of your college work.

Both the writer and the reader need the paragraph. Writers use paragraphs to focus their thoughts and to organize their material in a logical way, and readers use paragraphs to help them understand the writer's progression of thought. Here are the characteristics of a good paragraph.

1. **It focuses on one major idea called the controlling idea. It contains only material that pertains to the controlling idea so that the reader is not distracted by irrelevant details.**
2. **It provides enough details to develop and discuss the controlling idea so that the reader understands completely the writer's point.**
3. **It is logically organized so that the reader can clearly see (a) a controlling idea, (b) a body of supporting details, and (c) a conclusion.**
4. **It says something worth saying in precise and specific sentences and words.**

✓ Structure of a Paragraph

One simple model that will guide you in writing most of your paragraphs is called *the ministerial three.* The minister stands behind the pulpit and, in ringing tones, delivers his message to the congregation:

1. *He tells 'em what he is going to tell 'em.* (He introduces the subject, or topic, and indicates what he is going to say about it.)
2. *He tells 'em.* (He expands the subject, fills in details about it.)

The ministerial three.

3. *He tells 'em what he has told 'em.* (He sums up and reaches a conclusion about the subject.)

Just like this sermon that comes from the ministerial three, your paragraphs will come from the basic paragraph structure:

1. Beginning—TOPIC SENTENCE—*"Tell 'em what you are going to tell 'em."*
2. Middle—BODY—*"Tell 'em."*
3. End—CONCLUSION—*"Tell 'em what you have told 'em."*

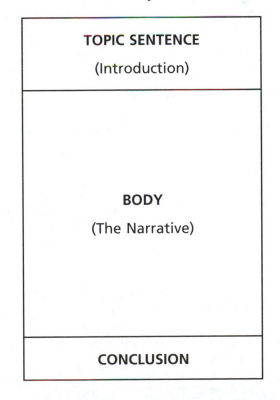

✏️ TOPIC SENTENCE

In expository writing, a good *topic sentence* is the key to a good paragraph. In expository writing, main ideas usually appear at the beginning of a paragraph in the topic sentence and are then explained in the rest of the paragraph.

A good topic sentence can

> *help writers organize* the details that they need to discuss an idea and prevent them from getting sidetracked from the main idea.
>
> *help readers understand* the material they are reading.

✓ Include Subject plus Attitude.

A good topic sentence presents both a *subject* and an *attitude* toward that subject.

> **Subject** = the topic that you will discuss
>
> **Attitude** = a statement that expresses an emotion, an opinion, an approach, or a commitment to your subject; attitude is what you say about your subject.

For example, "Dogs" is merely a subject, but "Dogs make good pets" is both a subject and an attitude.

The topic sentence (*subject* + *attitude*) states the **controlling idea** for the paragraph. All the sentences that follow the controlling idea must pertain to the controlling idea.

EXERCISE 1A: IDENTIFY SUBJECT AND ATTITUDE

In the following topic sentences, underline the subjects and circle the words or phrases that express attitudes.

1. Being in love is time-consuming.
2. Cults are scary.
3. The job of President of the United States is a thankless one.
4. The job of President of the United States brings many perks.
5. There are many advantages to belonging to a fraternity or sorority.
6. Belonging to a fraternity or sorority entails many costs, and money is only one of them.
7. Eating soup is good for the body, but making soup is good for the spirit.
8. Hate hurts only the hater.
9. My father's looks belie his personality.
10. Although I love being the center of attention, trying out for the church choir was terrifying.

✓ Be Specific.

The controlling idea must be as *specific*—to the point—as you can make it. Try to clarify your subject and attitude by choosing the most precise words possible. Use a specific word instead of a general one.

General: There is a picture on my desk.
Do you mean a painting, a drawing, a cartoon, or a photograph?

Specific: There is a color photo on my desk of my five-year-old son building a sand castle at the beach last summer.

General: I'm going to a show tonight.
Do you mean a play, a movie, an exhibit, a fashion show, or an opera?

Specific: I'm going to the 1999 Dealers' Car Show at the Expo Center tonight.

1. **If your controlling idea is specific, the reader will know exactly what you mean.** If you write "Painting is worthwhile," the reader will not know whether you mean painting a house or painting a landscape, or whether it is worthwhile for earning money or for personal satisfaction.

2. **If your controlling idea is specific, you have a better chance of proving your point.** If you write "No animal in the world does more for humans than the dog," the reader will wonder what you mean by "does more for." Do you mean work, protection, companionship, or, as in some parts of the world, a culinary delicacy? A specific sentence, however, such as "The drug-sniffing dogs of the U.S. Customs Service are both cost-effective and time-saving," tells the reader exactly what point you are trying to make.

3. **If your controlling idea is specific, the body of your paragraph will be more specific.** If you start with "Everything that lives on this earth needs nourishment," you will have to write a book to cover the subject. If, however, you start with "A so-called healthy breakfast ruins my morning," the body of your paragraph can be quite specific. Consider these specific details: "Mom's ham, eggs, toast, and juice taste great, but they make me sleep through my 8:00 class. A Surge and three glazed donuts, though, keep me awake, alert, and focused until lunch."

Your first try at a controlling idea: "I like the book *Huckleberry Finn*."
Nice try, but too general—not specific enough. One way to make your attitude more specific is to keep asking yourself "Why?" By doing this, you move from a general idea to a more specific one, as in the following example.

Ask yourself: **Why do I like it?**
Answer: *Huckleberry Finn* is interesting.

Ask yourself: **Why is it interesting?**
Answer: I don't know—it just is.

Ask yourself: **Think! Try harder! Why is it interesting?**
Answer: I like Huck's personality.

Ask yourself: **Why do I like Huck's personality?**
Answer: He seems real.

Ask yourself: **Why does he seem real?**
Answer: He is all mixed up. He thinks that he is sinful, but he is really a good guy.

Finally, ask yourself: **Now, can I write a topic sentence that says this?**
Answer: *Absolutely!*

Your second attempt: "A real joy of the book *Huckleberry Finn* is discovering the difference between what Huck thinks he is and what he really is."

Great! Once you began to ask "Why?" you change your subject from "I" to *Huckleberry Finn,* and that is exactly what you want to do. You want to discuss the book, not "I."

As you can see, a good topic sentence does more than just mention a subject. It provides a clear, specific guide that shows where the paragraph is headed.

✓ Narrow Your Controlling Idea.

Because most of the assignments in this text will be to write single paragraphs, you must limit and narrow each subject that you choose so that you can discuss it fully in one paragraph. Let's look at some ways to narrow the following broad topics:

Movies
movies of the 1940s and 1950s
film stars of the 1940s and 1950s
Humphrey Bogart's character, Rick, in *Casablanca,* portrayed mannerisms that are considered "cool" even today.

Sports
professional hockey
greatest players
Mario Lemieux's techniques of shooting the puck have made him the greatest hockey player of all time.

Automobiles
sport utility vehicles
The Jeep Cherokee and the Ford Explorer
Although the Jeep Cherokee and the Ford Explorer are both classified as sport utility vehicles, their construction designs are different.

Medicine
    nontraditional medicine
      herbal cold remedies
        The herbal extract, Echinacea, is considered by its many faithful users to be a potent fighter of the common cold.

After you have narrowed your broad idea to one that can be satisfactorily covered in one paragraph, be sure that your topic sentence expresses just **one** controlling idea. A topic sentence with two or three ideas is too cumbersome to develop in one paragraph and promises more than you can deliver.

Broad and vague:	"Television commercials are boring, misleading, offensive, and sexist." (You could write a book about this.)
Limited and focused:	"Television automotive product commercials often insult women's intelligence by portraying them in situations that make them appear naive and helpless." (A single paragraph could easily discuss three or four examples of this type of commercial.)

EXERCISE 1B: NARROWING A BROAD TOPIC

Using the three-step pattern just illustrated, narrow each of the following broad topics. Then, with your specific topic, write an interesting topic sentence.

1. Teams _____

    _____

    _____

2. Jobs _____

    _____

    _____

3. Violence _____

    _____

    _____

4. Politicians _____

_____

_____

5. Movie stars _____

_____

_____

EXERCISE 1C: MAKING SUBJECTS AND ATTITUDES CLEAR

Rewrite the following sentences so that the subject and attitude are clear and specific.

Example: Fishing is good for you. Obviously, <u>fishing</u> is the subject and <u>good for you</u> is the attitude, but neither is specific enough for the reader to know what you will discuss. The reader doesn't know whether you'll be explaining casting for trout in the stream behind your house or trolling for shark in the South Pacific from the back of a million-dollar yacht. And the reader won't know whether fishing is good for your body, your soul, your spirit, or your bank account.

1. Everybody knows I'm hardworking.

_____

_____

_____

2. My pet knows me very well.

_____

_____

_____

3. I think exercise hurts more people than it helps.

_____

_____

_____

4. "Cosby" is the best show on TV.

_____

_____

_____

5. Arguing is fun.

_____

_____

_____

6. When we moved to the farm, it fascinated me.

_____

_____

_____

7. Math is the pits.

_____

_____

_____

8. There is entirely too much emphasis on self-esteem.

_____

_____

_____

9. Stupidity is curable.

_____

_____

_____

10. Travel teaches people a lot.

_____

_____

_____

EXERCISE 1D: SUBJECTS AND ATTITUDES

Keeping in mind the need for a clear subject and controlling idea, put a check mark on the blank to the left of each statement that you think would make a good topic sentence. Rewrite those that you consider poor topic sentences. Try rewriting to improve even those sentences that you think are already satisfactory (about 98 percent of all writing could be improved).

_____   1. Best-selling author Stephen King is also a talented musician.

_____   2. You learn to write by writing.

_____   3. The KKK has the right to parade.

_____   4. Winning the high school basketball championship had a real effect on us.

_____   5. Michael Jackson is a different entertainer.

_____   6. The most exhilarating feeling in the world is running.

_____   7. Let me tell you about my day at the park.

_____   8. The world today has many problems.

_____   9. Nothing ever goes right.

_____   10. Some people do not respect their parents and think that they would be better off on their own.

◖▭▭▷ **BODY**

Once you have announced your controlling idea in the topic sentence, you must then develop and expand it. This occurs in the **body** of the paragraph. Here, you discuss, explain, support, or prove the controlling idea in a way that will best accomplish your purpose. You may use facts, reasons, examples, comparisons, contrasts, or definitions to develop your controlling idea. It makes no difference what method you select, so long as your development has these three essential qualities:

UNITY   COHERENCE   ADEQUATE DEVELOPMENT

✓ Unity

Unity **is staying focused, and a good topic sentence is the key to a unified paragraph.** If your controlling idea is vague, it will be difficult for you to focus; you can easily stray from your topic and destroy the unity of your paragraph by using irrelevant details.

Information not directly related to your controlling idea is distracting and even boring. A reader who doesn't see any connection between some of the details in your paragraph and your controlling idea may become confused and quickly lose interest. Write a topic sentence that states a clear, specific controlling idea, and use only information that *directly supports* that controlling idea.

In the following paragraph, for example, the italicized sentences do *not* support the controlling idea. A potentially good paragraph is spoiled because it lacks unity.

> The year was 1960. I was eighteen, a freshman in college, and without a car. Dad had been generous to a fault, so I always could borrow his "wheels" whenever I needed them. Unfortunately, I was too immature to respect the family car as I should have, and those beautiful vehicles took a pounding whenever I was behind the wheel. Two years earlier, at sixteen, while driving recklessly on a country dirt road, I consigned his '55 Mercury to the body shop after spinning out of control and bouncing off some very stubborn boulders. *Dad liked Mercurys; he owned three but became disenchanted with the dealer and switched to Pontiac.* Not long after that, I bent a front wheel on the parkway medial strip demonstrating an inability to neck with my girl and steer at the same time. *That was one relationship with no future, and fortunately I broke up with her before wrecking my Dad's car again.* Then there was the time that I raced a bread truck nose to nose from a stop light to see who would capture the single lane on the other side of the intersection. I almost won, but the feisty truck driver was not about to be outmaneuvered by a kid in his dad's '58 Mercury four-door. Fortunately, Dad was out of town and thanks to a speedy body man who could really handle putty and blend paint, Dad was never the wiser.

In retrospect, I suppose that I am lucky to be still alive. Perhaps, since I had managed to get into college, Dad figured that I had mellowed a bit, but in reality, it was probably self-defense. An old friend of his had a '56 Austin Healey 100-M LeMans for sale, somewhat of a classic even then. Just as Faust traded his soul for knowledge, mine went for the Healey. Through a series of miracles, yet unexplained, that car survived college, the Marine Corps, endless repairs, and years of prolonged neglect in dusty garages. *A couple of years ago, a man who was restoring one like mine wanted to photograph my Healey to help him restore his. I am certain that he thought I was crazy for allowing mine to languish for so long.* Today it sits forlornly on blocks, patiently waiting for its past-middle-age owner to bring it to life again. I have vowed to make this happen— for me, for the Healey, and most of all, for you, Dad.

✓ Coherence

Be sure that your sentences follow a logical, *coherent* sequence so that the reader can understand how you are developing the controlling idea. You might, for example, use time order (such as beginning to end) in telling a story, spatial order (such as left to right) in describing a location, or the order of importance (such as least to most important) in arranging a series of facts to prove your point. You cannot expect your reader to understand what you are trying to say if your sentences are not in some kind of logical order.

Notice how confusing the following paragraph is.

> Yesterday, my day was a mess. I hope that I don't have such a frustrating day soon again. Then my fan belt broke when I was on my way to work. The baby-sitter was sick, so we couldn't go to the movie that we were looking forward to. Because I was upset, I burned the steak that I had splurged on. We got off to a bad start because I had forgotten to buy coffee. When I finally got to work, I learned that the interesting project that I had been working on was canceled, so I spent the whole day doing boring filing. My husband forgot that I didn't have a car, so he failed to pick me up after work. Feeling that there was nothing else to go wrong, I flung myself on the bed—which immediately collapsed.

When the sentences are in order, however, the reader can easily follow the logical sequence.

> Yesterday, my day was a mess. We got off to a bad start because I had forgotten to buy coffee. Then my fan belt broke when I was on my way to work. When I finally got to work, I learned that the interesting project that I had been working on was canceled, so I spent the whole day doing boring filing. My husband forgot that I didn't have a car, so he failed to pick me up after work. Because I was upset, I burned the steak that I had splurged on. The baby-sitter was sick, so we couldn't go to the movie that we were looking forward to. Feeling that there was nothing else to go wrong, I flung myself on the bed—which immediately collapsed. I hope that I don't have such a frustrating day soon again.

✓ Adequate Development

Adequate development **is measured not by the number of words that you write, but rather by the quality and quantity of the information that you use to support your controlling idea.** Completeness, therefore, is not just a matter of length; it is the building up of your paragraph through the detailed development of your controlling idea.

Ask yourself these questions while you are writing:

1. **Do I have enough details to develop my controlling idea?**
2. **Do all of these details relate to my controlling idea?**
3. **Are these details specific and *not* vague or general?**

The following paragraph states a controlling idea but does not develop it adequately.

> The siren sounds, my blood pressure rises, I race to the station; this is what I am here for. The scene in the fire station appears to be total confusion, but everyone knows what he is doing. Lights flash and motors roar as the trucks are started. I pull on my bulky protective clothing, jump onto a truck, and strap in. We race down the street with our lights flashing and siren screaming. I am very excited and wonder if it will be a real fire or a false alarm. The truck stops quickly, and I see smoke and fire. It is now time to do my job. I am a volunteer firefighter; this is what I am here for.

Although this short paragraph has a specific controlling idea, there are not enough vivid descriptive details to interest the readers—to pull them into the excitement and drama of the situation.

In the following paragraph, with the same controlling idea, notice the difference when sufficient graphic details are added.

> The siren sounds, my blood pressure rises, I race to the station; this is what I am here for. As I near the station, the siren seems to scream at me, yelling at me to hurry. As I pull over to the curb, rush out of my car, and run into the huge fire station, I see many people scurrying about in an apparent state of chaos. I race to my tall, brown locker, ready to throw on my fire gear. In the background, bright yellow and red lights flash, motors roar; people are yelling and rushing everywhere. Firefighters try to complete their individual preparations as quickly as possible. The chief starts the motor of the Duplex, truck number one, while the assistant chief starts the engine of the Ford, the second truck. The first lieutenant opens the huge, white steel garage doors as the second lieutenant checks the fire trucks for safety. I grab my bright yellow fire helmet and throw it on, securing the tight leather strap under my chin. Next I pull on my heavy black and yellow jacket, clasping the thick metal hooks. The familiar smell of yesterdays' fires and smoke jolts my senses; my mind springs to life. I jump into my thick, black rubber boots, which are two

sizes too big and two tons too heavy. Then I reach down, grab my boot straps, and pull upwards, raising these clumsy things to my thighs. The chief yells at everyone to jump onto a fire truck. I obey him and leap onto the back of the Duplex. On each side of me stands another bulkily geared firefighter; we all hurry to pull the blue safety straps tightly around ourselves. When we are strapped in, I push the black safety buzzer twice, signaling to the chief that we are safely secured and ready to go. The large cherry red fire truck, with its brilliant lights flashing and its loud sirens wailing, pulls out of the station and races down the paved road toward a destination unknown to me. Now I finally have some time to think. My heart almost thumps out of my chest, cold sweat rolls down my back, and my hands tremble with excitement. I anticipate what the fire scene will look like. Will angry fire burst from a window, or will it only be a false alarm? Suddenly, I am shocked out of my personal thoughts as the fire truck screeches to a halt. I am afraid to look, yet eager to see the fire. My adrenalin pumps at full throttle as I see thick black smoke rising from the glowing red roof; fire blazes from a broken window. It is now time to do my job. I am a volunteer firefighter; this is what I am here for.

Angie Weister

CONCLUSION

To complete your paragraph, you need at least one or two sentences to end it effectively.

A conclusion achieves some or all of the following results:

1. **It signals the reader that you have finished the body of the paragraph.**
2. **It provides an ending to fit your purpose. Some options include**
   a summary of main points
   a conclusion based on the evidence that you have presented
   an emphasis of a key point
   a request for change
   a call for action
3. **It pulls your information together by reminding the reader, one last time, of the controlling idea expressed in your topic sentence.**
4. **It *ends* the paragraph and does *not* introduce new information.**

In the following paragraph, the writer presents carefully selected details to convince the reader that Kinsale is the most gracious town in all of Ireland.

Kinsale, or more appropriately in Gaelic, "Cionn-tsaile," county Cork, is the most gracious town in all of Ireland. I have visited that town three times in the past three years, but I have never really left. I was lucky enough to marry a daughter of the town, the daughter of Pat Jones. He stands and greets his guests from his balcony like a Roman emperor addressing his legions. Inside, Irene will have a perfectly prepared meal to go with their laughter and drinks. A few doors down is The Spinnaker. The proprietor could easily be described as the oldest teenager in history. Terry plays his rock and roll a bit loud for conversation, but to watch him carry on behind the bar is hysterical. In the off season, winter, the locals can be found in The Spaniard relaxing, drinking pints of Guinness and hot toddies, and singing Irish songs by the stone fireplace while seeking refuge from the lashing Irish rain. Just up the road is the historic inn, Scilly House. The Georgian fireplace is tended by Bill as he entertains his guests with a sing-along. Karin, the American expatriate, can be found creating classic breakfasts using her private garden and fresh local specialties. Downtown, in the oldest licensed premises in Kinsale, The White House's owners serve a steak that would make a Texas cattleman blush. Across the road sits Brian and Ann Cronin's Blue Haven. Brian can be found on the grounds or in the bar meeting, greeting, or working just as hard as any of his staff. After all of the indulging and fun has been paid for at Sunday morning mass, everybody gathers up their hangovers and ends the week at Acton's Hotel listening to Billy Crosby and the Cork City Jazz Band. The citizenry of Kinsale always greet new and old friends with the same hospitality: good food, good drink, and good times.

David P. Glass

His final sentence does more than simply end the paragraph. It reminds the readers that they *must* conclude from the evidence in the body that Kinsale's hospitality, its "good food, good drink, and good times," do indeed make it the most gracious town in all of Ireland.

✓ Paragraph Length

The length of a paragraph can vary according to its purpose and the type of writing that you are doing. There is no set paragraph length that a writer must adhere to.

How do you know if your paragraph is long enough? Abraham Lincoln is reported to have said that a man's legs should be long enough to reach the ground. A paragraph should be long enough to reach your readers, to tell them all they need to know in order to understand fully your controlling idea. At the end, your readers should be able to say, "Yes, now I understand exactly what you mean."

SUGGESTED ACTIVITIES AND ASSIGNMENTS

1. There are more than a hundred verbs in English that specify some particular kind of walking. Have each student suggest or demonstrate a specific verb for the general verb *walk*. For example, "He *strutted* down the street." Write the words on the blackboard. (Try to get sixty.)

Notice that by making the verb more specific, you create a picture not only of the way a person walks but also of the person walking. What or who might be likely to be *strutting* or *tiptoeing?* Try this same activity with *talk* and *laugh.* (Try to get twenty each.)

2. After you have gone over Exercises 1A through 1D, form into groups of four or five. Each group should try to improve the topic sentences. Put one or two of the improved sentences on the board to see if the class can improve them more.

3. Write a paragraph using what you have learned from this chapter. You should go through the writing process as outlined, at least for your first few assignments. First, think about possible topics that would be of interest to your classmates—things that have happened to you that taught you something, things you have done that were a real high point for you or that were funny or exciting in some way. Or discuss a subject that is very important to you, informing your readers about it or convincing them that you are right. Some possible topics:

Nothing infuriates me more than _____

I'll never forget the look on my mother's face when _____

I feel very strongly about _____

SENTENCES

A *sentence* is a group of words that expresses something that makes sense to the reader: a thought, a belief, an opinion, a fact, an observation. It must be complete enough for the reader to understand the message that the writer wants to send. A sentence contains at least two essential parts—a *subject,* which generally tells who or what the sentence is about, and a *verb,* which tells what the subject is or does (Samson laughed).

In writing any paragraph, you will use sentences. The sentence is the basic unit of thought, and each sentence must contain a complete thought. Before turning in your paragraph, make sure that each sentence is complete. Show your reader where each sentence begins and ends by capitalizing the first word and putting a period at the end.

✓ Fragments

A sentence fragment is an incomplete thought. It is called a *fragment* because it contains only *part of a thought.* Something is missing (usually a subject or a verb); therefore, a fragment usually fails to convey a clear message.

Sentence fragments usually result from one of the following causes:

The sentence has either no subject or no verb.

The sentence has only part of a verb.

The sentence is a dependent clause.

1. The sentence has either no subject or no verb.

Subjects and verbs are especially important in written English. When you are talking, you can often communicate a clear message without a subject or a verb, but only because the listener can figure out what you mean from the tone of your voice, or the expression on your face, or some other observable cue. For example, if you see two angry police officers charging down the sidewalk motioning for people to get out of their way, and you hear one of them say, "Out of my way!" you know what the officer means: "*You get* out of my way!"

You can easily supply the missing subject (*you*) and verb (*get*) from the officer's implied sentence. In written English, however, a fragment of a thought is rarely sufficient because a reader needs more information than a listener does. Things that can be implied in speech must be directly stated in writing. *You can't leave out important words and expect your readers to supply them.*

Therefore, to express a coherent thought in written English, a sentence needs both a subject and a verb (with the exception of short statements where the subject is clearly understood: "Stop" means "*You* stop"; "Wait here" means "*You* wait here").

2. The sentence has only part of a verb.

Incomplete verbs can also cause sentence fragments. The verb in a sentence does not always consist of just one word, because an action cannot always be expressed in just one word. To show a particular action taking place at a particular time, you often need several words to complete the verb. Consider the following:

Marmaduke *is diving* into the neighbor's pool again.

That dog *will be pleading* for his life when Mom finds out.

Neither of these sentences would make sense if it contained just the main verb without the helping verbs (*is* and *will be*).

Marmaduke *diving* into the neighbor's pool.

That dog *pleading* for his life.

One way to avoid this kind of fragment is to learn the difference between verbs and verbals. *Verbals* are incomplete verb forms that function as nouns, adjectives, or adverbs, but not as verbs. Note the following examples of verbals:

Fishing is his main hobby. (Verbal functions as a noun.)

The girl *dancing* is Ron's sister. (Verbal functions as an adjective.)

The boys came *to see* the pretty girls on the beach. (Verbal functions as an adverb.)

One of the most frequent types of sentence fragment is caused by using a verbal instead of a complete verb.

Fish *swimming.*

Fish *swimming* from the coast of Alaska to inland rivers every year.

Putting a period after these word groups does not make them sentences. Since their verb forms are incomplete, both are sentence fragments. Here are the correct versions:

Fish swim.

Fish swim from the coast of Alaska to inland rivers every year.

The following are also fragments:

Salmon *swimming* up the river to spawn.

Atomic power plants *operating* in the European countries.

The witness being *questioned* by the prosecutor.

These fragments can be made into complete sentences in several ways.

Salmon *are* (or *were*) swimming up the river to spawn.

Salmon *swim* (or *swam*) up the river to spawn.

Salmon *swimming* up the river to spawn overcome seemingly impossible obstacles.

3. The sentence is a dependent clause.

Fragments can also result from the failure to recognize *dependent clauses*. Placing a conjunction (*when*) before a subject and verb can make a sentence a fragment because it places the subject-verb unit in a dependent clause—the kind of clause that cannot stand alone. A dependent clause doesn't make sense until it is connected to a main idea.

Look at an example:

Fragment: When the queen went to Ireland. (dependent clause)

Sentence: When the queen went to Ireland, she attended several receptions. (dependent clause connected to a main idea)

Sentence: The queen went to Ireland. (conjunction eliminated)

EXERCISE 1E: IDENTIFYING AND CORRECTING FRAGMENTS

Mark fragments with an F and complete sentences with a C. Then convert the fragments into sentences.

_____ 1. It was terrific!

_____

_____

_____ 2. Going to college when there is no money.

_____

_____

_____ 3. The importance of learning how to write well.

_____

_____

_____ 4. That stinks!

_____

_____

_____ 5. The reason why all young men and women should have at least two years of military training.

_____

_____

_____ 6. Before I ever go to that brew pub again.

_____

_____

_____ 7. When I got picked for the soccer team.

_____

_____

_____ 8. Crippled by a bad back.

_____

_____

_____ 9. As I entered the prison.

_____

_____

_____ 10. The dark and gloomy night.

_____

_____

WORDS

English is a rich language. It is the language of scholars the world over. It is the international traffic-control language of pilots regardless of their native tongues. It has more words (500,000 not including technical terms) than any other language by far. The next largest language has 185,000 words.

Yet almost no word in the English language means only one thing; almost all words have several meanings—and very disparate meanings at that. Look at the following examples. Isn't it amazing that we can understand each other at all?

Stands can mean any of the following:

gets up	He *stands* when the teacher calls on him.
tiers of seats	The *stands* were full for the playoff game.
vending spots	We ate at the hot dog *stands*.
places to wait for taxis	We met at the taxi *stands*.
groups of trees	The *stands* of pines were beautiful.

Reserve can mean any of the following:

quiet dignity	He was a man of great *reserve*.
military person	He was a *reserve* officer in the Marine Corps.
extra	We always keep a little cash in *reserve*.
a back-up football player	He is a *reserve* on Notre Dame's team.
land set aside for a particular use	We vacationed at a nature *reserve*.

Present can mean any of the following:

gift	I got a *present* for my birthday.
to give	I will *present* my speech at two o'clock.
at this time	At *present*, we shall do nothing.
here	When the sergeant called my name, I answered, *"Present."*

So, you have many words to choose from. You are striving for clarity, so you want to be as specific as you can in order to communicate to your reader exactly what you mean. To do this, examine each subject and verb. Do not be satisfied with your first attempt; look at each sentence and change each word that is not as specific as you can make it. (One student reported that her grades went up dramatically after she began going through her paragraphs and eliminating all *to be* verbs.)

The words we select should be appropriate for our subject and our attitude. We usually can do this by choosing specific rather than broad terms.

Find two specific words for each of these more general words:

thing	_____	to say	_____
gadget	_____	to get	_____
instrument	_____	to do	_____
place	_____	to see	_____
circumstance	_____	to want	_____

Each of these words represents a broad class of things or actions. *Feature,* for example, could refer to a movie, a story, a special attraction, a nose, a chin, or an Adam's apple. It could also refer to a cartoon that appears regularly, or a special characteristic of a house, or a car, or an author, or an athlete.

Don't say *device* if you mean a can opener.
Don't say *vehicle* if you mean a Chevy Camaro.
Don't say *article* if you mean a T-shirt.
Don't say *movement* if you mean a karate chop.

The following lists illustrate the relationship between broad, general terms and specific words that point directly to objects. As you move down each list, you find that the words become increasingly more specific with each step. *Cow* is much more specific than *living creature,* and *motorcycle* is much more specific than *vehicle.*

Living Creature	**Vehicle**
animal	motor vehicle
quadruped	two-wheeled motor vehicle
cow	motorcycle
Jersey cow	Honda
Old MacDonald's Jersey Cow, Bossy	Honda CBR 1100XX Blackbird

EXERCISE 1F: CHOOSING SPECIFIC TERMS

Improve the following sentences by selecting more specific subjects and controlling attitudes.

> *Not specific:* One of my ancestors laid out the town down the river.
>
> *Specific:* My great-great-grandfather laid out Glen Arden, the beautiful suburb twelve miles down the Ohio from Cincinnati.

1. Circumstances have never been so encouraging for me.

   _____

2. The council responded to the citizens' suggestions.

   _____

3. Julie was so-so about her admirer's request.

   _____

4. The instructor's attitude concerned the students.

   _____

5. My car is fast.

   _____

6. George's pet is obnoxious.

   _____

7. That football player is enormous.

   _____

8. Since she was so old, the worker ignored her outburst.

   _____

9. While doing his work, he appreciated his wife bringing him a beverage.

   _____

10. My mother's face showed her feelings about the way Tom was dressed.

    _____

If you want your writing to be clear, be as specific as possible. If your subject is specific enough, all your readers will see the same picture. If your subject is too general, the meaning of your sentence will not be clear. For example, consider the following:

1. *Something* is floating in your soup. What do you see floating in your soup? A contact lens? A dandelion? A popsicle stick? Obviously, the word *something* is much too general.
2. A *creature* is floating in your soup. What do you see now? A monster? A mouse? A yellow-bellied sapsucker? You are probably thinking of something living, but that doesn't narrow the subject very much.
3. An *invertebrate* is floating in your soup. If you know that *invertebrate* means "without a backbone," you can narrow the picture down to a spineless creature, but you still don't know exactly what is floating in your soup. A clam? A bug? A coward?
4. A *bee* is floating in your soup. Now your subject is specific. The picture is clear; the only thing floating in your soup is a bee.

A bee is floating in your soup.

✓ Clear and Specific Verb

If you want your paragraph to make sense, you must learn to say exactly what you mean. Using the wrong word in a sentence can be just as serious an error as using the wrong number in a math problem. For example, suppose you had to describe an extremely intoxicated neighbor trying to reach his back porch after a night of bar-hopping. If you wrote, "My neighbor *walked* across the backyard," when you really meant, "My neighbor *staggered* across the backyard," then you would have conveyed an inaccurate picture to your reader. Changing the verb from *walked* to *staggered* creates a different image in the reader's mind. That's why it is so important to choose the right verb.

Look at the following sentences and see how the image in your mind is altered by the change of only one word in each sentence—the verb.

My neighbor *stomped* across the backyard. (Do you see an angry man?)

My neighbor *paced* across the backyard. (Do you see a nervous man?)

My neighbor *bounced* across the backyard. (Do you see a happy man?)

My neighbor *jogged* across the backyard. (Do you see an exercise buff in a gray sweatsuit?)

How does verb choice change the meaning of the following sentences?

Mary *looked* at John.	Mary *peered* at John.
Mary *glared* at John.	Mary *beamed* at John.
Mary *gazed* at John.	Mary *glanced* at John.
Mary *stared* at John.	Mary *leered* at John.
Mary *gawked* at John.	Mary *peeked* at John.

EXERCISE 1G: CHOOSING MORE SPECIFIC WORDS

For each italicized word or phrase in the following paragraph, choose a more specific term. Notice how the paragraph changes if you make the *something* a cat or a cat burglar.

Something jumped out of a *dark space,* and I *reacted.* It was *kind of large* and *it moved* past me *at a certain speed.* I *moved* after *it when my breathing stabilized.* I could hear some *noises* ahead of me coming from a *building.* As I neared the building, I recognized the *noises.* I *reacted* again. What an *unusual* experience, I thought.

chapter 2

Narrating

> What is a story? It is:
> a clarification of life—not
> necessarily a great clarification,
> but . . . a momentary stay against
> confusion.   Robert Frost

WHAT IS A NARRATIVE?

A *narrative* is a story. Long before man could write, he could tell stories. Thousands of years earlier than the Egyptian pyramids, which record the accomplishments and the destiny of the pharaohs, cave paintings told stories. Cave paintings may have had religious meaning, but they most certainly recreated hunt scenes from the daily life of the cavemen. Through all the centuries since, the storytellers have entertained and taught their audiences out of their experiences. People still share the ancient fascination with the telling of tales.

✓ Two Kinds of Narrative Writing Today

1. FICTION.   *Fiction* is made up essentially of novels and short stories. Fiction does not say explicitly what it means; it allows the reader to decide its meaning, its significance. Often, fiction expands to the related media of television and movies.

Storyteller.

2. EXPOSITION. *Exposition,* too, tells a story, but it announces its significance. Exposition tells the reader explicitly what it means. Usually, exposition announces its meaning in the topic sentence, which is first in the paragraph and is echoed in the conclusion. Occasionally, however, meaning is not revealed until the conclusion.

The verb *to narrate* means tell, to give an account of. Probably few days pass when you don't say, "Let me tell you what happened to me." Writing a narrative is really just putting on paper what happened.

✓ The Expository Narrative

An *expository narrative* not only tells your readers what happened but also why the happening was meaningful to you. Remember that you are not going to tell them your whole life history—certainly not in one paragraph—so you focus on one event and its meaning to you.

Perhaps you can prod your memory with questions like these:

> Does anything stand out in my recollection?
> Do I recall something frequently?
> Why did I do . . . ?
> Why is . . . an important person in my life?
> Did I change because of what happened?
> Did I learn something from it?

The answers to such questions will help you arrive at your controlling idea. What happened will be your subject, and how you responded to it will be your attitude. As soon as you have your controlling idea in mind, write a sentence that gives your general subject and expresses clearly your attitude toward it. For example, consider this topic sentence:

> Perhaps the funniest thing I ever saw was two policemen trying to catch a cow in a shopping center.

The funniest thing I ever saw is, of course, your attitude. *Two policemen trying to catch a cow* is the event, or subject.

Stories must make a point and usually must make it in the topic sentence. Once you have your topic sentence, you are ready to tell the story that illustrates it. Remembering that the body of your narrative essay is a story, you select only details that advance that story. Keep your story moving to its climax with every sentence you write.

ASSIGNMENT. Your assignment for this chapter is to write a narrative paragraph about a personal experience.

HOW TO WRITE A NARRATIVE PARAGRAPH

1. Choose a memorable personal experience to write about, one that had a significant effect on you.
2. Ask yourself, "What point do I want to illustrate with my story?"
3. Write a sentence that makes the point of your story clear to your reader.
4. Place that sentence either at the beginning of your paragraph (topic sentence) or at the end (concluding sentence).
5. Make sure that the details of your story are vivid enough to enable the reader to feel as though he was right there with you when it happened.
6. Make sure that your last sentence is a conclusion and not the last detail of your story.

ORGANIZATION OF A NARRATIVE PARAGRAPH

The narrative paragraph has the same three-part organization discussed in the first chapter: **beginning, middle,** and **end.**

1. **Beginning (*Introduction*)** Here, the reader is introduced to the story situation.
   a. You may begin with a topic sentence (subject + attitude)

or

    b. You may begin by relating actions or events that build toward a
       climax, holding back your topic sentence until the end to add
       suspense or drama.

2. **Middle (*Body*)** The body contains the narrative details that support your
   topic sentence.

3. **End (*Conclusion*)** The conclusion echoes the controlling idea stated in
   the topic sentence and reaffirms the significance of the narrative in the
   body of the paragraph.

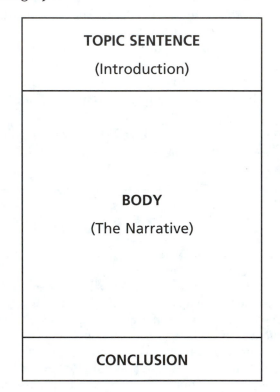

✓ Some Tips on Narrative Writing

1. HAVE A CENTRAL PURPOSE—MAKE A POINT!

Telling a story is not just listing a sequence of things that you have done or
that have happened to you. Your narrative must be important for some reason; it must make a point. Your reader should understand why you feel that
the experience you have selected is worth writing about.

2. ABOVE ALL, CHOOSE AN EXPERIENCE THAT IS WORTH WRITING ABOUT!

Suppose a friend decided to tell you about what he did yesterday:

      I got up about 7:00 and took a hot shower. Then Spike and I took a quick
    walk in the rain before breakfast. There was just enough time for a cup of

coffee and some Raisin Bran before I had to leave for class. My last class ended at 3:50, and I was starved. After a Whopper with cheese and a large order of fries, I headed home to do some studying. I did a few math problems, reviewed my sociology notes, and then fell asleep at my desk. After waking up, I picked up Lori and we ate a pizza. I dropped her off because she had homework and went home. Instead of studying as I had planned, I fell asleep on the couch in the middle of Jay Leno.

Do you find yourself saying, "So what!" and asking yourself, "Why is he telling me this? What is the point of this boring sequence of events? If he didn't have anything more important to say, why didn't he just keep quiet?"

If your readers react this way to your narrative, you do not have a clear central purpose. You are not making a point.

The student writer of the following paragraph has a clear central purpose—to share with the reader the satisfaction of a personal victory.

> **When I entered the Labor Day Rodeo, I had no idea that the luck of the draw would challenge me with the meanest bull of the rodeo company.** Named Spot On, he had a reputation of throwing cowboys off and whirling back to plow them over. When I heard about him, I wondered if I had what it takes to ride him, but when the chutes were loaded, my confidence returned. It was time to let my reflexes take over. I climbed up into the chute, tied my bullrope tightly around my hand, sat down, and nodded my head. At that instant, the roar of the crowd became a whisper. All I heard was the latch click and the groan of the metal gate swinging open. Suddenly in an explosion of man and loose-skinned, bellowing Brahma bull, we flew out of the chute. Beyond the chute, the bull turned left, the man leaned right. I countered his move by grabbing a new hold with my right foot. The bull continued leaping left, and I spurred him at every jump. After about six seconds, we both began to weaken, but I leaned farther and farther to the outside of the spin. Spot On set straight out for the other end of the arena, and I was able to right myself by throwing my hips and upper body to the center of his back. Somewhere in the background the buzzer sounded. I bailed off to the left with my feet pumping even before they hit the ground. I knew Spot On was searching the arena, so I had to get to a fence before he got to me. Lunging for the top rail and pulling myself up, I glanced over my shoulder to see my conquered foe glaring at me. We both knew we would meet again and the outcome might not be the same, but, for me now, I was victorious over the meanest bull at the rodeo.
>
> T. J. Higgs

3. BE HONEST AND SINCERE!

Write honestly and directly in natural language. Don't try to impress your reader with stilted, phony wording. Be honest with yourself, too, and don't try to hide your own failing and doubts. After all, is there a human being who has never done anything selfish or stupid or frivolous?

4. KEEP YOUR STORY MOVING!

Remember, the narrative paragraph portrays action. It is like a moving picture in which objects are in motion from one moment to the next. The writer must capture that action for the reader; your sentences must have a sense of direction and carry your controlling idea forward. If your controlling idea does not progress as you develop your narrative, the reader will lose interest, but by keeping the story moving, the reader will stay with you.

In the following student paragraph, the writer recalls the longest, slowest, and most terrifying ride of her life. Her fears are even more intense because of her husband's occupation and her limited knowledge of his whereabouts. With each narrative detail, suspense mounts as her story moves steadily toward its climax in the conclusion. Note that she uses two sentences to fully express her controlling idea.

> **While I was merging into traffic onto Route 60 South from Center Township, I looked to my right and saw a large column of black smoke fill the air. As a former flight attendant, I had a premonition as to what might have just happened.** As I drove cautiously down the road, the blackness and the smell of smoke nearly overcame me. Traffic slowed, and I came to a stop about five hundred yards from the Aliquippa exit. Then I heard a man yell, "A plane just went down!" At that moment, I said a little prayer for my husband, John, a pilot for USAir who had been flying in and out of Pittsburgh all day. I retrieved my bag from the back seat and quickly pulled out his trip sheet. My hands shook as I looked up his trip number and prayed that he was safe somewhere else. To my horror, I saw that he was due to land at Pittsburgh, inbound from Columbus, Ohio, at 7:15 P.M. I looked at my watch; it was about 7:20 P.M. Suddenly, I heard sirens and saw several emergency vehicles approaching. Straining to hear a few more details through my open window, I heard an eyewitness say, "I believe it was a 737." A knot formed in my stomach, for John was flying the Boeing 737/300-400. A police officer then pulled over on the median and instructed everyone to keep moving. Slowly, traffic began to move, and I prayed for John's safety the whole way home. That two mile drive was the longest drive of my life. As soon as I arrived, I ran to the answering machine. After five previous messages and several hangups, I finally heard the voice that brought tears of relief to my eyes. Unfortunately, my premonition of the crash was correct, but thankfully my prayers were answered. John was not one of the pilots on Flight 427, which had no survivors.
>
> Kirsten R. Fry

5. FIND YOUR VOICE!

All good writing has a clear voice. Not only does good writing say something, but it also says it in a distinctive tone of voice. The voice of a writer is his **style.** And, as a great French writer once observed, "Style is the man." Even technical writing, which tries to avoid any expression of personality, achieves an impersonal style suited to its own purpose. It is easily recognized for what it is: It has a voice.

Just as you can recognize a friend's voice on the telephone, you can recognize an author well known to you by his voice, his style. Even if you cannot identify the voice, you are frequently aware of its individuality. The author's voice reflects his beliefs, his philosophy, his sense of humor—or lack of it—his dreams, his loves. In short, the style *is* the man.

If you want your writing to influence your readers, you need to find a voice to come through your writing. You almost undoubtedly have a style of your own; therefore, it will take no great effort to let it shine through in your writing.

Here are several individualized voices that you may or may not be able to identify but that you will certainly perceive as highly unusual or even unique.

Perhaps the best-known voice among American writers is Mark Twain's. He is funny, but just below his comedy lies his heart-wrenching wryness. He loves but deplores what he calls the "damned human race." Above all else, he despises pretension.

The voice of the following excerpt, taken from *Puddin'head Wilson,* is immediately identifiable by every reader familiar with Twain.

> Courage is resistance to fear, mastery of fear—not absence of fear. Except a creature be part coward, it is not a compliment to say it is brave; it is merely a loose misapplication of the word. Consider the flea!—incomparably the bravest of all the creatures of God, if ignorance of fear were courage. Whether you are asleep or awake he will attack you, caring nothing for the fact that in bulk and strength you are to him as are the massed armies of the earth to a sucking child; he lives both day and night and all days and nights in the very lap of peril and the immediate presence of death, and yet is no more afraid than is the man who walks the streets of a city that was threatened by an earthquake ten centuries before. When we speak of Clive, Nelson, and Putnam as men who "didn't know what fear was," we ought always to add the flea—and put him at the head of the procession. . . .

> Mark Twain, *Puddin'head Wilson*

Winston Churchill, prime minister of England, and one of the greatest men of our century, was a prolific writer and master stylist. He was a living symbol of the free world's resistance to Nazi brutality during World War II and personified for all English-speaking peoples resistance to tyranny. He lightened and brightened not only his personal life but also his statesman's career by his wit and humor. His style projects equal quantities of self-esteem and appreciation of others.

> Shortly before World War I, Nancy Astor, the American-born wife of Waldorf, Viscount Astor, visited Blenheim Palace, the ancestral home of the

Churchill family. In conversation with Churchill, she expounded on the subject of women's rights, an issue that was to take her into the House of Commons as the first woman member of Parliament. Churchill opposed her on this and other causes that she held dear. In some exasperation Lady Astor said, "Winston, if I were married to you, I'd put poison in your coffee." Churchill responded, "And if you were my wife, I'd drink it." . . .

In the summer of 1941, Sergeant James Allen Ward was awarded the Victoria Cross for climbing out onto the wing of his Wellington bomber, 13,000 feet above the Zuider Zee, to extinguish a fire in the starboard engine. Secured only by a rope around his waist, he managed not only to smother the fire but also to return along the wing to the aircraft's cabin. Churchill, an admirer as well as a performer of swashbuckling exploits, summoned the shy New Zealander to 10 Downing Street. Ward, struck dumb with awe in Churchill's presence, was unable to answer the prime minister's questions. Churchill surveyed the unhappy hero with some compassion. "You must feel very humble and awkward in my presence," he said.

"Yes, sir," managed Ward.

"Then you can imagine how humble and awkward I feel in yours," said Churchill. . . .

Churchill was accosted at a wartime reception by a rather overbearing American lady. "What are you going to do about those wretched Indians," she demanded. "Madam," replied Churchill, "to which Indians do you refer? Do you refer to the second greatest nation on earth, which under benign and munificent British rule has multiplied and prospered exceedingly? Or to the unfortunate North American Indians, which under your present administration are almost extinct?"

Clifton Fadiman, *Anecdotes*

Not only professional writers or great persons have a "voice." *Every* writer can develop a voice, a distinctive style that personalizes his writing. That style—how he says things—stands for the man, his attitudes toward himself and toward others, what he loves and what he dislikes, what he thinks about. What can you deduce about the personality of the student who wrote the following essay?

In the Lion's Den

I peeked around the door that led to the schoolyard, and I knew that from that point on, it was going to be a horrible day. I did not want to cross that ever present threshold which divided safety from almost imminent danger, but the beckoning voice of a nearby yard supervisor forced me through the archway looming overhead. As I inched out from the great wall of a door, the only wall protecting me, I braced for what was to come, waiting for those tormenting words: "There's the dork. Get him!" I had finally passed into the amphitheatre where the ravenous lion, my peers, were about to engage in mortal combat. I was expecting my whole existence to be torn limb from limb by the never-ending barrage of insults that were the lion's claws and teeth, but there was nothing. My whole outlook on the period suddenly changed, "Was I actually going to have fun at recess today?" I asked myself in disbelief. Were they finally going to leave me alone? Then, strolling unknowingly away from the guardianship of the supervisor, it began, taking me completely by surprise: "You loser" and "Now you're mine," now familiar chants, stung me with every cascading word, like salt on an open wound. Then came the subtle tripping and the "accidental" stray tennis balls hitting me. I quickly ran back to the roaming eyes of the supervisor and sat there on the step for the rest of the period. Looking back on this vivid memory of my grade-school years, I realize now that had I fought back early in my school career and not allowed myself to be bullied, things might have turned out differently. I would not have dreaded waking up on a school day or going out for recess. I might have even had a few friends. Who knows? Of all the events in my life that I have regretted, it is my submission to these grade-school bullies. I wish that I would never have given my classmates the chance to transform me into the whipping boy I had become for so many years. The happiest day of my life was the day I graduated from eighth grade because this was the day I would see my classmates for the last time, along with the anguish that accompanied their fearful aura. As I left the amphitheatre that day, I was suddenly struck with an ironic sense of accomplishment: I survived, yet the lion had defeated me.

Ryan Shadis

6. RE-CREATE—DON'T RELATE!

Try to remember exactly what you saw and how you felt, and then carefully choose words that will most accurately enable the reader to *re-create* your experience in his imagination. Choose words that make you and your reader one person so that he can visualize the experience through your eyes and feel its emotional impact. This sharing of the same vibrations is called *empathy,* the most desirable response in narrative writing.

After reading the following student paragraph, analyze your immediate reactions to it.

At the age of nineteen, I had a horrifying, gruesome experience. The nightmare occurred in the barracks at Fort Gordon, Georgia, where we were preparing for an inspection. Four girls were assigned to various duties in the latrine. Shivbby, our barracks sergeant, and Debbie Howell volunteered to strip the latrine floor using turpentine and a buffer. Meanwhile, MacDonald and I waited outside until they were finished so that we could go in and complete our work details. Suddenly there was a blast followed by a flash fire, and both MacDonald and I were thrown backward from its impact. Debbie Howell came tearing out of the latrine screaming like a banshee, and I saw that both of her feet were burning. Immediately, MacDonald and I threw her to the floor and quickly extinguished the flames which engulfed her feet. Then, as we turned and looked at each other, horror filled our eyes. MacDonald screamed—her eyes filled with disbelief. "Oh my God, Bessie, Shivbby is still in there; she is still in the latrine!" We both ran to the latrine and were horrified as Shivbby, who was burned black from head to toe, came staggering out of the latrine and collapsed into MacDonald's arms. After witnessing this gruesome sight, I went into shock, unable to believe that the figure before me, burned beyond recognition, was once my barracks sergeant. The sight and smell of burning flesh and hair almost made me vomit, but I held it back. However, when the ambulance attendants arrived and lifted Shivbby, some of her burned flesh remained on MacDonald's arms. That was my breaking point. I dashed out of the building and did not care where I went, for I was running away from the scene of a nightmare. Still, to this day, seven years after her death, I can see Shivbby's burned body and smell the rancid flesh and hair. This nightmare will linger in my memory forever.

Bessie Young

1. Did you empathize with the feelings of the writer? If so, why?
2. Does this paragraph have a topic sentence? Identify the subject and attitude.
3. Is the paragraph unified? Do all of the narrative details support a single controlling idea?
4. Is the paragraph coherent? Do the narrative details unfold in a logical progression?
5. Did the writer use words that expressed feelings and emotions? What are some of them?
6. Did the writer use language that depicted any of the five senses: touch, taste, smell, sight, hearing? How many can you count?
7. Did the writer use words that portrayed visual imagery? What are some of the more vivid ones?
8. Does the conclusion echo the controlling idea in the topic sentence?
9. Was the writer's purpose clear, and did she make her point?
10. Does the writer have a voice, or style, that reveals something about the person she is?

If you answered these questions with a firm "yes," then we can conclude that this paragraph was indeed a successful narrative.

✓ What Can I Write About?

At this point, you may still be saying to yourself, "I can't think of anything! My life has been a drag. What could I possibly write about that anyone else would want to read?"

Don't panic. Think about your past and remember that your life is unique. No one else has lived a life exactly like yours; therefore, you have had some experiences that no one else has had. Even if someone did have a similar experience, like giving birth for the first time or being involved in an automobile accident, *your* responses to those experiences will be different and very personal. The key to the beginning of a good narrative paragraph lies in choosing an experience that is right for you.

Think about the events of your childhood. What was it like growing up? How did you get along with your parents, brothers, and sisters? Where did you live, and what was that like? Where did you go to school? What were your friends like, and what did you do together?

Think about life as an adult—your relationships, your jobs, your children, your attempts to reach your goals and dreams.

THINK ABOUT SOME POSSIBLE "FIRSTS."

Your first date	Your first taste of defeat or glorious success
Your first love	Your first day on a new job
Your first child	Your first Christmas away from home

THINK ABOUT TYPES OF EXPERIENCES.

Unforgettable experiences	Sentimental experiences
Lessons learned from experiences	Terrifying experiences
Embarrassing or funny experiences	Heartbreaking experiences
Successful or triumphant experiences	

Now, after reviewing these possibilities, can you honestly say, "I can't think of anything!"?

TOPIC SENTENCE

✓ Choosing a Workable Topic Sentence

The topic sentence for a narrative paragraph is supported by details that tell about a single incident.

1. **A narrative topic sentence can be the first sentence in the paragraph, expressing both subject and attitude.**

   Being arrested and booked is a frightening experience, especially if one is a victim of mistaken identity.

2. **It may take more than one sentence to express fully the controlling idea for a narrative paragraph.**

   While baling hay in the upper pasture, I looked up and saw a small plane heading straight for me, smoke pouring from its engine. As I dived from the tractor, I knew that this was not going to be another typical day on the farm.

3. In some narratives, the controlling idea may not be expressed until the conclusion.

> As I stared with anguish at the body of the Marine to whom I had been talking just thirty minutes before, it suddenly hit me like a hammer that I would be dead too had I not taken that short walk for some fresh air.

Be sure to write a topic sentence that can be developed or supported by a *single* narrative incident. The following topic sentences, for example, cannot be illustrated by a single incident or story. Why not?

> "While working as a waitress at the Lone Star, I have encountered several types of irritating customers."
>
> "Students in my English class can be divided into three groups: the alert, the indifferent, and the comatose."
>
> "Attending a community college has many advantages over attending a large university."

BODY

The body of a narrative paragraph is a single story told in chronological order—that is, events are told in the order in which they occurred according to time sequence. In a narrative paragraph, just write the topic sentence and then tell the story that supports the topic sentence.

In the following paragraph, the writer has a clear purpose in mind and makes his point up front by putting his topic sentence first. If the writer clearly states his opinion in the first sentence, the reader does not have to ask, "So what? Why are you telling me this?" Also, note that immediately after the topic sentence, the writer adds two sentences of introductory material before actually beginning the story.

> **Although most people think that horses are beautiful, but stupid, I'm an expert who knows better.** I was teaching Baron, my own horse, some of the tricks of "high dressage," a special training in which the horse learns to dance, walk on his hind legs, kneel down, and do a lot of showy things like that. Baron was doing very well, but he was still my saddle horse, too. One December 24, I rode Baron over to take a friend his Christmas present. Once I was there, my friend and I decided to have a little Christmas cheer. Time sped past, but suddenly I realized that dusk had fallen and so had about three inches of snow. Hurriedly jingling out a few last Christmas wishes to my friend and his family, I mounted Baron and trotted down the drive. My wife would be seething that I was late for dinner on Christmas Eve. If I cut through the woods on a little trail only Baron and I knew, I could save about four miles. So, I curved left to the trail. At first, it was beautiful in the woods, white and silent. That horse and I could have been alone in the world.

Then, crash! Baron stumbled over a deadfall branch, and we both thudded to the ground. Baron struggled to his feet and bolted fifty yards away. But I knew I wasn't going to get up without help; something important was broken. There I was, helpless, in the middle of the woods with the snow filling up the hoof marks, the one clue that led to me. It would be hours, maybe days, before anyone found me—too long, anyway. It was up to Baron and me. I called him, softly. He came and nuzzled me. Then I commanded, "Kneel, kneel." He'd done it in the ring, but would he do it now in the snow and underbrush? I couldn't reach him to give him the hand signals, just the words over and over and over. But he did it! He kneeled. Then, somehow, half-fainting, I draped myself across the saddle. On command, he rose. On command, he followed the path home, walking. Baron probably saved my life that night. I'll agree that horses are beautiful, but I'll never be convinced that they are stupid; Baron and I know better.

In the following paragraph, the writer has chosen to hold his topic sentence until the end to create suspense, drama, or an emotional climax.

It happened to be the first day of hunting season, one of those crisp, clear November days when the tips of the grass are covered with frost and the steam is rising from the fields. Sneaky, our little beagle, had just jumped a rabbit. My heart pounded as the dog brought the bunny around in a fatal circle, back toward me and the other hunters, friends of my father's. We were strung out in single file at the edge of the woods, facing a field of tall elephant grass. We could see the rabbit coming toward us from our left, bounding through the grass, heading for a fence on our right and safety in the woods beyond. Four of the hunters were to my left, my father a few yards to my right. As the rabbit came into firing distance, the hunters, one by one, began taking shots at the frightened, bounding ball of fur. Four shots. Four misses. Now, the rabbit was nearing the fence. My father, one of the best marksmen in the country, didn't even raise his gun. He was waiting for me to shoot. I did, and I hit the rabbit a few yards in front of the fence. All Dad said was "Good shot," but I knew he was proud, especially since all of his friends had missed it. What wings of fancy my mind has taken about that experience. I can be sitting in a meeting with clients, attending the theater, engaging in a discussion, driving, lying awake at night—any time. **I can spend what seems like an eternity reminiscing about that moment and the feeling that welled up inside of me when I knew that I had pleased my father.**

Larry Werner

CONCLUSION

The narrative paragraph must have a conclusion, just like the other types of paragraphs that you will be writing. If your topic sentence comes first, as in the paragraph about Baron and his rider, then the conclusion should echo the controlling idea or central impression expressed in that topic sentence.

Topic sentence expressing controlling idea:

Although most people think that horses are beautiful but stupid, I'm an expert who knows better.

Concluding sentence echoing controlling idea:

I'll agree that horses are beautiful, but I'll never be convinced that they are stupid; Baron and I know better.

If the writer chooses to build a sequence of events that culminate in a central impression, he can put the topic sentence at the end, as in the narrative about the hunting trip. Here, the topic sentence appears only once, both as topic sentence and concluding sentence.

Combined topic and concluding sentence:

I can spend what seems like an eternity reminiscing about that moment and the feeling that welled up inside of me when I knew that I had pleased my father.

EXERCISE 2A: IDENTIFYING CLEAR CONTROLLING IDEAS

Put a check mark before each of the following topic sentences that you think could be successfully developed by the narrative method.

_____ 1. My mother-in-law seemed boring until she started recalling her college days.

_____ 2. Last winter's storms shattered the trees around my house as if they had been blasted by heavy gunfire.

_____ 3. John and James are twins.

_____ 4. My bedroom furniture is shabby.

_____ 5. Because my bedroom furniture is shabby, I decided to refinish it.

_____ 6. When I decided to refinish my shabby bedroom furniture, I almost ruined my marriage.

_____ 7. I made three phone calls last night.

_____ 8. The three phone calls I made last night were to old friends.

      _____ 9. My three phone calls last night were to friends I hadn't seen for years.

      _____ 10. My three phone calls last night to friends I hadn't seen for years made me realize how lucky I am.

✓ Some Do's . . .

1. *Do* limit your subject and narrow its scope to a single significant event or possibly a single thread of closely related events.
2. *Do* arrange the details of the narrative in *chronological order*—the order of the time in which things happened.
3. *Do* use the past tense. There are exceptions, of course, but usually the *simple past tense* will serve you best in telling your story: "We *strolled* toward the lake." "We *saw* the speedboat." "Then we *heard* the boy in the water scream." If you need to include some detail that occurred before the action of your story takes place, all you need to do, in most instances, is to add *had* or *had been* to the simple past form: for example, "I *had been* told." "I *had* heard." "I *had* looked."
4. *Do* make sure that your paragraph of personal experience is unified. To achieve this unity, you must first write a clear and specific topic sentence containing a controlling idea that introduces a story. Next develop a body of narrative details that support your topic sentence. Finally, write a conclusion that sums up your story and restates your controlling idea.

✓ . . . and Don'ts About the Narrative

1. *Don't* try to cover too much. Remember, you are not writing your autobiography.
2. *Don't* write a pointless account of boring, everyday events. Also, no matter how dramatic your details may be, you must show how and why they were significant for you. You have to *make a point about your experience* and relate all your details to that point.
3. *Don't* include details that are not required to support your main point. You must be very selective. If your narrative is about something that happened to you late at night, don't start by talking about what you had for breakfast unless it has some direct reference to your nighttime adventure.

SUGGESTED ACTIVITIES AND ASSIGNMENTS

1. Telling tall tales is an American tradition carried on today by such organizations as the Liars' Club and by countless hunters, fishermen, and yarn spinners. Taking no more than two minutes for the telling of each story, see who can come up with the biggest whopper.

2. Relate an experience that you feel has some interest for your reader. Make sure your topic sentence can be supported by telling a single incident. You undoubtedly have experiences that are embarrassing or frightening, that are funny or sad, experiences that are significant for you. If they are meaningful for you, you can make them meaningful for others.

3. A good storyteller is never without friends because the art of the narrative is something that everyone appreciates. Our most cherished childhood memories, in fact, are usually preserved in story form:

> Dad, remember the first time you took Larry hunting up at Brushcreek? It's a wonder either one of you came back alive. . . .

> Your great-grandmother will never live down the day she got caught in the speak-easy with Reverend Felcher's son. . . .

✏️ SENTENCES

COMMON SENTENCE BOUNDARY ERRORS

COMMA SPLICE: Placing a comma between two sentences

Example: Robert Peary was an Arctic explorer, he led the famous expedition to the North Pole.

FUSED SENTENCE: Fusing two sentences together with no punctuation

Example: The name Matthew Henson is not as well known as Peary's he was Peary's assistant.

RUN-ON SENTENCE: Forcing too many main ideas into one sentence: e.g., connecting a string of clauses together with "ands" or "buts"

Example: Most people don't know Matthew Henson but he was a very skilled African-American explorer and he was Robert Peary's assistant and he was actually the first man to set foot on the North Pole but the history books never talk about Henson.

Because of your concentration on an interesting subject and a convincing attitude, you may overlook the necessary boundaries between sentences and sentence parts. After all, you know what you mean. And, indeed, the earliest writing did get along without such boundaries.

Punctuation is by no means as old as writing, but written communication is much easier to understand now that we have those little signs and symbols to indicate relationships between sentences, clauses, phrases, and words.

Remember your reader! The narrative paragraph is usually fast-paced. You are telling a story, and you are probably reliving the experience as you write. Don't go so fast that you forget your reader; he doesn't know the story. Make sure that your reader can follow your thoughts by dividing your story into recognizable units of thought-sentences. Use the correct linking words or phrases to show the relationship between your thoughts.

You must show where one thought ends and another begins.

If you have completed a thought, show the reader with a period (.).

If you are asking a question, show the reader with a question mark (?).

If you are making an extremely emotional statement, show the reader with an exclamation mark (!).

These three marks all show that a sentence has been completed.

✓ Comma Splices

If you mistakenly put a comma at the end of your thought, your confused reader will assume that you have not completed it but have more to say. For example:

The coach sent Bobbie in with a play, when he reached the huddle, he had forgotten it.

The conductor punched the ticket, when the passenger got it back, she crammed it in her pocket.

When two thoughts are coupled together with a comma, the error is called a *comma splice*. Comma splices are serious mistakes because they are errors in logic, not just in punctuation.

The basic rule concerning the comma splice is that independent clauses (complete subject-verb units that could be separate sentences) cannot simply be spliced together with a comma. For example:

The French Club is meeting at six, all members unable to attend should see the president before leaving school.

The English I test will be given on Friday, that is the only time it will be given.

✓ Fused Sentences

Similarly, if you fuse two complete thoughts together without any punctuation at all, the reader will become even more confused:

> The coach sent Bobbie in with a play when he reached the huddle he had forgotten it.

When two complete thoughts, especially if they are not very closely related, are run together without any punctuation, as in the second sentence about the punched ticket, the error is called a *fused sentence.* **Here are some more examples:**

> The big money is in computers that is what I want to major in.
>
> Our family had a cat for twenty-one years that is the record for long-lived felines.
>
> The local steel mill is downsizing they have to compete with foreign companies.

Comma splices and fused sentences such as these can usually be corrected in several ways.

1. **Make two separate sentences.**

> The coach sent Bobbie in with a play. When he reached the huddle, he had forgotten it.
>
> The French Club is meeting at six. All members unable to attend should see the president before leaving school.

2. **Use connecting words, such as** *and, but, or, for, nor, yet, so,* **preceded by a comma.** These words, called *coordinating conjunctions,* are discussed later in "Punctuation Between Clauses."

> The coach sent Bobbie in with a play, but when he reached the huddle, he had forgotten it.
>
> The big money is in computers, so that is what I want to major in.

3. **Use a stronger mark of punctuation, the semicolon (;).** You might think of the relative strength of these marks of punctuation as a formula: comma (,) + coordinating conjunction = semicolon (;).

> The coach sent Bobbie in with a play; when he reached the huddle, he had forgotten it.
>
> The big money is in computers; that is what I want to major in.

4. Use a *conjunctive adverb,* a linking word or phrase, such as *therefore, moreover, consequently,* and *as a result.*

> The coach sent Bobbie in with a play; however, when he reached the huddle, he had forgotten it.

> The big money is in computers; therefore, that is what I want to major in.

Notice that you need the stronger mark of punctuation, the semicolon, when you connect two thoughts with a conjunctive adverb. Place a semicolon before the conjunctive adverb and a comma after it.

5. **Make one of the independent clauses subordinate** by using *subordinate conjunctions,* such as *because, before, after, since, while, until, if, so that, as, as if, as though, once, as long as,* and *so on.* (Coordination and subordination are dealt with more fully in Chapter 3.)

> Although the coach sent Bobbie in with a play, when he got to the huddle, he had forgotten it.

> Because the big money is in computers, that is what I want to major in.

6. **Separate two independent clauses into two sentences with a conjunctive adverb at the beginning of the second sentence.**

> The coach sent Bobbie in with a play. However, when he reached the huddle, he had forgotten it.

✓ Run-On Sentences

The *run-on sentence* consists of several main clauses loosely joined together by a series of coordinating conjunctions, such as *and, so, for,* and *yet.* A reader who is forced to read a long string of thoughts without pausing can easily become confused. For example:

> Jack decided to take Karen dancing and he needed some money so he stopped at the bank on his way home but it was closed and he started getting desperate because this was her birthday and he had promised to take her out so, as a last resort, he borrowed fifty dollars from his dad but to get the money he had to agree to clean out the garage the next day.

A run-on sentence can be corrected by separating it into short sentences. Notice how much clearer the meaning becomes when you can pause at the end of major thought groups.

> Jack decided to take Karen dancing, and he needed some money. He stopped at the bank on his way home, but it was closed. He started

getting desperate because this was her birthday, and he had promised to take her out. As a last resort, he borrowed fifty dollars from his dad. However, in order to get the money, he had to agree to clean out the garage the next day.

It is important to remember that, although run-on sentences are long, not all long sentences are run-ons. *A run-on sentence is not determined by the number of words in a sentence. Rather, it is determined by the way those words are strung together in loosely connected clauses.* Run-on sentences are ineffective not because they are long but because they *obscure meaning.*

Notice that the excerpt from Clarence Day in Exercise 2J is written in long sentences, but they are perfectly clear because his phrases and clauses are so precisely put together.

PUNCTUATION BETWEEN CLAUSES

If you use a coordinating conjunction—*and, but, or, for, nor, yet,* and *so*—between two independent clauses, always put a comma *before* the conjunction. Remember, an independent clause states a grammatically complete thought and can stand alone.

> (independent clause), *and* (independent clause).
>
> (independent clause), *but* (independent clause).
>
> (independent clause), *yet* (independent clause).

These conjunctions are used at other times *without* commas, as in the following examples:

> Jack spends his mornings playing golf and his afternoons swimming.

In the preceding sentence, *and* does not join two independent clauses. There is no comma in front of the *and* because "and his afternoons swimming" is simply an additional phrase, not an independent clause.

> The boss *and* the secretary were driven to the airport.

In this sentence, *and* simply joins the two parts of a compound subject. Use no comma.

> Jack bought a new car *and* promptly wrecked it.

In this sentence, *and* does not join two independent clauses; it simply joins the two parts of a compound predicate, *bought* and *wrecked.*

A comma is needed before the *and* in a series of three or more terms.

> The colors of the flag are red, white, *and* blue. (a series of three or more words)

Smiling faces, clean fingernails, *and* polished shoes were what he looked for in his morning inspection. (a series of three or more phrases)

When Jack will arrive, what he will have to say, *and* when he will have to leave are the only questions on her mind. (a series of three or more clauses)

If the ideas in two independent clauses are closely related, you can incorporate both independent clauses into one sentence and separate them with a semicolon (;). The semicolon indicates that both ideas are closely related, but it provides enough of a pause to keep them from running together.

(independent clause); (independent clause).

If you use a conjunctive adverb, such as *therefore, moreover, besides, nevertheless,* and others, between two independent clauses, use a semicolon before the conjunctive adverb and a comma after it.

(independent clause); *therefore,* (independent clause).

(independent clause); *moreover,* (independent clause).

(independent clause); *besides,* (independent clause).

A common error is the comma splice that sometimes occurs with the use of conjunctive adverbs such as *consequently, however, besides, nevertheless, then, thus, still,* and others.

Comma splice:	We had lunch at the Woodman, then we went out to Lake Pomeran.
Correct:	We had lunch at the Woodman; then we went out to Lake Pomeran.
Comma splice:	We were sure we would be late, nevertheless we got there before the curtain went up.
Correct:	We were sure we would be late; nevertheless, we got there before the curtain went up.

The short conjunctive adverbs *then, thus,* and *still* don't always need a comma *after* them, but they always need a semicolon *before* them.

John studied hard; *still* he failed the test.

It is important to know the distinction between the various kinds of conjunctions, or connecting words.

First are the coordinate conjunctions—*and, but, or, nor, for, yet, so.* This is the complete list; there are no other coordinate conjunctions.

Second are the subordinate conjunctions—*before, after, when, while, although, because,* and others. These connect clauses that are not independent. We will discuss them fully in a later chapter.

Third are the conjunctive adverbs—*also, besides, consequently, however, therefore, likewise, nevertheless, then, thus,* and *still.*

What is the difference? The words in the first and second groups are always used as conjunctions, but the words in the third group are *not* always used as conjunctions. When they are used as adverbs, their location in the sentence can shift.

> *However,* his boss told Jerry to finish the job by noon.
>
> His boss, *however,* told Jerry to finish the job by noon.
>
> His boss told Jerry, *however,* to finish the job by noon.
>
> His boss told Jerry to finish the job, *however,* by noon.
>
> His boss told Jerry to finish the job by noon, *however.*

Do you see how adverbs can be moved around in the sentence? Now notice that the coordinate conjunctions—*and, but, or, nor, for, yet, so*—do not have this mobility. Try moving an *and* around in a sentence. You quickly see that it cannot be moved around.

A conjunctive adverb, then, is just an adverb used to provide a connecting link between independent clauses.

> The boss told Jerry to finish the job; *however,* he couldn't get it done that day.
>
> He thought she was being wasteful; *besides,* he was saving up for a new car.

A number of phrases, such as *in fact, as a result, to be sure, after all, for instance, for example,* can be used to perform the same function as the single-word conjunctive adverbs.

> Nature has a way of taking care of its mistakes; *as a result,* no living species should be considered useless or dispensable.

When words such as *however, consequently,* and *nevertheless* do not join independent clauses, do not use a semicolon. Simply put a comma before and a comma after the word.

> *Wrong:*   The senator's wife; *however,* did not want him to run again.
>
> *Correct:*   The senator's wife, *however,* did not want him to run again.

Wrong:	All the avid fishermen; *to be sure,* would be out on the lake before dawn.
Correct:	All the avid fishermen, *to be sure,* would be out on the lake before dawn.

Read the following examples, and observe why each is punctuated differently.

Sally has the flu; therefore, she cannot attend class today. (*Therefore* separates two independent clauses.)

John is, therefore, the best player we have on the team. (*Therefore* does not join independent clauses.)

It seems to me, however, that your plan does not consider every alternative. (*However* does not join independent clauses. The "that" clause is dependent.)

I would like to go; however, there is no available transportation at that time of day. (*However* separates two independent clauses.)

To punctuate correctly, you need to know the difference between coordinate conjunctions and conjunctive adverbs. You also need to remember the difference between an independent and a dependent clause. (Look again at *fragments* on pp. 16-18).

EXERCISE 2B: USING VARIOUS METHODS TO CORRECT SENTENCES

Select the method you consider best and correct the following sentences. Explain why you think that the method you chose is the best.

1. When she went to California to whale-watch my cousin decided to go there to college.

   _____

   _____

2. She wants to become an environmental scientist she is especially interested in marine life.

   _____

   _____

3. If she can get a scholarship she would like to spend her senior year in New Zealand.

   _____

   _____

4. The Great Coral Reef almost circles New Zealand it has more marine life than anywhere else in the world.

   _____

   _____

5. Many people think the large sea creatures are dangerous and are poisonous that they are even man-eaters.

   _____

   _____

6. That's totally wrong most are harmless to man even friendly.

   _____

   _____

7. Even the unfriendly ones run away if they are not cornered.

   _____

   _____

8. Kate is not afraid of any of them she respects them all.

   _____

   _____

9. She is not careless with any no matter how gentle they seem.

   _____

   _____

10. I have a wonderful snapshot of her California trip she is kissing a whale.

_____

_____

EXERCISE 2C: PUNCTUATING COMMA SPLICES AND FUSED SENTENCES

Supply the correct punctuation for the following comma splices and fused sentences.

1. The pup had run away we had failed to shut the gate.

_____

_____

2. The critics said that the book had a plot like King Lear's the author disagrees.

_____

_____

3. During Prohibition my grandfather made his own home-brewed beer once it blew up all over the cellar.

_____

_____

4. The student was disappointed he hadn't gotten the *A* he wanted.

_____

_____

5. We went on the cable suddenly our television viewing doubled.

_____

_____

6. Janie was embarrassed she didn't understand the opera.

_____

_____

7. Jason was very happy that the new girl had accepted his invitation he had tickets for the rave.

_____

_____

8. The street lights were very bright we could see the comet clearly.

_____

_____

9. Your plan does not include every alternative many are left out.

_____

_____

10. He hadn't talked to his friend for ten years he recognized his voice immediately.

_____

_____

EXERCISE 2D: PUNCTUATING RUN-ON SENTENCES

Punctuate or rewrite to correct the following run-ons.

1. My psychology class is a disappointment to me I guess I expected it to be more practical it really is a history of psychological ideas.

_____

_____

2. We have a riding lawn mower it has to be tuned up every spring by the time it's ready the grass is ten inches high.

_____

_____

3. I have a job as an auto mechanic it's just part-time my young sister makes more money baby sitting.

_____

_____

4. The weather was awful last winter there wasn't enough snow to make good skiing often storms wrecked roofs and broke huge branches off trees.

_____

_____

5. A misguided committee in our town tried to bring back "the good old days" they had sleigh rides and hayrides and dances around a maypole it didn't work nobody came.

_____

_____

EXERCISE 2E: RECOGNIZING FRAGMENTS, COMMA SPLICES, AND FUSED SENTENCES

On the lines below the following sentences, identify the errors you find and correct them.

1. The dog was romping on the lawn the cat was looking on.

_____

_____

2. The dog was romping on the lawn the cat looking disdainful.

    _____

    _____

3. Even though spring is late.

    _____

    _____

4. The melting snow gurgling in the downspouts.

    _____

    _____

5. The mother comforted her little boy he had been frightened by the
    storm.

    _____

    _____

6. The clown amused the children their parents laughed a lot too.

    _____

    _____

7. The circus parade created much enthusiasm many people decided to
    go to the show.

    _____

    _____

8. Many scholars are convinced that people cannot think.

    _____

    _____

9. Without words to think with.

_____

_____

10. The dinner was excellent roast beef mashed potatoes asparagus raspberry sherbet.

_____

_____

WORDS

To write clearly and convincingly, you need to consider not only your paragraphs and sentences but also your *words*. Words are the identifiers of your thoughts. Words are the building blocks of everything you construct verbally. Through words you specify what you intend to talk or write about, what you are going to say about it, and what you think and feel about it.

✓ The Actor-Action Sequence

In the narrative paragraph, you, the writer, are telling a story, moving from the first action to the second, on to the next and the next. In order to give movement to your paragraph, you should use the **actor-action sequence and strong verbs:** *I recoiled, he shouted, they stormed, my mother screamed.* Try to eliminate the weak verbs from your paragraph. (The weakest are the *to be* verbs—*is, was, were, are, has been, have been,* etc.) The following section will tell you how to do this.

Two essential elements of good writing are **precision** and **economy.**

precision: being exact
economy: saying it in the fewest possible words

To help you achieve precesion and economy, use, whenever possible, the actor-action sequence in sentence structure. The basic sentence structure is the simple, active sentence.

Owls cry.
The instructor praised the class.
The river overflowed its banks.

Active Voice:	The subject is doing something.
Example:	*Clemente* (subject) hit a home run.
Passive Voice:	Something is being done to the subject.
Example:	A *home run* (subject) was hit by Clemente.

The important thing to notice here is the *actor-action sequence.* Somebody or something *does* something—cries, praises, overflows, works, plays, or performs some act. This is called the **active voice.**

Whenver the context permits, have somebody or something do something: Make the subject of your sentence the actor and use an active verb. (*Context* refers to the overall meaning of the passage in which you are using either active or passive voice.)

Suppose, for example, that you wanted to tell someone what Tom did this morning. The most logical and direct word sequence would be to begin with Tom (the actor) and then immediately tell what he did (the action):

Active Voice:	The subject is doing something.
Example:	Tom (subject) milked the cow this morning.

Sometimes, however, the focus shifts, and the cow is emphasized instead of Tom:

Passive Voice:	Something is being done to the subject.
Example:	The cow (subject) was milked by Tom this morning.

Notice what happened. The actor (Tom) is no longer so important, and Old Bessie steps into the spotlight. In effect, the actor-action sequence has been reversed, so that the reader now pays more attention to the cow than to Tom. This type of sequence is called **passive voice.**

Which of the two do you think is the more direct and less wordy? Active voice is better, of course, because it puts Tom (the actor) first and immediately tells your reader, in fewer words, what Tom is doing. Does this mean, then, that you should never use passive voice? No, but try to use active voice whenever possible because it places the emphasis on the actors and does not bury them somewhere in the sentence.

In some cases, it is correct to use passive voice. For example, sometimes the actor is unknown or unimportant. In a sentence such as

The road was built in 1867.

the actor—who built the road—is unknown. In a sentence such as

The Populist Party was defeated.

the actors—who did the defeating—are unimportant. In both situations, therefore, it is appropriate to use passive voice.

EXERCISE 2F: USING THE ACTIVE VOICE

Revise the following sentences to the active voice, where possible.

1. The schoolboard meeting was attended by a majority of irate parents.

   _____

2. The fact that the football coach was fired angered them.

   _____

3. A chance to defend himself had never been given to him.

   _____

4. The new book was damned by the critics and so it was ignored by the readers.

   _____

5. The letter was answered by me and also replied to by my sister.

   _____

6. The ordinance was voted into law.

   _____

7. The store was closed because the business area was too far away from it.

   _____

8. Its replacement was disappointing to its old customers.

   _____

9. The job was well done by the committee and its sponsors were pleased.

   _____

10. The blossoming of the fruit trees was making the entire neighborhood smell wonderful.

_____

EXERCISE 2G: MAKING WORDY SENTENCES SHORTER AND CLEARER

When possible, put the following sentences in actor-action sequence. Then replace general or cumbersome terms with more precise terms.

1. Conan Doyle is a writer of mystery stories and mystery novels who has created a detective named Sherlock Holmes who appears in all his detective stories.

_____

_____

_____

2. Many writers have created characters who turn up over and over again in their mystery stories where they are always a detective who solves the mystery.

_____

_____

_____

3. Some of the detectives who are the good guys and always figure things out so that they are able to solve the problems any detective like Sherlock Holmes and Hercule Poirot and Inspector Morse.

_____

_____

_____

4. Another thing that is always a feature of the detective stories which have the same detective in them is that the detective always has a pal who is a stooge.

_____

_____

_____

5. This pal always has a title, like Dr. Watson or Captain Hastings or Sergeant Lewis, that shows he's important but he doesn't know much because the detective who solves the problem has to explain everything to him.

_____

_____

_____

6. Sergeant Lewis is smarter than the others which is a good thing for otherwise he'd be fired or else retired like Dr. Watson and Captain Hastings who really don't have anything to do.

_____

_____

_____

7. Dr. Watson is supposed to be a working doctor because he says once in a while he must see a patient, but he forgets them when Holmes has a case to solve.

_____

_____

_____

8. These three detectives don't seem to have any interest in women or really any life of their own at all except what happens when they are working on a case.

_____

_____

_____

9. They do have certain strange odd manners or habits like Sherlock playing the violin and Poirot drinking his tea and fiddling with his mustache and Morse listening to classical music.

_____

_____

_____

10. Although I like the books that have been written about them, I like even better to see the television programs that they are on.

_____

_____

_____

✓ Replacing Weak Verbs

The most common weak and imprecise verbs are the *be* verbs: *is, was, were, have been,* and so forth. For example:

The impurities *are in excess of* EPA standards.

Note the italicized words, *are in excess of*. Which word in that group could serve as a new verb to replace *are*? If we replace *are in excess of* with one word, *exceed*, we have made the sentence clearer and less wordy.

These impurities *exceed* EPA standards.

Here is another example:

The fifth chapter *is an explanation of* Henry George's economic theory.

Here again, it is not difficult to find a new verb to replace *is*. Just look at the phrase *an explanation of*.

The fifth chapter *explains* Henry George's economic theory.

To replace the generally weak and wordy *be* forms, look for another word in the sentence to serve as an active verb.

Weak: The claim of the investigator *is* that the cargo door flew open.

Strong: The investigator *claims* that the cargo door flew open.

Using other weak verbs, such as *provide, make, use, serve,* and *give,* usually weakens your writing. Wherever possible, replace these weak verbs with verbs that show action.

Example: Paddle fans provide gentle circulation of air.
Improved: Paddle fans gently circulate the air.

Example: This type of heating and cooling system makes fewer demands on energy.
Improved: This type of heating and cooling system demands less energy.

Example: A heat pump is used for heating and cooling the house.
Improved: A heat pump both heats and cools the house.

Note that these revisions cut down the number of words. As a result, every word works harder and the meaning of the sentence stands out more clearly.

EXERCISE 2H: REPLACING WEAK VERBS

1. These alumni give many gifts to the college of which they are graduates.

   _____

2. The parents always had an excuse for their son's bad grades.

   _____

3. His teachers, they say, never take into consideration the fact that he is a very delicate child.

   _____

4. When he wrote about the play, the dramatic critic said in his review that he was of the opinion that the play was too long.

_____

5. The instructor tells us in his lectures the same things we have already read in our textbooks.

_____

6. The word processor provides an easy way to make changes in your writing to make it better.

_____

7. The students who are already in our school are helpful to new students.

_____

8. There is a belief by some members of the tribe that it may cause you harm or even kill you to have your photograph taken.

_____

9. I feel that cramming for exams doesn't really help you very much unless the exam is taken right away.

_____

10. The request is made for a worthy cause and by respectable citizens.

_____

chapter *3*

Describing

The ability to describe is a valuable skill that helps to make writing more effective:

> Description can **communicate** the thoughts and emotions of the writer to the reader.
>
> Description can **explain** technical equipment and technical processes.
>
> Description can **enliven and strengthen** other forms of paragraph development, especially narration.

In addition to special needs in writing, description also plays an important role in everyday communication. Few of us can make it through the day without describing something—an exam, a romantic date, an incident at work, the weather, a child's behavior, a new pet. In this chapter, you will learn some effective techniques for describing that will improve your writing.

In the following paragraph, Frank Norris describes the southwestern town of Guadalajara at the turn of the century to give his readers a sense of place and time. Although this paragraph is pure description, he uses it to set the stage for the narrative of his novel.

> It was high noon, and the rays of the sun, that hung poised directly overhead in an intolerable white glory, fell straight as plummets upon the roofs and streets of Guadalajara. The adobe walls and sparse brick sidewalks of the

drowsing town radiated the heat in an oily, quivering shimmer. The leaves of the eucalyptus trees around the Plaza drooped motionless, limp and relaxed under the scorching, searching blaze. The shadows of these trees had shrunk to their smallest circumference, contracting close about the trunks. The shade had dwindled to the breadth of a mere line. The sun was everywhere. The heat exhaling from brick and plaster and metal met the heat that steadily descended blanket-wise and smothering, from the pale, scorched sky. Only the lizards—they lived in chinks of the crumbling adobe and in interstices of the sidewalk—remained without, motionless, as if stuffed, their eyes closed to mere slits, basking, stupefied with heat. At long intervals the prolonged drone of an insect developed out of the silence, vibrated a moment in a soothing, somnolent, long note, then trailed slowly into the quiet again. Somewhere in the interior of one of the 'dobe houses a guitar snored and hummed sleepily. On the roof of the hotel a group of pigeons cooed incessantly with subdued, liquid murmurs, very plaintive; a cat, perfectly white, with a pink nose and thin pink lips, dozed complacently on a fence rail, full in the sun. In a corner of the Plaza three hens wallowed in the baking hot dust, their wings fluttering, clucking comfortably. And this was all.

Frank Norris, *The Epic of the Wheat*

The following paragraph describes the writer's loved and laughed-at father who does a homely chore with his own particular flair.

When I was still living with my parents, my father and I customarily washed the dinner dishes—unless my mother dissuaded him because we had eaten from the "good" dishes. The "good" dishes were old and beloved and fragile. With the "good" dishes, my father, lost in his own exuberant conversation, might absentmindedly dry the handles right off the cups. But most nights he and I did the dishes. One of his customs was to spread newspapers on the kitchen floor and collect the trash on them. Now, as all dedicated readers know, any printed thing is to be read. (One of my own dogs once bit me because, in a distrait moment, I was reading the dog bone box before I fed her.) Therefore, as he tidied up the kitchen, my father would read a snatch or two to me and if he found it really interesting, he would shout such snatches to my mother in the living room. He usually prefaced his readings with, "I see by the garbage, . . ." He did a lot of reading that way. The Disposall is much more efficient, but it lacks the charm of my father's dramatic productions from the garbage.

OBJECTIVE VS. SUBJECTIVE DESCRIPTION

Objective Description

is literal and outwardly focused.

is impersonal and detached.

tells readers what something looks like, what it does, how it works.

focuses on the object being described rather than the observer's personal perceptions.

Technical writing uses **objective description** almost exclusively.

✓ Subjective Description

is personal and introspective.

conveys opinion, attitude, and empathy.

TOPIC SENTENCE FOR DEVELOPMENT BY SUBJECTIVE DESCRIPTION

The following student paragraph is a **subjective description** of his teacher's office. Note that this writer began his paragraph with some introductory background details. His topic sentence (subject + attitude) is actually the fourth sentence in the paragraph:

Last week in English class, we studied the art of description. Then each member of the class had to go to a room on campus and record the most significant descriptive details about the room, those details that conveyed the central impression of the room. I chose my English professor's office, and boy, did I have fun! **After observing the room ["my English professor's office"] for only a few seconds, I had no trouble arriving at a clear central impression: what I saw could best be described as *an organized mess.*** The first thing I noticed after entering the room was that her office was no bigger than an overgrown closet, so her desk just kind of jumps out at you. There was a huge stack of blank videotapes piled on the left-hand side of the desk because there was no room for anything on the bookshelf. It was overflowing with miscellaneous stacks of papers that even God couldn't sort out, and every other inch of possible space was filled with documentary videos she uses in class, Native American artifacts, cards from friends and students, Kleenex, fruit, trinkets, coffee mugs, and books of all sorts: writing texts, history books, dictionaries, biographies, educational reports, sociology texts, essay collections, and American Indian anthologies. The workplace on her desktop had a calendar filled with notations that she had obviously written in a hurry: birthdays, meetings, class assignment deadlines, etc., and her filing cabinet was dotted with family photos and a message from Albert Einstein: *"Excellent ideas have always encountered violent opposition from mediocre minds."* To the right of her desk sat another small desk with an old Selectric typewriter on top, followed by another stuffed bookshelf that hugged the adjacent wall. Then stacked and thrown in the corner were seven or eight cardboard boxes, making the limited space even more cramped. Her bulletin board was like none I have ever seen. It was more like a time capsule than a bulletin board, complete with cartoons, department memos, and progressive years of class syllabi going back at least three years. It was as if nothing was ever taken off of that bulletin board unless gravity was kind and pulled it to the floor. And I noticed one more thing before I left: although my English professor puts her health food in plain view, her trash can was half full of fast food from McDonald's and in the top left drawer of her desk lies a stash of junk food hidden to all but her. I decided that after this discovery, I would stop before I got into trouble.

Chris Hoffman

Notice the differences between an objective and a subjective description of the same machine:

Objective: The Franklin 120 videotape machine is an autofocus camera encased in tempered steel and lightweight aluminum. It is equipped with a black and white cathode-ray-tube optical viewfinder, a solid-state image detector, and two omnidirectional mikes. It also has a 4-inch single-speed power zoom and a 2-1/2 inch adjustable eyepiece focus.

Subjective: The new Franklin videotape machine is an intimidating piece of equipment that looks more like a space weapon than a movie camera. If someone pointed it at me, I would be too terrified to smile.

Remember: It is important to be specific in both objective and subjective description. Referring to an optical viewfinder as "a little shiny contraption" or "that funny-shaped thing on the back of the camera" does not help readers to form a mental picture of the object.

ASSIGNMENT

Your primary assignment for this chapter is to write a paragraph that subjectively describes a person or a location or an object.

A PERSON (OR A PET)

Describe someone who has made a distinct impression on you.

Begin with a topic sentence that gives the reader a central impression of that person.

The body should include descriptive details about physical characteristics, behavior or mannerisms, and attitudes.

All details in the body should relate to your central impression of that person.

Your conclusion should also reinforce the central impression.

A LOCATION

Describe a place that leaves you with a sense of sadness, joy, loneliness, contentment, or some other distinct feeling.

Begin with a topic sentence that conveys the mood or central impression that the location holds for you.

Be sure that all descriptive details in the body contribute to this mood or central impression.

Finally, your conclusion should also reinforce the central impression, your overall emotional response to that location.

AN OBJECT

Describe an object, using subjective details and observations to complement any details of physical description.

Choose an object that you can respond to emotionally, such as your first car, a favorite childhood toy, a hideaway you played in, a house or cottage, a prized possession, heirloom, or collectible.

Begin with a topic sentence that conveys a meaning or central impression that the object holds for you.

Be sure to relate all observations in the body to your central impression.

Focus on *subjective* descriptive details; don't lapse into purely objective description.

> ***Example:*** The fire-gutted old warehouse loomed against the glare of the stormy sunset.

Your conclusion should re-echo the central impression, which conveys the special meaning that object has for you.

HOW TO WRITE A DESCRIPTIVE PARAGRAPH

1. Use *all* of your senses to observe descriptive details about the person, place, or thing you are describing.
2. Ask yourself specific questions, such as "What do I see?" "What do I hear?" "What do I smell?" to help you focus on important details.
3. Record all of these details in your notebook.
4. Examine your details and see what kind of central impression emerges from your observations.
5. State this central impression in an interesting topic sentence.
6. Choose those descriptive details that most clearly convey your central impression (eliminating irrelevant details) and arrange these details effectively in the body of your paragraph.
7. Add a concluding sentence that permanently fixes the central impression in your reader's mind.

✓ Describing Through the Senses

Good subjective description allows the reader to experience the same emotional and sensory responses that you have felt. To create a clear, vivid picture for the reader, use language that allows him or her to share your feelings and to see, hear, taste, smell, or touch, as if the reader were in your head and in your shoes. **Words can convey and enhance sensory perceptions:**

> Bells *"clang."*
>
> Unseasoned potatoes taste *"bland."*
>
> Old milk smells *"sour."*
>
> A dog's tongue is smooth—it *"slurps,"*—but a cat's tongue is rough—it *"scrapes."*
>
> My poison ivy *"itched"* so incessantly that I felt like hacking off my arm.
>
> Julia Roberts' (or Richard Gere's) performance in *Pretty Woman* activated every pleasure producing hormone in me.

Don't just tell the reader—*Show her!* Think of your reader's imagination as an empty VCR player and your paragraph as a full cassette. Once you load the VCR and push "Play," you and your reader become one until the end of the tape.

OBSERVE YOUR SUBJECT ACCURATELY

1. *Focus on your subject,* just as a photographer would do to capture birds in flight, children at play, a glamorous fashion model on a runway, or an old man sleeping on a park bench.

Get your subject into focus and limit your description.

2. *Limit or narrow your description of the subject in terms of time, place, spatial perspective, and point of view.*

Time—*when* your observations occurred
    Considerations: Time of day?
                       Time of year?
                       Over an extended period of time?

Place—*where* your observations occurred
    Considerations: Inside?
                       Outside?
                       At a specific location?

Spatial perspective—the *visual* and *distance orientation* toward your subject
    Considerations: A total view?
                       Emphasis on specific details?
                       The whole subject, then "zooming in" to a specific feature?

Point of view—the *approach* or *attitude* that you adopt toward the subject
    Considerations: Favorable?
                       Unfavorable?
                       Fair?
                       Biased?

3. *Formulate responses to your subject.* After you have focused, limited, and narrowed your subject, list your original responses to the subject as quickly as they come into your mind.

Now you are ready to write your descriptive paragraph using the three-part structure: beginning, middle, and end.

✏️ ORGANIZATION

✓ Topic Sentence

All of the descriptive details that you have assembled should point toward a *central impression,* which will form the nucleus of your topic sentence. For example, if you are describing a person, carefully select descriptive details to form a central impression of that person (central impression = controlling idea). After using your senses to gather impressions about a person, ask yourself:

What can I say about this person after observing all these details?

Does the person appear to be a rigid, conservative soul or an independent, free spirit?

Does his or her appearance project a feeling of warmth and compassion or a feeling of coldness and insensitivity?

Certain details will create impressions. For example, the following description of George Washington as a young man creates a definite impression. After observing Washington, a fellow Virginia officeholder recorded these details:

> Straight as an Indian, measuring 6 feet 2 inches in his stockings, and weighing 175 pounds
>
> Well-developed muscles, indicating great strength
>
> A well-shaped head, gracefully poised on a superb neck
>
> Blue-gray, penetrating eyes overhung by a heavy brow
>
> A face that terminates in a good, firm chin
>
> A pleasing and benevolent though a commanding countenance, regular and placid features with all the muscles of his face under perfect control, though flexible and expressive of deep feeling when moved by emotion
>
> Deliberate and engaging in conversation, looks you full in the face
>
> Graceful movements, a majestic walk

Henry Bragdon, "George Washington:
Monument or Man?"
American History Illustrated

These descriptive details lead to a central impression—that of a strong, calm, dignified man. The observer concluded that Washington's demeanor, his outward appearance, was "at all times composed and dignified." If this observer had been writing a descriptive paragraph about Washington, this central impression would have formed the basis of this topic sentence:

> George Washington was a dignified-looking young man.
>
> *or*
>
> George Washington's appearance as a young man projected an aura of composure and dignity.
>
> *or*
>
> George Washington's appearance projected all the attributes of a born leader.

Note, however, that topic sentences such as

> George Washington was a *good* man.
>
> *or*
>
> I have a *positive impression* of George Washington.

would *not* be good topic sentences because they are vague. Your topic sentence must present a clear, specific central impression.

Now contrast the descriptive details about Washington with those about Captain Henri Wirz, commander of Andersonville, the South's most notorious military prison during the Civil War.

> An undersized, fidgety man with an insignificant face and a mouth that protruded like a rabbit's
>
> Bright little eyes, like those of a squirrel or rat, which assisted in giving his countenance a look of kinship to the family of rodents
>
> A little gray cap perched upon his head
>
> Stepped nervously about
>
> Gnat-brained and cowardly
>
> A snarling little temper
>
> Sputtered in very broken English

> John McElroy, *Andersonville: A Story
> of Rebel Military Prisons*

Based on these details, write a topic sentence that expresses a central impression about Captain Wirz on the following line:

_____

If you are describing a place or location, you also gather details from your senses to form one central impression—an atmosphere, a mood. What do you see or hear or smell? Where is it? Is it at the shore or in your backyard? Is it in a building? If so, what kind of building? What time of day is it, and what time of year?

Details create the atmosphere, the central impression. For example, let's look at the descriptive details of two very dissimilar rooms.

One Room

Place: a living room
Where: an old farmhouse in the country
When: a cool evening in late autumn
Sights: soft, upholstered sofa and chairs in warm colors of rust, yellow, orange, and brown
a thick rust-colored tweed carpet
an old brick fireplace with a carved wooden mantel
an oak coffee table covered with a newspaper, a pipestand, and a child's coloring book
an old wicker basket filled with freshly picked flowers
a handmade quilt lying over the back of a rocking chair
antique paintings in wooden frames on the walls

Sounds: the laughter of children
            the crackling of burning logs
Smells: aroma of homemade bread baking in a nearby kitchen
            the scent of cherry logs burning in a fireplace

Another Room

Place: a living room
Where: a high-rise apartment building in a city
When: a rainy day in March
Sights: black and white shiny leather sofa and chairs
            white globe lamps with hard black plastic bases
            a gray tile floor with white shag rug in the center
            a glass coffee table with narrow steel legs
            a glass end table covered with an arrangement of silk flowers
            abstract prints on the wall in slim black metal frames
            a china closet filled with crystal and sterling silver
            nothing out of place
Sounds: rinse cycle of the automatic dishwasher in the kitchen
            outside traffic—beeping horns, screeching brakes
            the lonesome wail of an outbound steamship
Smells: a hint of expensive perfume
            a reminiscent whiff of floor wax

How do these two sets of details make you feel? What atmosphere or mood do they create?

Sum up the mood or atmosphere of each room in a central impression.

_____

_____

Write a topic sentence for each.

_____

_____

EXERCISE 3A: TOPIC SENTENCES FOR DESCRIPTION

Put a check mark in front of each sentence you think would make a good topic sentence for a descriptive paragraph. Rewrite the others to improve them as topic sentences.

_____   1. All the time I was growing up, we lived in the last house on
                a dead-end street.

_____ 2. Although I haven't been in it since I first left for college, I still lovingly remember every detail of my old home on Harbaugh Street.

_____ 3. That Harbaugh Street house holds my fondest memories of my parents.

_____ 4. My cousin Charlie, who lived with us for a couple of years, is the kindest, most intelligent man I know.

_____ 5. In the house next door lived a series of three families whose children are still my good friends.

_____ 6. Stanley, Betty, and Mary Evelyn, and Jim were and are real pals.

_____ 7. I never really knew the people who lived across the street.

_____ 8. They were the Stanhopes and they were stiff and formal even though we'd been neighbors for years.

_____ 9. My mother, who believed that people felt more friendly if they did you a small favor, phoned them to ask to borrow a little salt.

_____ 10. They agreed, but when she went over to get it, carrying half a dozen freshly baked rolls, she found half a tin cup of salt outside the closed door.

✓ Body

The body of your descriptive paragraph supplies the details that support your topic sentence.

CHOOSING DESCRIPTIVE DETAILS

Choose only those descriptive details that *most clearly* convey your central impression and arrange them effectively in the body of your paragraph.

Choose *clear* and *specific* details

Choose *vivid* details that project visual imagery and evoke sensory responses

Which of these two sentences is more effective and why?

After I fell out of the raft and went under, I was sure that I would drown.

or

After being catapulted from the raft and sucked under, I tumbled end-over-end on the river bottom like a towel in a dryer. "What a stupid way to die," I thought, as the icy water numbed my consciousness.

In the following paragraph, the student writer uses language to evoke a sensory response from his readers. The locker room that he is describing doesn't have to be any one in particular, yet his choice of vivid, specific details makes the room real in our imaginations.

One of the most distinctive, and perhaps most easily recognizable, atmospheres is that of an athlete's locker room. As you enter, the unmistakable odor of perspiring bodies, damp leather, and dirty clothes hits you; it is a familiar one for the athlete, but sometimes unbearable for others. The room is usually large, dim, and long enough to be lined with rows of army-green lockers. The dryers hum in the background while the steam from the showers settles and penetrates every nook and cranny, making the floor and walls seem dripping wet. We bring our emotions into this sanctuary, away from prying eyes and ears, to release our joys and jubilation, disappointments and discouragements, and sometimes our tears. The language would make an English professor cringe, yet nothing could ever change it. It may sound offensive in many respects, but to an athlete it is part of his life that he cherishes and never forgets when those days are set aside for a different kind of life.

John Navage

In another student paragraph, the writer has selected details intended to develop sympathy for a caged gorilla that is forced to endure our world.

Seeing the gorilla at the zoo was a troubling experience. Protected by heavy iron bars, I stood with my group of kindergartners, over whom I had been affectionately appointed homeroom mother, and stared open-mouthed at the huge beast. Inside his bleak, narrow cage, the wheezing ape ruled over one fake rock and a worn-out tire. This tire he lugged intermittently from spot to spot to rest on. Hunched on his treadless throne, he clutched at his shiny, black cheeks as he peered cautiously at the amazed faces of his child visitors. As my own bulging eyes wandered from the metal sign on the cage, which warned, "Dangerous Animal—Do Not Feed," to the darting eyes of this miniature King Kong, I wondered if he was as much in awe of me as I was of him. Several hoodlums from another group of visitors shouted, "You're ugly" and "You stink." Ignoring their ugliness, I could not help feeling a little motherly sympathy for this innocent alien in his hot fur jumpsuit. His gargantuan appearance was frightening, but his guileless expression was as lovable as those on the faces of my hypnotized six-year-olds.

Connie Susich

Read the following passage from *Cannery Row* carefully. Notice how well American author John Steinbeck uses image-making language to create clear, vivid pictures. Underline the words and phrases that make you feel that you can almost reach out and touch the various creatures.

Doc was collecting marine animals in the Great Tide Pool on the tip of the Peninsula. It is a fabulous place: when the tide is in, a wave-churned basin, creamy with foam. . . . But when the tide goes out, the little water world becomes quiet and lovely. The sea is very clear and the bottom becomes fantastic with hurrying, fighting, feeding, breeding animals. . . . Starfish squat over mussels, and limpets attach their million little suckers and then slowly lift with incredible power until the prey is broken from the rock. And then the starfish stomach comes out and envelops its food. Orange and speckled and fluted nudibranchs slide gracefully over the rocks, their skirts waving like the dresses of the Spanish dancers. And black eels poke their heads out of crevices and wait for prey. . . . Hermit crabs like frantic children scamper on the bottom sand. . . . Here a crab tears a leg from his brother. The anemones expand like soft and brilliant flowers. . . .

Then the creeping murderer, the octopus, steals out, slowly, softly, moving like a gray mist, pretending now to be a bit of a weed, now a rock, now a lump of decaying meat while its evil goat eyes watch coldly. It oozes and flows toward a feeding crab, and as it comes close its yellow eyes burn and its body turns rosy with pulsing color and anticipation and rage. Then suddenly it runs lightly on the tips of its arms, as ferociously as a charging cat. It leaps savagely on the crab, there is a puff of black fluid, and the struggling mass is obscured in the sepia cloud while the octopus murders the crab. . . . And down to the rocks come the black flies to eat anything they can find . . . the smells of life and richness, of death and digestion, of decay and birth burden the air. And salt spray blows in from the barrier where the ocean waits for its rising-tide strength to permit it back into the Great Tide Pool again. And on the reef the whistling buoy bellows like a sad and patient bull.

John Steinbeck, *Cannery Row*

Note: Sometimes fiction writers modify the rules of punctuation in order to achieve certain effects. We recommend that you follow established rules of punctuation for your assignments in this text.

EXERCISE 3B: USING SPECIFIC AND DESCRIPTIVE DETAILS

Rewrite each of the following sentences in specific descriptive terms to create a vivid mental picture.

1. That movie was a real scream.

   _____

   _____

   _____

2. Her do was a fun thing.

   _____

   _____

   _____

3. The garage is jammed with stuff.

   _____

   _____

   _____

4. The whole joint is an awful mess.

   _____

   _____

   _____

5. She ought to redo everything.

   _____

   _____

   _____

✓ Ordering Details

Once you have chosen the best details to support your central impression, you must arrange them in a logical order. Whether your paragraph describes a person, a place, or an object, you cannot list details at random. There must be a sensible pattern of progression.

When you, the writer, observe something firsthand, you see a picture of the whole thing. The order in which you think about its different parts or effects doesn't really matter. Your reader, however, cannot visualize the whole as you did. Therefore, you must provide a pattern into which your reader can logically fit the details and re-create the whole in his or her own imagination.

✓ Patterns of Organization

1. Spatial arrangement

> Arrangement of details in a predictable sequence that the eye can easily follow.
>
> The main pattern for descriptive writing.

Your location in relation to what you are describing can help you to arrange details effectively.

From a fixed position:

You can sweep around a room.

You can scan an object from top to bottom.

You can examine someone from head to toe.

You can observe a landscape from the horizon to where you are standing.

You can choose a particular characteristic and extend your pattern of details outward from it.

While in motion:

You can relate your impressions as objects come into view.

You can describe something as you travel past it.

You can describe something while walking around it.

2. Chronological order

> Arrangement according to time sequence.
>
> Used primarily for narration and explaining processes.

3. Order of importance

> Arrangement according to degree of importance.
>
> Movement from the least to most important details is the most effective sequence.

Note: Although spatial order is more prevalent in descriptive writing, chronological order and order of importance are also used in some descriptive situations.

In the following paragraph, observe how the writer has positioned his subjects. What special patterns of orientation and movement are evident as we observe one subject through the eyes of another?

T.A. Slade's appearance and demeanor radiated the casual self-assurance of a man completely satisfied with himself and in harmony with his world. As I noticed him striding my way across campus, showing moves that only John Wayne could match, I felt the draw of his imposing, solitary presence. Shoulder length black hair, flint green eyes, bare arms, bronzed and tattooed, broadcasted "lean and mean," but I knew the *real* Slade. The whole package was held together with a leather thong headband, a tight black leather vest (very open at the chest), and extra tight vintage Levis poured over chewed up heavy duty cycle boots. As soon as he spotted me—it didn't matter how far away he was—a knowing grin slowly spread across his weathered, pock-marked face. A sizable flash of gold indicated that he was not into cheap or fashionable dental work. As he sauntered into earshot, the usual "Hey man, what's goin' down?" rasped through the air. Soon, I was lost in a Camel cloud, offset by whiffs of Old Spice, one of Slade's few concessions to social propriety. Tossing his head to keep unruly hair out of his face, along with a sly wink, signaled that I would soon hear about the latest coed who had tested his restraint. If it wasn't about women, it was usually a salvo launched at his "demented" English teacher for "trashing" his latest poem, or perhaps a rhapsody on his aging Harley. No one else could tell it quite like Slade, and he relished spreading the word as much as I did getting it. Finally, his diatribe concluded, he ambled past me down the walk seeking other disciples to inspire. His usual "adios," a quick "solidarity" gesture into the afternoon sky, ended our short encounter. Turning to watch this prince of enchanters disappear through an archway, I reluctantly shook off the spell he had cast and headed for my car.

EXERCISE 3C: USING LOGICAL ORDER FOR DESCRIPTION

Rearrange the following details to make sense of what a young child might feel about a disruption in his family. Put the numbers of the sentences in the correct sequence on the line below.

1. However, as far as I was concerned, my mother and I were a complete and whole unit.
2. What was wrong with my mother?
3. In addition, there were lots of kids—lots and lots of kids—for those times my mother and I wanted to play.

4. When I was a little kid, during the Korean War, I scarcely knew I had a father.
5. My mother trotted across the lawn to protect me, I assumed.
6. But one day, out of the blue, a terrible thing happened.
7. There were no fathers there.
8. She had never cried when she kissed me.
9. My mother and I lived in a community of mothers and kids.
10. To my shocked surprise, my mother hugged that man and kissed him and cried.
11. A man rushed up our walk, a lean and sun-burned man.

✓ Conclusion

Effective description provides details that form a central impression—a feeling or effect that you want your reader to share with you. The conclusion of a descriptive paragraph should be

> A detail of observation that permanently fixes the central impression in the reader's imagination.
>
> A final opportunity to leave a desired effect on your reader.

In the following paragraph, this student writer concludes by drawing his details together to provide a final unifying impression.

> **The fall season signals a coming of happier times for the lovers of winter and its associated activities. However, to me it appears as the end of a more pleasant climate, with no more gathering of family and friends for summer picnics, and the long wait for the cycle to begin again.** Gazing from the kitchen window, I can see the towering locust trees, their foliage now colored halfway between a dull green and brown. The leaves, aided by a gentle breeze, make a slow fluttering descent to the ground, and the rich, strong, acrid smell of burning leaves hangs in the air. The lawn, pockmarked by patches of dead grass caused by the heat and dryness of the past several months, now tries to make a recovery in growth but seems almost passive in its attempt and ready for a period of dormancy. The flower gardens, now in their faded glory, have lost much of the splendor of spring and summer. They wish only for someone to rescue the fittest of the species for survival indoors. A few neighbors, after hearing the forecast of possible frost in our area, scurry about to bring their prize plants indoors and leave the remainder outside for "nature" to deal with. Autumn, to me, is a solemn time of the year. Yes, it is here again and almost time to find a good book, a relaxing chair, turn up the thermostat, and wait.

Harvey Estep

✓ Some Do's . . .

1. *Do* make use of *all* of your senses to observe. Use your sense of touch, smell, taste, and sound, as well as your sense of sight.
2. *Do* make sure that your central impression is clear. Use *specific* words to state your controlling idea.
3. *Do* limit your description of a place in terms of time of day and season of the year. Get your subject into focus before you start describing.
4. *Do* choose your words with care. Use words and phrases that convey sharp, descriptive images, and remember that you can create vivid images with many kinds of words, not just adjectives and adverbs.

✓ . . . and Don'ts About Describing

1. *Don't* describe a person by simply compiling a list of his or her physical characteristics. Clarify your central impression of the person and then develop that central impression with clear, descriptive details.
2. *Don't* rely on just a few descriptive details to convey your central impression. Make sure that you have provided enough details so that your reader can actually see what you see and feel what you feel.
3. *Don't* confuse objective description with subjective description. Remember that in objective description (technical writing, for example), the object being described is more important than your perception of that object.

SUGGESTED ACTIVITIES AND ASSIGNMENTS

1. Choose a well-known place on campus—cafeteria, library, gymnasium—and have the students provide sensory details of the area. Put these on the board. Encourage the students to include details of sound, smell, taste, and touch as well as sight. The teacher should write headings on the board: What Do I See? What Do I Hear? What Do I Smell? What Do I Feel? What Do I Taste? When enough details are listed, have the class select a central impression.
2. Divide the class into two groups of equal number (if the groups are unequal, the teacher may take part or may pull a student out to help as a judge). Have each group turn its desks to face an opposite wall. Give each group a simple drawing. Being careful not to let the other group see its drawing, each group should write directions on how to draw the figure. Then the groups will exchange their directions and attempt to draw the figure as directed. This is a sure test of the value of the directions.
3. One good way of developing your descriptive skills is to sharpen your senses. Choose an item to observe (a flower, a banana, a leaf, a piece of

pizza) and watch that object change over a period of time (5–7 days). Observe it closely every night and record your observations. Be alert for even the most minute change in color, texture, and smell, and notice how these changes affect the overall appearance (and thus your central impression) of the object.

4. Reread the section in Chapter 2 on Finding Your Voice and then try to apply that principle to description. Description, as you know, is seldom written to stand on its own but is usually a complement to other modes of writing. Thus it is usually brief. Recall some sensory experience of your own—it need not be visual—and let your memory speak. For instance:

> When my baby was about three months old, he got a nasty, bumpy rash. I was assured that it wasn't serious and would go away soon, but I still felt awful. Putting him to bed one evening, I realized that he was totally covered with those red bumps except for his feet. I stood leaning over his crib, feeling one little foot in each hand. "He's got satin feet," I said to myself over and over. "He's still got satin feet."

5. Choose an object from your home or your workplace and write a technical description of that object. Focus only on what you see. Then think about how the object makes you feel and write a subjective description of the object (an appliance, a photograph, an office machine, a piece of furniture).

SENTENCES

In any writing you do, you want the ideas to flow smoothly, the relationships between the ideas to be clear, and the relative importance of each idea to be apparent. To accomplish these goals, you combine sentences into independent and dependent clauses and connect them in such a way that the reader can follow your line of thought easily.

In your descriptive paragraph, there is movement—you are describing someone or something from top to bottom, from left to right, from far to near, or by some other pattern. By combining your sentences carefully and correctly, you can take your reader with you.

The Independent Clause

The **independent clause** contains the main idea of the sentence; it can stand alone. That is, an independent clause is a simple sentence. For example:

John studied his English last night.

This sentence makes sense because it gives you a clear and complete statement of John's doing something. Any independent clause can be a sentence.

Sally lost her comb.

The pitcher dropped the ball.

I like beer.

✓ The Dependent Clause

The **dependent clause** contains an idea of secondary importance and does not express a complete thought. Frequently the dependent clause begins with a word that warns you that the clause cannot stand alone. For example, if someone says to you, "Because he had a test today," you would wait to hear the rest of the sentence. A dependent clause *depends* on an independent clause to make sense.

John studied his English last night *because he had a test today.*

When you join a dependent clause to an independent clause, the relationship of the two ideas is clear. This type of joining is called **subordination.** You can even join them in reverse order. When you put the dependent clause *before* the independent clause, you usually separate them with a comma.

Because he had a test today, John studied his English last night.

Remember: A dependent clause cannot stand alone. It can only be used to help an independent clause. The independent clause contains the main idea. The dependent clause helps to explain the main idea or adds information to it.

✓ Coordination

Sometimes a sentence is made up of two or more independent clauses, and a dependent clause is not used.

I jogged down the road, *and* Sue followed on her bike.

The process of joining independent clauses is called **coordination.** Words used to link independent clauses are called **coordinating conjunctions.** You should memorize them.

and   but   or   for   nor   yet   so

If you use one of these words to join two independent clauses, a comma should go in front of it:

(independent clause), *and* (independent clause)

CONNECTING CLAUSES EFFECTIVELY

To Connect Two Main Ideas:

Use a COORDINATE CONJUNCTION

I liked the book, *but* I hated the movie.

Use a CONJUNCTIVE ADVERB

The actors were inexperienced; *furthermore,* they were clearly miscast.

To Connect a Main Idea with a Subordinate Idea:

Use a SUBORDINATE CONJUNCTION

The director could have made a far better film *if* he had read the book.

or

If the director had read the book, he could have made a far better film.

Remember that coordination gives the same rank or level of importance to each of the independent clauses. Joining independent clauses with *and, but, or, for, nor, yet,* or *so* implies *equality in value and emphasis.* Coordination is the right structure or grammatical form only when the two ideas expressed in the clauses are relatively equal in importance.

Bill joined the army, but Sam joined the navy.
Thunder filled the air, and black clouds rolled across the sky.

You must also select the right coordinator.

and—To indicate an additional fact of equal importance

Mary washed the dishes, *and* Tom made the salad.

but—To indicate an exception, qualification, or reversal

I love the music, *but* I can't dance.

for—To indicate an explanation of the first clause

> She refused to testify, *for* she was terrified of the defendant.

or—To indicate an alternative to the first clause

> Jack can return to school, *or* he can go to work.

yet—To indicate an exception, qualification, or change

> He said he had no money, *yet* he went to Florida last week.

nor—To carry over a negative idea from the first clause

> The money was never received, *nor* was the monument ever built.

so—To indicate a result of the statement made in the first clause

> I studied all night, *so* I was ready for the test.

FAULTY COORDINATION

Most faulty coordination results from the misuse of **and.** *And* should not be used if another coordinating conjunction shows the relationship better.

> *Faulty:* She had little formal art training, *and* she managed to become successful as an artist.
>
> *Improved:* She had little formal art training, *yet* she managed to become successful as an artist.

Another misuse of *and* is in connecting two ideas that are not of equal value or importance. If the ideas are unequal, you must use *subordination.*

> *Faulty:* The field had just been plowed, and John soon found a perfectly preserved arrowhead.
>
> *Improved:* Because the field had just been plowed, John soon found a perfectly preserved arrowhead.

✓ Conjunctive Adverbs

Independent clauses can also be connected with **conjunctive adverbs.** Conjunctive adverbs are used primarily to show special relationships other than those expressed by a simple *and* or *but.* **Be sure to choose the right**

conjunctive adverb to show the relationship that you intend. Here are commonly used conjunctive adverbs to suit various purposes.

Purpose	Use	Example
To show time:	*afterward* *later* *finally* *meanwhile* *then* *at the time* *soon* *now* *next* *thereafter* *last*	Jimmy smashed in the grill of his dad's car; afterward, he did a lot of hitchhiking.
To show addition:	*in addition* *furthermore* *moreover* *besides* *again* *too*	The cost of building an atomic power plant is enormous; furthermore, we still haven't solved the problem of disposing of atomic waste.
To show reason, result, or conclusion:	*thus* *consequently* *therefore* *surely* *in fact* *as a result*	All indications pointed toward his defeat; consequently, he withdrew from the race.
To show condition, qualification, or alternation:	*otherwise* *still* *anyhow* *however* *nevertheless* *instead*	She appeared to have little chance of getting the job; nevertheless, she was determined to apply.
To show comparison or contrast:	*similarly* *likewise* *conversely* *still* *however* *on the other hand*	Your investment could prove profitable; on the other hand, you could lose every cent.
To indicate an illustration or example:	*for example* *for instance*	Many of the inventions that have altered our daily lives have come from the laboratories of giant corporations; for example, Bell Laboratory scientists have received more than 19,000 patents.

✓ Subordination

Subordination enables you to arrange your ideas in terms of value and emphasis. Whereas coordination links the two clauses on the same level of importance and emphasis, subordination enables you to make clear other relationships between the clauses, such as *when, where, why, how,* or *under what conditions.*

The words introducing the dependent clauses and indicating the relationship between clauses are called **subordinating conjunctions.**

> *Whenever* the cowboys came into town, there was sure to be a brawl. (when)
>
> *Wherever* Mary goes, you can be sure to find Jack with her. (where)
>
> *Because* he was almost broke, he decided to stay home. (why)
>
> *As if* he hadn't a care in the world, Jack kept right on spending his money foolishly. (how)
>
> *Although* he was dead tired, he got up and dressed quickly. (under what conditions)

The part of the sentence beginning with the subordinate conjunction is a dependent clause. "Although he was dead tired" is not a complete thought; by itself, it would be only a sentence fragment. The part of the sentence that gets the most emphasis is the complete thought, "he got up and dressed quickly."

In the following two sentences, the main (independent) clause, italicized, expresses the main idea; the subordinate (dependent) clause expresses an idea of lesser importance. Which of the two versions is correct? The answer depends on what the writer intends to emphasize. The first version puts the emphasis on the California earthquake, a major disaster. The second sentence, on the other hand, puts the emphasis on a bit of personal information. Which is empathized depends on what the writer wants. Obviously, the earthquake is of more general importance, yet it may be correctly put in the subordinate clause if the writer wishes to emphasize a personal fact.

> When I was taking my nursing exams, *the California earthquake struck.*
>
> When the California earthquake struck, *I was taking my nursing exams.*

Note: When a subordinate clause precedes a main clause, put a comma after the subordinate clause.

FAULTY SUBORDINATION

Faulty subordination occurs when we can't decide which idea is more important. If the more important idea is misplaced by being put in the subordinate clause, the meaning of the sentence is distorted.

Faulty: As I witnessed the bank robbery, I waited for Joe Fritz to make a phone call to an old girlfriend.

Correct emphasis: As I waited for Joe Fritz to make a phone call to an old girlfriend, I witnessed the bank robbery.

Do not overload a sentence with too many subordinate clauses.

Overloaded: Big cars like the Cadillac Fleetwood and the Lincoln Town Car which were very popular in the 70's and 80's that were rear wheel drive and which were "gas-guzzlers" were what senior citizens liked because of their spacious, comfortable interiors.

Revised: Big rear wheel drive "gas-guzzling" cars of the 70's and 80's, such as the Cadillac Fleetwood and the Lincoln Town Car, were very popular with senior citizens who preferred their spacious, comfortable interiors.

THE SUBORDINATE CONJUNCTION

COMMONLY USED SUBORDINATE CONJUNCTIONS

after	even though	since	whatever	which
although	how	so that	when	whichever
as	if	that	whenever	while
as far as	in order that	though	where	who
as if	just as	till	whereas	whoever
as long as	now that	unless	whereby	whom
as soon as	once	until	wherever	whomever
because	once that	what	whether	why
before	provided that			

All these words are subordinate conjunctions, but they can also be used as other parts of speech. (In the sentence "I left *before* the dance," *before* is a preposition.) They are subordinate conjunctions only when they introduce a subordinate clause and show its relationship to the independent clause.

To show the precise relationship between the subordinate clause and the independent clause, you must choose the right subordinate conjunction.

Purpose	Use	Examples
To indicate time:	*before* *after* *since*	Since Bobby went away, Freda has been unhappy.
	when *while* *as* *just as* *as soon as* *as long as* *whenever*	When the teacher lectured, Frank took copious notes.
To indicate cause:	*because* *since* *so that* *in order that*	He practiced constantly so that he could make the team. Since the pool was contaminated, the swim party was canceled.
To indicate condition or concession:	*if* *though* *even though* *how* *although* *provided that* *whether* *even if* *unless* *as far as* *as long as*	Unless I get a raise in March, I'll quit. As long as Ron is in charge, his brother-in-law will get all the overtime.
To indicate manner:	*as if* *as though*	He acted as though he were the coach rather than the trainer. As if I didn't know better, I accepted the chairmanship.
To indicate place:	*where* *wherever*	I don't know where I left my textbook. Wherever Julie went, Charles was sure to follow.
To indicate contrast:	*whereas*	Whereas the other nations have agreed, France remains adamant. He is a prosperous attorney, whereas his brother is a criminal.

This list indicates only the general purpose of the common subordinate conjunctions. **The correct subordinate conjunction is the one that shows the logical relationship of your ideas as accurately as possible.** You must

8. A few minutes into the play my grandfather remarked to my grand-mother that some people might be frightened by it. After another few minutes the police siren sounded. From his house my grandfather could see the entrance to the police station. He looked out and saw dozens of people hurrying up the steps of the police station.

_____

_____

9. Dozens more were on the sidewalk. Some were gazing at the sky. Some were peering behind them. Mothers were carrying sleeping children. Older children were crying and clinging to their parents.

_____

_____

10. This scene of terror was repeated all over the country. Orson Welles had to interrupt his performance to assure people it was only a play. It was not true. Other radio stations helped by announcing that Mars was not attacking us. "The War of the Worlds" was never played again. Welles had thought it would be fun. Half his audience didn't see the joke.

_____

_____

WORDS

In your descriptive paragraph, you are attempting to *show* the reader what you saw or heard or felt. You cannot do this unless you are specific and concrete. The reader will not "see" what you are feeling if you say, "I feel bad." He may "see" and empathize with you if you say, "My head is pounding; my eyes feel like they're bulging out of my head; if I move I get dizzy; even my hair hurts."

The success of your paragraph depends on your organization and your sentences, which in turn depend on your selection of words. Part of the paragraph, primarily the topic sentence, depends on general ideas or concepts. General ideas must be expressed in general words—not so general that they are cloudy or vague, but they must be general enough that all your supporting details can fit under them.

General words stand for a whole classification or group of things. Words like *medications* are general, as are words like *trees* and *books* and *citizens*.

> Even a small hospital must stock many *medications.*
> *Trees* line both sides of the main street in my town.
> *Books* tumbled out of the shelves and spilled over the desk.
> The council called on all *citizens* for financial aid.

Yet, even when they are used in topic sentences, the words must be as specific as they can be to fit the meaning of the paragraph.

> *Maples* and *buckeyes* lined both sides . . .
> The council called on all *senior citizens* . . .

Once you have your general idea in mind, you then want to support it with more specific details.

> **General words** indicate classifications or broad categories of things, like *trees.*
>
> **Specific words** indicate individuals within that classification, like *elm, maple, pine, oak.* Of course, it is possible to become increasingly specific. There are Dutch elms and Chinese elms, sugar maples and Norway maples and red maples.
>
> **Abstract words** indicate ideas that are understood intellectually, like *color* or *noise.* Abstract words name qualities *(intelligence, patriotism),* concepts *(evolution, progress),* and conditions *(illness, poverty).*
>
> **Concrete words** are understood through the five senses of sight, sound, smell, taste, and touch because concrete words refer to things in the physical world like *orange* or a *peanut butter and jelly sandwich.*
>
> Her dress was *red* and *navy blue.* (sight)
> My skin felt *clammy.* (touch)
> The drum went *boomlay, boomlay, boom.* (sound)
> The pickle was *bitter.* (taste)
> The *stench* of uncollected garbage was overpowering. (smell)

✓ A Clear and Specific Modifier

For the precise and concise choice of words, three techniques have already been discussed:

> Choosing active verbs rather than passive verbs
> Choosing a clear and specific subject
> Choosing a clear and specific verb

A fourth technique is choosing clear and specific modifiers. A **modifier** is any word or group of words that changes the meaning of another word. It changes meaning by making more complete the picture given of the modified word.

The boy ran down the street.

There's no modifier for *boy*. Is he two years old or sixteen?

The *young* boy (or The *four-year-old* boy) ran down the street.

We now know more, but what does he look like?

The *red-headed four-year-old* boy ran . . .

The *freckled, red-headed, four-year-old boy* ran . . .

The *crying, freckled, red-headed, four-year-old boy* ran . . .

All the italicized words are modifiers acting on the word *boy,* so that the reader gets a more complete picture of him. Like subject and verb, modifiers must be as specific as you can make them.

Modifiers complete the picture.

✓ Adjectives and Adverbs

Differences Between Adjectives and Adverbs

ADJECTIVES: Words that describe nouns

my *devoted* husband (What kind of husband?)

numerous awards (How many awards?)

ADVERBS: Words that clarify verbs or modifiers

He yelled *frantically.* (How did he yell?)

a *remarkably* quiet child (How quiet?)

Modifiers fall into main groups: those that modify nouns and those that modify other parts of the sentence. Modifiers of nouns function as **adjectives.** Modifiers of other parts of the sentence function as **adverbs.** The following examples illustrate the confusion that arises when *adjectives* are not specific.

Mary is a *strange* child.

Does that mean that Mary is neurotic, unpredictable, old-fashioned, suspicious, quiet, isolated, frightened, or insecure?

Mr. Anderson is a *nice* man.

Does that mean that he is kind, warm, sincere, thoughtful, patient, or generous?

Senator Thompson is a *bad* politician.

Is the senator dishonest, incompetent, or unsuccessful?

Adverbs that are not specific are vague and confusing.

It was a *poorly* developed paragraph.

What is inadequately developed or illogically developed?

The money was *improperly* distributed.

Was the money distributed illegally, immorally, or haphazardly?

That magazine is published *periodically.*

Is it published weekly, monthly, or annually?

Nouns and verbs and adjectives and adverbs can all combine to add vivid descriptive detail.

Moonlight creeping silently between the shadows revealed a mossy staircase leading down to the river.

Once you have your general idea in mind, you then want to support it with specific details. It takes effort to write a good paragraph, but your choice of words—words that tell a tale, that draw a picture, that create emotions—will let you communicate successfully with your readers.

EXERCISE 3F: USING SPECIFIC AND CONCRETE TERMS

Occasionally you don't want to be specific. If you intend only to give your generalized feeling about a subject, you have no need for specifics. You might say, "He's a good man," or you might remark, "I sort of enjoy old movies."

Usually, however, you want to convey more than just a general attitude and so you need specific and concrete terms.

In the following exercise, make the italic terms more specific.

1. The *book* was *sort of blah.*

_____

_____

_____

2. The parents were *kind of good people.*

_____

_____

_____

3. Their *kids,* on the other hand, were a *real mess.*

_____

_____

_____

4. Joe *took part* in *all sports,* and he was particularly *good* in *some of them.*

_____

_____

_____

5. The *meal* and the *place* were *all right,* but it *was too far to go.*

_____

_____

_____

EXERCISE 3G: SELECTING VIVID WORDS

In the following paragraph, blanks are left unfilled. For each blank, there is a word list below the paragraph suggesting comparable terms. Although all the words would do, some are preferable to others. Choose the one you think suits best and tell why you think so.

All changes of seasons are welcome. We hail the (1) _____ of the new and only slightly regret the (2) _____ of the old. Perhaps, however, autumn seems to us most (3) _____. Today, at (4) _____ the sky brightened with a (5) _____ glow. Clouds, (6) _____ in the east, obscured the (7) _____ of the sun. A (8) _____ rooster (9) _____ morning. Rabbits, their families almost (10) _____, (11) _____ in the (12) _____. Squirrels, as usual, (13) _____ in the trees. Bird (14) _____ is muted to a (15) _____. But more than anything else, fall is (16) _____. Early morning frost is (17) _____, while frost in the evening is (18) _____. When the sun shines, the entire world is (19) _____. The air is (20) _____. The trees are (21) _____. Summer was wonderful and will be again, but now I'm refreshed and glad to avoid its (22) _____.

(1)	arrival	(2)	passing	(3)	satisfying
	coming		terminating		satisfactory
	occurring		elapsing		acceptable
	reaching		ending		pleasing
	achieving		stopping		desirable
(4)	sunrise	(5)	warm	(6)	gathered
	dawn		golden		collected
	4:19 A.M.		mellow		massed
	daybreak		yellow		piled up
			bright		
(7)	light	(8)	early rising	(9)	announced
	heat		ambitious		celebrated
	glow		vocal		foretold
	brightness		cheerful		foreshadowed
	sight		loud		promised
(10)	grown	(11)	played	(12)	meadow
	independent		hopped		field
	mature		frolicked		yard
					lawn
(13)	climbed	(14)	calls	(15)	murmur
	scampered		song		whisper
	romped		chattering		burble
					mumble
(16)	exuberant	(17)	gray	(18)	silver
	flamboyant		bluish		glistening
	variegated		pewter		moonstruck
	rampant		shining		gray blue
	glorious		glinting		
(19)	golden	(20)	soft	(21)	various
	rosy		sweet		many
	afire		caressing		vibrant
	ripe				like Joseph's coat
					vivid
(22)	heat				
	languor				
	lassitude				
	sluggishness				

chapter 4

Explaining

a Process

ORGANIZATION

Process writing explains how to do something, or it explains how a particular result was achieved. Process writing is *instruction:*

It can be *simple*—how to build a small campfire for cooking, explained in a single paragraph

It can be *complex*—how to clone farm animals by gene splicing, explained in a bulletin of several hundred pages

Common characteristics of all processes

A process follows an ordered sequence.

A process consists of a series of steps or stages.

A process has a particular purpose or end product.

Some uses of process writing—On the job

Explaining steps in construction

Explaining how to operate machinery

Explaining progressions of steps or events in reports and analyses

Process writing in business and industry is usually done by a **technical writer,** who is specially trained to explain complex, technical processes in clear, precise English.

Elsewhere

Explaining how to do something or how to make something

at home   for a hobby
at school   in sports

"How-to" process writing is the type that most of us are familiar with. Each day we read how-to instructions in newspapers, in magazines, in books, in manuals of instruction, and on the Internet. We follow processes to accomplish tasks, and we explain processes to help others in all aspects of our daily lives.

✓ Assignment

Your assignment for this chapter is to write a paragraph that explains a process. Choose one of the following options:

1. Write a paragraph in which you explain *how to do something*. For example, explain how to

paint a room   restore a lawn
deal for a new or used car   adopt a foreign child
shop for quality bargains   make a jack-o-lantern
organize a garage sale

2. Explain a *process of transition (progression)* from one stage or state of being to another. For example, explain the process you went through to get

from a "C" student to an "A"   from carefree teenager to responsible
   student   parent
from Christian to Muslim   from depression to contentment
from indebtedness to solvency

Some Tips for Choosing a Process to Explain

1. Choose a process that you can cover fully in one paragraph.
2. Choose a process that is interesting and informative.
3. Choose a process that you already know how to do correctly (or have experienced).
4. Choose a process that you can learn by doing library research and/or consulting an expert.

For more ideas, see the lists of possible topics in the Activities and Assignments section of this chapter.

Although most people expect most process paragraphs to be instructional and technical, notice how the following student paragraph touches the heart.

The transformation from businessman to Syria Shrine clown appears to be simple, but, in fact, it is a complex and magical process. The briefcase carried by this somewhat paunchy, three piece suited man is often filled with a variety of makeup rather than contracts and memos. The garment bag hanging in his closet does not hold a clean suit and fresh white shirt, but rather, a colorful baggy costume. Like an artist at work, he arranges the various bottles, jars, paints, and brushes. Soon, the smell of grease paint fills the room. Sitting down in front of a lighted mirror, he picks up a black pencil and begins to sketch the outline of his eyes and mouth. Using a dampened sponge, he next applies a smooth layer of pancake makeup. The practiced hands achieve a satin finish any woman would envy. With each step in his metamorphosis, the man's demeanor changes. He grins and smiles as flashes of Emmett Kelly fill his mind. In a manner similar to Rembrandt's, a paint brush is used to stroke on the white makeup, and a candy apple red paint stick colors in the big curving smile of his mouth. As the costume is taken from its bag, the story book animals printed on the fabric seem to return the smile of the man as he dresses. Oversized pockets are filled with candy and balloons. A frizzy red wig hides the last trace of the businessman; thus the clown, the funny man, is born. After practicing the magic flower trick one more time, he pushes open the door to the children's chemotherapy ward. The kids start to laugh and cheer while Artie, the clown, chokes back a tear and starts his act.

Kerren Hunter

How to Write a Paragraph that Explains a Process

1. Ask yourself: "Who is my audience?" "How much information will they need to understand the process I am explaining?"
2. Write a topic sentence that clarifies the purpose of the process or that conveys the value of the process.
3. Tell the readers exactly what they will need in order to complete the process (tools, materials, an unending supply of patience, etc.).
4. Clearly explain each stage of the process step by step.
5. Go back and review your explanation to make sure that you have:
   a. Let the reader know exactly what to expect at each step.
   b. Warned the reader of any potential problem that could occur.
   c. Given the reader enough explanatory details to clarify each step of the process.
6. Decide whether the reader needs a diagram or some other visual aid to understand the process fully (a technical process, for example).
7. Write a concluding sentence that refocuses the reader's mind on the value of the process.

✓ Topic Sentence

The paragraph that explains a process, like any other paragraph, needs a *controlling idea:* **subject** + **attitude**.

> **Subject**—*identifies* the process that you are going to explain.
>
> **Attitude**—*states* the results of the process
>
> ### *and/or*
> the advantages of the process
>
> ### *and/or*
> the benefits gained from the process

Be sure to *narrow* your subject to one that you can explain in a single paragraph:

Too broad:	The journey from unknown, starry-eyed adolescent to Miss America finalist requires as much planning as a presidential campaign.
Focused:	Because she had a hearing impairment, Heather Whitestone had to devise a unique strategy in order to win the Miss America crown.

Note the following examples:

Subject (process):	using a backfire to control a forest fire
Attitude (results achieved):	saves lives, property, and resources
Topic sentence:	The use of backfire to control a forest fire is a risky process, but it often saves lives, personal property, and natural resources.
Subject (process):	following the correct steps in waxing a car
Attitude (results achieved):	beauty and protection
Topic sentence:	To give your car a waxing that both beautifies and protects, carefully follow each step in the preparation and application process.
Subject (process):	following four steps to prepare for a test
Attitude (results achieved):	saves time

Topic sentence: Following four basic steps can help to save you time when studying for a test.

Subject (process): following a few proven techniques at a job interview

Attitude (results achieved): make a favorable impression

Topic sentence: Following a few proven techniques can help you to make a favorable impression at your next job interview.

EXERCISE 4A: CHOOSING EFFECTIVE CONTROLLING IDEAS

Which of the following statements commit the writer to explaining a process? Put a check (mark) beside those that could introduce a process paragraph.

_____ 1. Few people realize that preparing mentally for a game is every bit as difficult as preparing physically.

_____ 2. Writing a term paper is not difficult once you learn the required parts and understand the steps in writing each of them.

_____ 3. There is nothing in this world so good as a pizza.

_____ 4. Riding a horse is not so difficult as the procedure that must be followed for getting on the animal.

_____ 5. I have never seen anyone look so beautiful as Irene did on her wedding day.

_____ 6. I am sure most teachers who stay in the business have ways of handling the class clowns, but Miss Weison's three-step program never failed.

_____ 7. Preparing to travel to a foreign country requires careful planning and execution.

_____ 8. It is not nearly so difficult to entertain friends at a party at your house once you have mastered the system.

_____ 9. Getting into college required a whole series of steps, designed, I think, to discourage the faint at heart.

_____ 10. Before serving a ball in tennis, before attempting a putt in golf, before stepping up to the plate in baseball, you should put yourself through a series of movements designed to relax the body and prepare the mind.

✓ Body

The body contains the sequence of steps that the reader must follow in order to complete the process. *Accuracy* is the most important requirement for explaining a process. You must

> *know the process thoroughly before explaining it to someone else.*
>
> *follow the prescribed sequence carefully.*
>
> *use precise wording.*
>
> *explain steps in enough detail.*

To organize the body, break down the process into *logical* steps. Ask yourself the following questions as you write:

1. Whom are you explaining the process to? To communicate successfully, obtain some basic information about your reader, such as the following:

> educational level
>
> degree of expertise or knowledge about the process
>
> any limitations that might affect your reader's ability to understand or to complete the process

For this assignment, assume that your reader is one (or all) of your English classmates.

2. Have you listed all of the essential steps? If you are not sure, then do more research on your topic.

3. Can you discuss all of the steps in a single paragraph? If you have too much information, narrow your subject or choose a less detailed process.

4. Do you understand each step well enough to explain it clearly and precisely? If not, *review* the process by doing it yourself, or doing library research, or consulting an expert.

Caution: Never guess or bluff when explaining how to complete a process. Anything less than total accuracy could be, at the least, embarrassing; at the most, disastrous.

5. Have you listed the steps in a logical sequence that the reader can follow? The sequence of steps that you prefer may not be clear to the reader *or* easy for him to follow.

> The reader must see not only how step A relates to step B, but also how A, B, and all following steps relate to the completed process.

Use only the prescribed sequence when explaining a process.

If you omit a step, do not assume that the reader will know intuitively to add it himself.

6. Have you used transitional (linking) words and phrases to make each step flow smoothly into the next? Smooth transition from one point to the next

moves the reader forward smoothly and steadily from one point to the next.

enables the reader to see more clearly how the steps of the process relate to each other without being distracted by choppy, uneven writing.

Although the following student paragraph is somewhat longer than the recommended length for your paragraphs, it is an excellent example of process description.

1. It is *unified* and *coherent:* All steps of the process directly support the controlling idea and follow a logical sequence toward a final result.
2. It uses *detailed secondary support* to describe and clarify the various tasks that fall under each primary step. The rich visual imagery in these supporting details creates vivid word pictures in the reader's imagination.
3. It maintains *continuity* (flows smoothly from beginning to end) by skillfully using (a) transitional words and phrases, (b) coordination, and (c) subordination to link primary steps and details of secondary support.

As you read, underline all of the transitional words and phrases that you can find.

There are four primary steps in the making of a New England shade-grown cigar: field work, shed work, processing, and production. The most demanding and time-consuming step in the whole process is the field work. First, tiny dull-green tobacco seedlings are placed into freshly tilled dirt by machine. These seedlings are protected by large cheesecloth tents and are watered by an overhead sprinkling system. As the plants begin to mature, and with the tents still in place, single-engine airplanes spray the fields with a white powder insecticide. Then male and female field workers are each assigned several rows in a field, and, using their hands (the most important tool), they tie the tobacco from the bottom of the stock to a wire six feet above the ground with a ball of twine. The string works like a bean pole, helping the tobacco to grow straight and tall. When the plant is three feet tall, suckering begins. The field worker lies on his back, working his way through the rows, pulling the immature leaves from the bottoms of the plants. Within a week after suckering, picking begins, and the leaves are placed into large rectangular canvas boxes on runners that are pulled up and down the rows of tobacco. Then, as the workers are picking the leaves, the shed work begins. The canvas picking boxes are transported to huge barns, where the tobacco is stacked on tables. Here the tobacco leaves are machine sewn by two workers onto lathes of wood twenty-four inches long; twenty-two pairs of leaves are twined along the lathes. These lathes are then placed on beams extending from the ceiling to the bottom row, approximately six feet from the ground. After the shed is filled, the next step, processing, begins with a stage called curing. Huge round burners are connected by pipes to tanks of propane; the heat from the burners dries out the tobacco, which adds flavor to the leaves. After curing, stems are removed, the leaves are washed, and the tobacco is graded according to size and shape. The final step, the production process, now begins. Top-grade leaves are used for the wrappers of the cigars, and the lower-grade tobacco is used for the inner makings of the cigar. The top-grade leaves are then wound tightly around the "filler," either by hand or by machine. This final step produces the shade-grown cigar and is the culmination of three to five months of back-breaking work.

Trina Gonzalez Friend

✓ Using Secondary Support

When explaining most processes, just listing the main steps, the primary support, is not enough. For your reader to understand the process thoroughly, you must explain the main steps more precisely by using the added details of secondary support.

Secondary supporting details make the primary steps of your process clearer and more specific:

They can specify needed tools, equipment, and materials.

> To strip this chest, you will need a quart of stripper, rubber gloves, a 2-inch paintbrush, a putty knife, four pads of 00 and three pads of 0000 steel wool, two sheets of 100 grit sandpaper, a sanding block, and one pint of mineral spirits.

They can provide special instructions.

> Blend the eggs, butter, and flour with a wooden spatula for approximately one minute; *do not* use an electric mixer.

They can tell the reader why a particular step is important or what might happen if a step is omitted or not followed correctly.

> When benchrest shooting, allow the rifle barrel to cool for one to two minutes between shots. If you do not, the barrel will overheat, and the resulting expansion of lands and grooves will destroy your accuracy.

They can provide warnings of possible hazards.

> Before opening the main breaker panel, be sure that your tools, ladder, and footwear are insulated and nonconductive, for this stage is the most dangerous.

They can let the reader know what to expect at various steps of the process.

> When your new zucchini plants reach 3 to 10 inches in height, they become irresistible, succulent hors d'oeuvres for rabbits and woodchucks. This is the time to cage your plants, spray them with insect powder, or sit for long hours looking through the scope on your .22.

The following example further illustrates the importance of using secondary supporting details. When a reader is only partially informed, even a simple process can become complex.

What if a friend of yours who has never changed a tire before and who is intimidated by instruction manuals is about to drive across the country with his family? Knowing you to be an automotive expert, he asks you to write down simple instructions for changing a flat that he can understand. Eager to help him, you draft the following "easy" instructions:

> All you have to do is follow these five simple steps. First, secure the vehicle. Second, check the spare. Third, jack up the car. Fourth, remove the flat, and last, mount the spare. You should have no problem if you follow these instructions carefully. Have a nice trip!

Because you know how to change a tire, having done it many times, you may think that you are doing him a big favor by providing this explanation. *Wrong!* Too many questions are left unanswered. He could spend hours in utter confusion, asking himself:

> Why do I have to secure the vehicle? (No one wants to steal a car with a flat tire.)
>
> What do I check on a spare tire?
>
> Where do I place the jack, and how does it work?
>
> How do I remove the lug nuts?
>
> Why do I mount the spare? (This is a car—not a horse—or maybe that's how I tell if there is any air in it.)
>
> How do I get the jack out from under the car once the tire is changed?

All that you have given your friend is a rough outline of the process—a much too brief chronological list of the main steps in the process. If this was all he had to rely on, your unlucky friend would wish that he had joined AAA instead of listening to you!

Fortunately, after reading your "easy" instructions before leaving, your friend begins to ask you many questions. Wisely, you write a new set of instructions using secondary supporting details to supplement the primary steps of your first version.

> First, pull as far off the road as you can, and, for safety reasons, *secure the vehicle:* Put the transmission in park, set the emergency brake, turn on the flashers, and shut off the engine. If you are on a hill and can find a rock, for added safety, use it to block one of the wheels to prevent the car from drifting. Next, *check the spare tire* to see if it is inflated and be sure that you have all the tools: jack, handle, and lug nut wrench. The owner's handbook will tell you how to assemble the jack and where to place it. Before jacking the car, remove the hubcap with a screwdriver or prybar and loosen the lug nuts with the wrench, counterclockwise. Next, place the jack in the correct position and carefully *jack up the car* until the bottom of the flat is about three inches off the ground. This will allow enough clearance to remove the flat and put the spare on. Next, *remove* the lug nuts and then *the flat. Mount* the spare on the hub, replace the lug nuts, and tighten them by hand until all are snug against the wheel. Now, carefully lower the jack according to instructions in the handbook. Remove the jack, and, using the wrench, tighten all lug nuts securely in an X pattern. This ensures uniform tightness of the wheel on the hub. Tighten each lug nut again following a clockwise pattern to ensure that you didn't forget any. Next, replace your hubcap securely so that it won't fall off. If it is loose or won't stay on, put it into the trunk until later. Put all of your tools back where they belong and put the flat tire where it is accessible. Finally, remove any wheel blocks, and be sure to stop at the next service center to have your flat repaired or replaced.

Your friend should now be able to change a flat successfully because *the secondary supporting details that you added clearly explain the rationale or significance of the primary steps in the process.*

✓ Explaining a Technical Process

In our increasingly technological world, more and more on-the-job writing involves complex technical explanations. Explaining how a new computer system works, illustrating the proper way to repair damaged equipment on a space station, analyzing the process of radon microscopy for a class of medical lab technicians—all of these tasks require *technical writers* who can explain detailed processes clearly and specifically. Technical writers have no margin for error when the success of their companies or the safety of human lives depends on their expertise. If you decide to explain a technical process for your assignment, then you are a technical writer and must think like a technical writer.

First, you must be especially accurate in the areas common to *all* process writing:

> Explaining steps in a logical sequence
>
> Using transitional words or phrases to link ideas
>
> Using specific details to clarify main points

Second, you must consider the following additional factors when explaining technical processes:

KNOWING YOUR READERS' TECHNICAL EXPERTISE

All writers should know the characteristics of their audiences so that they can adapt their writing to those readers. *If writing is not adapted to the reader, effective communication cannot occur.*

A technical process writer must be especially aware of the readers' characteristics because technical writing is often highly specialized and complex.

1. Determining the readers' level of expertise.   The technical writer has two basic types of reading audiences: (1) the general reading audience and (2) the technically aware reading audience.

The *general* **reading audience**

> may represent a wide range of educational levels.
>
> usually has little or no specialized technical knowledge.
>
> has diverse background and interests.
>
> may have differing degrees of interest in the process.

The *technically aware* **reading audience**

> has a specialized technical orientation (often more so than the technical writer does).
>
> is profession-oriented, whereas a general reading audience's interests are more diverse.

2. Adjusting your level of complexity.

The general reading audience will understand technical processes more clearly when provided with the following:

> Background and/or supplementary information about the process
>
> Reasons why the process is important or relevant to them
>
> Working definitions of technical terms
>
> Clear explanations in simple, nontechnical language
>
> Some repetition and/or emphasis of key points
>
> **whereas**

The technically aware reading audience can assimilate complex technical information more easily than the general audience because

> It has more comprehensive prior knowledge about the process to be explained.
>
> It understands sophisticated technical language.
>
> It grasps technical concepts quickly.
>
> It is more strongly motivated to master the process.

Caution: When in doubt about the technical level of your readers, it is always better to risk explaining too much rather than too little.

but

Do not oversimplify explanations so much that you insult your readers' intelligence.

USING VISUAL AIDS

The nontechnical reading audience, in particular, often needs to *see* a process both visually *and* mentally.

Visual aids can

> make concepts clearer and more understandable.
>
> help readers to remember facts and details.
>
> eliminate the need for long, complex explanations.
>
> show the results of a process.

Some tips on using visual aids.   First, evaluate the process and your reading audience *objectively.* Then ask yourself, Would a visual aid make *this* process any clearer or any simpler for *this* reading audience? If the answer is *yes,* then

> Use a clear and simple visual aid that directly supports your controlling idea.
>
> Use a visual aid that complements, enhances, or clarifies what you are explaining.
>
> Avoid using a visual aid that detracts in any way from your explanation.
>
> Avoid using more than one visual aid if one will do the job.

Remember: You do *not* have to use a visual aid if you determine that your explanation is just as effective without one.

A good visual aid, like the diagram on the next page, can help your reader to understand better a major concept within the process.

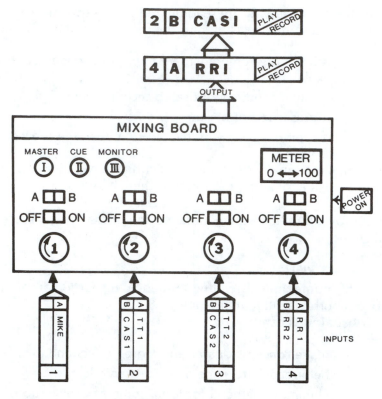

How to use a sound mixer.

USING PRECISE LANGUAGE

All forms of technical writing demand precision. Whether you are defining a term, comparing, contrasting, describing, or analyzing—in explaining a process, precise words, calculations, and measurements are crucial. For example:

> If structural beams are not *precisely* aligned, even if just one beam is off by a fraction of an inch, a bridge could eventually collapse.

> *or*

> If a welding textbook did not *precisely* explain how structural stress occurs, a welder who studied that book could cause hundreds of people to die because he received unclear or inexact information.

Precise technical process explanations can be as necessary at home as on a construction site or in a medical research laboratory. Imagine, for example, that you never had to change a fuse because all of your former residences had circuit breaker panels. In fact, you don't even know what a fuse box looks like, but here you are, alone, with a dark TV screen in your new house. You just blew a fuse when you turned on the microwave to make some popcorn. Calmly, you call the previous owner, who tells you that he has left a set of written instructions in the kitchen cupboard. Much relieved, you unfold the piece of paper and begin to read:

> First, turn everything off. Then find the damaged one and replace it with the same type. Last, turn everything back on.

By attempting to follow sketchy instructions like these, you could place yourself in a very dangerous situation—and you still wouldn't know how to replace a blown fuse. What does the writer mean by *everything?* What, exactly, is *damaged?* How does one recognize a blown fuse and safely remove one?

How to change a fuse.

The reader should have received the following, more precise instructions, which explain in greater detail and use specific terminology.

> First, find a strong flashlight so that you can examine the fuses that are in the fuse box. Also, there is a box of spare fuses on the shelf beside the fuse box. Be sure that the floor beneath the fuse box is dry. If it is wet or damp, put a board or other nonconducting material on the floor so that your feet will not contact any water. Next, move the main power switch, which is the large metal lever on the side of the fuse box, to the "off" position. Now open the fuse box door, and you will see two vertical rows of round screw-in fuses, each approximately one inch in diameter, with a little window on the end. Now use your flashlight to locate the blown fuse, which will have either (1) a scorched window or (2) a clear window with a broken metal strip inside. After locating the blown fuse, remove it by turning it counterclockwise with your fingers. If it sticks, use a dry cloth or rubber gloves to get added leverage. (If you still can't remove the blown fuse, switch the power on and call an electrician later.) After

unscrewing the blown fuse, check the amperage capacity that is written on the fuse (5-10-15-20-30) and screw in tightly (clockwise) a spare fuse having an equal or lower number on it. If you use a new fuse with a higher number, the circuit could overload and cause a fire. Last, close the fuse box door, and move the main power switch back to the "on" position. Be sure that the power is fully restored to prove that you replaced the blown fuse and not a good one. Throw the blown fuse away so that it doesn't get mixed up with the spare fuses.

This revised technical process instruction is obviously much more detailed and much more precise than the original version. Because the writer of the first set of instructions knew the process so well, he failed to evaluate fully the needs and limitations of his reader relevant to the blown fuse situation.

✓ Conclusion

The conclusion of a paragraph that explains a process should, like other assigned paragraphs in this text, (1) re-echo the controlling idea and (2) end the paragraph. Depending on the type of process, the purpose of the writer, and needs of the reader, the process conclusion is highly flexible and can achieve one or more of the following purposes:

> Restates the intended results of the process.
>
> Confirms total process completion.
>
> Guarantees specific results if steps are correctly followed.
>
> Verifies that steps were followed in correct sequence.
>
> Encourages the reader to try the process.
>
> Promotes the advantages and/or benefits of the process.
>
> Expresses personal impressions of satisfaction, relief, or well-being that result from completing the process.
>
> Emphasizes the importance of the process to the reader and/or others.
>
> Provides expert or professional advice concerning the process, to include cautions, warnings, restrictions, and exceptions before, during, and after the completion steps.

In the following paragraph, the student writer uses humor, creativity, and logical sequencing of details when explaining his process for coping with a "Big Mac Attack." Note his appropriate, highly creative conclusion.

> **I will readily admit that I am a man of many vices.** Smoking, profanity, and sleeping late are just a few, but I am quite sure that with a little willpower, I could be persuaded to give these up. There is one habit, though, which I refuse to break. That is my incomparable lust for the towering culinary masterpiece commonly known as the "McDonald's Big Mac." I have, for the past

four years, been intermittently stricken by the infamous "Big Mac Attack." Just the sight of a McDonald's commercial on television, or the mere humming of the Big Mac theme song, "two all beef patties, special sauce, lettuce, etc. . . ." send my gastric juices into a frenzy. When I reach this point, I do not *want* a Big Mac,—I *need* one. I grab the keys to the family car and sprint out the door, not giving a thought to my appearance or the weather; I start the car, gun the engine, and leave the driveway so fast that my tires squeal. I begin to salivate as my thoughts turn to indulging my monstrous pangs of want. I drool as I think of the two beef patties being fried on the grill. I can almost taste the special sauce that adds a bit of mystery to the Big Mac (although I've always suspected this was merely thousand island dressing). Next, I contemplate the unique taste created by the contrast between the crispy lettuce and the creamy cheese. There are also visions of pickles and onions, as the whole appetizing mess is placed between a triple-decker sesame seed bun. My stomach hits overdrive when I spot the golden arches which identify my destination. As my stomach continues to sing its hungry song, I reach the parking lot, run inside, and blurt out my order. I receive my food and quickly find a place to sit. I then tear open the box and torture my stomach for one final second, as my nostrils eagerly absorb the aromatic vapors that rise toward my face. I slowly pick up my Big Mac with trembling hands and raise it to my open mouth. The culmination of my frantic rush to this small booth is even more than I had anticipated. Whoever said, "Nothing tastes as sweet as victory," must have lived before the creation of the "McDonald's Big Mac."

Wally Quinn

✓ Some Do's . . .

1. *Do* explain every step in the process. When you are thoroughly familiar with a process, you may unknowingly underestimate or downplay the importance of minor steps in the process when explaining it to someone. You must never assume that your reader can always follow your explanation accurately if these steps are omitted or not fully clarified.
2. *Do* place your steps in logical order; use transitional words or phrases to build a bridge from one step to the next.
3. *Do* recognize the importance of visual aids in helping your reader understand a technical process. Even a well-written explanation of a highly technical process can seem complicated to readers until they see an illustration of how the object works.
4. *Do* have a purpose in mind. Ask yourself, "Why am I explaining this process? What do I want my readers to learn from this process?"

✓ . . . and Don'ts About the Process Paragraph

1. *Don't* choose a topic that can't be adequately explained within the terms of your assignment. Don't commit yourself to more than you can deliver.

2. *Don't* use vague, general terms to explain a technical process. Use simple, precise language, and remember to define technical terms that might be unfamiliar to a general reading audience.

3. *Don't* forget the importance of secondary supporting details in explaining a process—any kind of process. Without specific secondary details, your readers cannot fully understand the process you are explaining.

SUGGESTED ACTIVITIES AND ASSIGNMENTS

1. Divide the class into small groups and distribute one sheet of heavy-bond typing paper to each student. Have a volunteer from each group to give directions to the rest of the group on how to make a paper airplane. Be sure the students understand that

    The student giving directions cannot repeat an instruction.

    The students taking directions cannot redo any step (refold the paper). After the students are finished, have each group give their models a test flight and see which group constructed the best plane. If any of the groups' planes perform badly in the flight test, ask the group to discuss aloud what went wrong during the direction-giving process.

2. Think of a process related to your major field and explain that process to two different audiences: (1) students in your major who are familiar with most of the technical terms you are using; and (2) students outside your major who know nothing about the process.

3. Write an explanation of some technical process with which you are very familiar. It doesn't have to be a process related to your career. It could be a technical process related to recreational pursuits, repair of household appliances, or automobile maintenance. Explain the process as simply as possible, and then give your explanation to a group of students unfamiliar with the process. See if they can draw a diagram of the process based on your written explanation. After they have finished, examine their diagrams and see how accurate they are. Then discuss the diagrams with them. Were there any particular points at which your explanation seemed unclear? Did more than one student have a problem illustrating a certain step in the process? Did one student know more than another about the type of process you explained, and was this reflected in that student's diagram? Which step was easiest for the students to illustrate? Which was the most difficult? How could you improve your explanation?

4. Try to write your own how-to paragraph on topics such as how to: buy a used car, avoid tension, perform CPR, study for a test, rebuild a piece of machinery, or choose a doctor.

▱▷ SENTENCES

In writing a process paragraph, your first responsibility is to be clear. After all, if you are telling your readers how to do something, you defeat your purpose if they can't follow your instructions or see your direction.

Surprisingly to new writers, shorter is clearer. The more concise your paragraph, the easier it is for your reader to comprehend. Of course, you can't leave anything out, but you can shorten your sentences by combining your ideas. When you combine two or more ideas into one sentence, you show the reader the relationship between the two and also show the relative importance of each. The following examples will show you how to do this effectively.

✓ Combining Sentences Using Relative Pronouns

One method of combining sentences is by using *who, whose, which,* or *that* to tuck the subordinate clause inside the main clause.

Separate:	Rachel had dreams of becoming a Broadway star. She came from Enid, Oklahoma.
Combined:	Rachel, who came from Enid, Oklahoma, had dreams of becoming a Broadway star.
Separate:	The fifty-dollar gift certificate surprised Ellie. The certificate was tucked inside the wallet.
Combined:	The fifty-dollar gift certificate, which was tucked inside the wallet, surprised Ellie.

EXERCISE 4B: COMBINING SENTENCES USING RELATIVE PRONOUNS

Combine the following parts of sentences by making one a *who, whose, which,* or *that* clause.

1. My doctor is a competent physician. She is also one of the most caring persons I know.

   _____

   _____

2. Salvatore Gravano was a high-ranking member of the Cosa Nostra. He was called "Sammy the Bull."

   _____

   _____

3. Sammy had been underboss, second in command of the Gambino family. He has admitted to killing nineteen people for "the family."

   _____

   _____

   _____

4. The Richmond family gave the party. It was a real blast.

   _____

   _____

   _____

5. I had never met Carlos before the concert. He became a true friend.

   _____

   _____

   _____

6. The team seemed lethargic and inept during the first half. It caught fire during the last quarter.

   _____

   _____

   _____

7. Gloria finds time to belong to many of the school's clubs. She commutes from a town thirty miles away.

   _____

   _____

   _____

8. The mile race will be the most exciting event in this year's track meet. It will be the final event.

_____

_____

_____

9. My fiance's mother is an extremely thrifty woman. She bought a beautiful, but expensive, dress for our wedding.

_____

_____

_____

10. The playground is in the middle of the town. It is a meeting place for children, senior citizens, and everyone in between.

_____

_____

_____

✓ Reducing Clauses to Phrases

Usually, *who, which,* or *that* clauses can be further reduced.

Separate:	Carmen wanted to have a big party for Freddy. She was always ready to celebrate.
Reduced:	Carmen, who was always ready to celebrate, wanted to have a big party for Freddy.
Reduced:	Carmen, always ready to celebrate, wanted to have a big party for Freddy.

Note the words eliminated from the following sentences without any loss of meaning.

1. Shuffleboard, (which is) the favorite sport of many senior citizens, is especially popular in Florida.

2. The Susan B. Anthony dollar, (which was) launched with much fanfare, never did gain favor with the American public.

3. The company (which was) charged with polluting the river was eventually fined $300,000.

✓ Using Verbal Phrases to Combine Sentences

Subordination enables you to combine sentences and, at the same time, express the relationship between ideas more precisely than separate sentences would. Frequently, the subordinate idea can be further reduced to a *verbal phrase*.

Separate:	Greg stared into the water along the edge of the coral reef. He suddenly saw what looked like an ancient cannon embedded in the sandy floor of the bay.
Combined:	Staring into the water along the edge of the coral reef, Greg suddenly saw what looked like an ancient cannon embedded in the sandy floor of the bay.
Separate:	Robbie searched the stores for a Harris Tweed jacket. He finally found one in Brooks Brothers at a bargain price.
Combined:	Searching the stores for a Harris Tweed jacket, Bobbie finally found one in Brooks Brothers at a bargain price.
Separate:	Lucie gazed out the window at the snow-swept prairie. She wished she could be in some exotic place like Twenty-nine Palms.
Combined:	Gazing out the window at the snow-swept prairie, Lucie wished she could be in some exotic place like Twenty-nine Palms.

EXERCISE 4C: COMBINING SENTENCES USING VERBALS

Combine the following pairs of sentences, reducing one of the sentences to a verbal phrase.

1. I returned from the rest room to pick up the straw hat I had left on the table. I finally saw it on a nearby table filled with hot rolls.

_____

_____

_____

2. Sheila read the medical dictionary. She was convinced that she had several rare and exotic diseases.

_____

_____

_____

3. Jimmy finally signed a letter of intent to a Division II school. He felt a great sense of relief.

_____

_____

_____

4. I read Stephen King's book, *Cujo*. I wouldn't go near my dog for weeks.

_____

_____

_____

5. I saw twenty-one-year-old Tiger Woods play golf. It was an exhilarating, yet humbling, experience.

_____

_____

_____

6. My friends and I saw the movie *Huckleberry Finn*. We immediately went home and started building a raft.

_____

_____

_____

7. I began getting a lot of junk mail on retirement homes and brochures on long-term care insurance. I had just turned sixty-five.

_____

_____

8. Many Hong Kong natives were nervous. They realized that the city would soon be under Chinese rule.

_____

_____

9. I found it was much easier writing a paragraph than it had been. I had learned the process.

_____

_____

10. I do a lot of decorating for Christmas. It is fun for me.

_____

_____

✓ Combining Sentences Through Appositive Words and Phrases

Appositives are words or phrases that restate another word or phrase and define, explain, or expand upon its meaning.

                                        appositive
1. The Nord, *a short alley leading to the shipyard,* was crowded with workers.

                                              appositive
2. Dwight D. Eisenhower, *thirty-fourth president of the United States,* was the descendant of German immigrants who had originally settled in Pennsylvania.

The *appositive* often provides a way of tucking subordinate details neatly into a single sentence instead of using two or three sentences. Note how the following groups of sentences illustrate the use of appositives in combining sentences:

> Oklahoma is known as the Sooner State. It was admitted to the Union in 1907.
> Oklahoma, *the Sooner State,* was admitted to the Union in 1907.

> Jacob grew up in Enid, Oklahoma. Enid is known as the wheat capital of Oklahoma.
> Jacob grew up in Enid, *the wheat capital* of Oklahoma.

> Tulsa is one of the nation's leading oil centers. It is Oklahoma's second largest city.
> Tulsa, *Oklahoma's second largest city,* is one of the nation's leading oil centers.

EXERCISE 4D: COMBINING SENTENCES THROUGH APPOSITION

Use appositive phrases to combine the following pairs of sentences into one clear sentence.

1. Stalin was a leader of the Soviet States.
   He had thousands of his own people killed, some because the barking of their dogs annoyed him.

   _____

   _____

2. Some songs never go out of date.
   "Twilight Time" is an example.

   _____

   _____

3. My son, Andrew, is an accomplished pianist.
   He is angry because I won't let him play football.

   _____

   _____

4. Ann Landers is an advice columnist whose articles appear in many newspapers.
   Some of the letters she receives are hilarious.

   _____

   _____

5. One of the five best books I've ever read is James Clavell's *Tai-Pan*.
   It tells the story of one man's dream of making Hong Kong the center of England's Oriental Empire.

   _____

   _____

WAYS TO ELIMINATE CHOPPY WRITING

Combine short simple sentences into one more interesting sentence by

1. Turning one sentence into a *relative clause*.

   Abraham Lincoln often experienced depression and severe headaches. He may have actually been suffering from manic depression.

   Lincoln, who often experienced depression and severe headaches, may have actually been suffering from manic depression.

2. Turning one sentence into a *verbal phrase*.

   I skimmed through Kay Jamison's autobiography yesterday. I can understand why the critics described it as an "extraordinary" book.

   Skimming through Kay Jamison's autobiography yesterday, I can understand why the critics described it as an "extraordinary" book.

3. Turning one sentence into an *appositive phrase*.

   Notre Dame is one of the world's most beautiful Gothic cathedrals. It was built in Paris between 1163 and 1345.

   Notre Dame, one of the world's most beautiful Gothic cathedrals, was built in Paris between 1163 and 1345.

✓ Combining Sentences to Eliminate Choppy Writing

Choppy writing is not only monotonous and wordy, but it also fails to show the exact relationship between one idea and another.

Choppy: Albert Camus is a French writer. He was born in Algeria. He was born in 1913. His father was a farm laborer. His father was killed in World War I. Camus studied at the University of Algiers. He became a journalist. He championed economic and social reforms for Algerians. Local colonial authorities considered him an agitator.

Improved: The French writer Albert Camus, son of a farm laborer who was killed in World War I, was born in Algeria in 1913. He studied at the University of Algiers and became a journalist who championed economic and social reform for Algerians. Local colonial authorities considered him an agitator.

EXERCISE 4E: COMBINING SENTENCES TO SHOW RELATIONSHIP OF IDEAS

Applying what you have learned about sentence combining, rewrite the following paragraph. Try to combine short, simple sentences in a variety of ways so as to show the logical relationship of ideas. You may add conjunctions and other connective words where necessary.

My friend went to a bingo game last Friday. Her name is LaRue. She hates bingo. She only went because her sister wanted to go. LaRue does not like to give money away. When she gives someone money, she wants "to take something home with me, in a bag," she says. She was hesitant to buy a lot of Bingo cards. They cost money. She played all evening with two cards. Other people had twenty or thirty. She began to feel embarrassed about this. She bought two cards for the big finale. It was Double bingo. LaRue won. The caller came to her table and gave her one hundred and eighty-eight dollars! LaRue could hardly drive home. She asked her sister when the next bingo was to be held.

✏ WORDS

✓ Wordiness

When you are writing your process paragraph, remember that effective sentences are concise. This is really true of all paragraphs, but it is particularly vital in explaining a process. The reader needs to learn the process; he does not need or want excess verbiage to slow him down or confuse him. Each detail that you use should say exactly what is necessary *and no more*. Needless words never improve a paragraph—and they won't impress your instructors; they will depress them. Whether you are writing a paragraph in English class, or doing a term paper in biology, or taking an essay exam in history, or drafting a résumé for a potential employer, you must choose precise words that say *exactly* what you mean. Writers often repeat details needlessly, or they use five or six words to say something that could have been said in one or two words.

It is easier to avoid saying too much if you recognize a few key areas where you can cut out excess words.

1. Reduce wordy phrases to a single word.

due to the fact that	because or since
in the event that	if
at that point in time	then
is in agreement with	agrees
at the present time	now
during the time that	while
through the use of	by or with
in many cases	frequently
in view of the fact that	since
in this modern day and age	today
for the purpose of	for
in spite of the fact that	despite

2. Eliminate *redundancies,* the senseless repetition of the same idea in different words.

audible ~~to the ear~~	adequate ~~enough~~
green ~~in color~~	~~important~~ essential
rectangular ~~in shape~~	7:00 A.M. ~~in the morning~~
~~completely~~ eliminated	seniors ~~in their last year of school~~

3. Eliminate the unnecessary *it*.

In the Bible it says . . .	The Bible says . . .
In the U.N. Charter it says . . .	The U.N. Charter says . . .
In the movie it shows . . .	The movie shows . . .
In the book it tells . . .	The book tells . . .

4. Eliminate some modifiers by using precise nouns, verbs, and modifiers.

The cat with the long white silky hair	The angora cat
The old, beat-up, rusty car	The bomb
He clapped his hands together	He applauded

She was whiny, complaining, fault-finding	She was querulous
The boy who picked on smaller boys	The bully

5. Eliminate the timid phrase.

It seems to me that we are out of dog food	We are out of dog food.
In my opinion, blue is not Sue's color.	Blue is not Sue's color.
It is my opinion that too many of our tax dollars are wasted.	Too many of our tax dollars are wasted.

6. Eliminate unnecessary subjects.

The sensation of pulsing, throbbing pain	Pulsing, throbbing pain
The sound of loud, cackling laughter	Loud, cackling laughter
The smell of the stale odor of cigarette ashes	The odor of cigarette ashes

7. Use actor-action sequence (active voice).

Laughter from the class next door was heard by all of us.	We all heard laughter from the class next door.
Soccer was the game played by most of the boys in our neighborhood.	Most of the boys in our neighborhood played soccer.

8. Avoid the use of vague phrases such as *sort of* and *kind of*.

The house was *sort of* a grayish color.	The house was a weather-beaten gray.
He was *kind of* a strange old man.	He was an eccentric old man.

9. Avoid the use of intensifiers such as *very, quite, really,* and *real*. They are meaningless.

> Now that was a *real* horse. (Do you mean a *sleek* horse, a *spirited* horse, a *powerful* horse, a *winning* horse? Do you mean a live horse as opposed to a rocking horse?)

> Sara had a *really very serious* accident. (Is there any difference between a *serious* accident, and a *really serious* accident, and a *really very serious* accident?)

10. Eliminate wordy negatives.

I did not remember to call my boss.	I forgot to call my boss.
Max did not pay any attention to me	Max ignored me.

Note that although you must eliminate every unnecessary word, this does not mean that you should eliminate words necessary for clarity. Be sure *all* the words you use tell your reader something.

EXERCISE 4F: ELIMINATING USELESS WORDS

Eliminate the deadwood from the following sentences:

1. I honestly and sincerely believe that people who have communicable diseases that are easily spread to other people should be isolated from other people even if they don't want to be.
2. People who own their own businesses, work day and night, and don't have much time to spend with their parents or kids or brothers and sisters are at the risk of becoming isolated permanently from their families and loved ones.
3. I fully intend to pursue my education in the field of English in graduate school.
4. At this point in time, I am a student in a community college; I am majoring in business and I am specializing in accounting.
5. There are thirty students who are planning to try out for the basketball team of the school.
6. I wrote this paper by myself; no one assisted me, and I got no help from anyone.
7. Stan really likes golf, which is his favorite outdoor recreation, and he relishes the theater, which is his favorite indoor activity to watch or go to.
8. My speech class, in which we learn to write and deliver speeches is my favorite class, the one I enjoy the most of all the classes I am taking.
9. I truly believe that my boss acted in ways that anyone would think was foolish.
10. Doris's father, who worked as a laborer all his life, made sure that all of his three children went to college and graduated with degrees.

✓ Reducing Sentences and Clauses to Verbal Phrases

A **verbal** is a verb part that cannot stand alone as a verb; that is, it cannot complete a statement about the subject (see the Sentences section of Chapter 1). Verbal phrases, however, can often be used to replace subordinate clauses, coordinate clauses, or even separate sentences. Study the following examples carefully.

subordinate clause

Original: Since the salespeople had not met their quotas, they were forced to work late every night until Christmas.

changed to verbal phrase

Revised: *Not having met their quotas,* the salespeople were forced to work late every night until Christmas.

coordinate clause

Original: He was given no better choice, so he took the job cleaning auto parts.

changed to verbal phrase

Revised: *Given no better choice,* he took the job cleaning auto parts.

coordinate clause

Original: Chavez had defied the court order. He was sentenced to thirty days in jail.

changed to verbal phrase

Revised: *Having defied the court order,* Chavez was sentenced to thirty days in jail.

or

Chavez was sentenced to thirty days in jail for *defying the court order.*

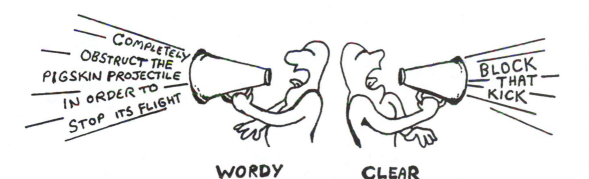

Avoid wordiness.

Note that the verbal phrase may come before the main clause, within the main clause, or, rarely after the main clause, but it should be set off by commas.

Knowing the truth, Mrs. Harriman refused to be intimidated by the lawyer's threats.

EXERCISE 4G: USING VERBAL PHRASES

Reduce each of the following sets of sentences to one sentence by combining a verbal phrase with an independent clause:

> *Example:*   Fred was hammering away in his basement workshop. He could not hear the doorbell.
>
> verbal phrase   independent clause
>
> Hammering away in his basement workshop, Fred could not hear the doorbell.

1. When Carlos noticed how much weight he had gained. He started an exercise program.

   _____

   _____

2. Julie was frightened out of her wits. But she continued to climb the steps to the high-dive platform.

   _____

   _____

3. I volunteered to work at a geriatric hospital. It was one of the best things I ever did for me.

   _____

   _____

4. I learned to read. It was very difficult for me as an adult, but it was also the most rewarding thing I had ever done.

   _____

   _____

5. Jerry decided to open his own business. He was disgusted with the treatment he got working for other people.

   _____

   _____

6. Bennie worked as a cab driver for four years. He helped to pay his way through college.

   _____

   _____

7. Trina was strapped for cash. She decided to sell her beloved BMW.

   _____

   _____

8. Trina sold her car. She had to walk to school and to work.

   _____

   _____

9. Trina discovered that she lost some unwanted weight and became much more fit. She decided not to buy another car.

   _____

   _____

10. Martin was suffering from a severe allergy. He couldn't concentrate on the test.

    _____

    _____

chapter 5

Explaining with Examples

ORGANIZATION

✓ Using Examples to Explain

Exposition is writing that explains. Much of your daily communication is explaining how something works, why something happened, what something is, or how a thing is like or unlike something else. Explaining occurs in all aspects of our lives:

> Your teacher explains how to write clear paragraphs.
>
> You explain goal defense to a six-year-old soccer player.
>
> Your teenager explains why she got home at 1:00 A.M. instead of 11:30 P.M.
>
> Your boss explains her new plan to increase your productivity.
>
> You explain why your homework assignment is a week late.
>
> Your doctor explains how a daily diet of cheeseburgers and fries is making you a candidate for coronary bypass surgery.
>
> You explain to your wife (or try to) why you forgot her birthday for the third year in a row.

These sentences are examples of typical situations that use explaining to convince, to inform, or to instruct. In each chapter, this text uses examples to help you understand paragraph writing more clearly.

Good examples clarify writing that explains. Just as this text uses numerous examples to explain and clarify paragraph writing techniques, you can use written examples to inform, to persuade, to clarify your ideas more effectively.

✓ What Is an Example?

When used in expository writing, an **example** is a unit of information that illustrates, clarifies, or illuminates a controlling idea. Examples can be both *primary support* and *secondary support* in a paragraph that explains. See pages 144–148 Organizing Your Examples.

In the narrative paragraph, you shared an experience; in the descriptive paragraph, you shared your impressions. In this writing assignment, you will share your knowledge by explaining with examples. For most of us, examples come naturally when we are asked to explain something:

Question: Why don't you like him?
Answer: On our first (and last) date, he was a cheap, conceited "jerk" from beginning to end. It all started when he . . .

Question: What will taking Psychology 101 ever do for me?
Answer: Well, here is how it helped me to get the best of you.

Question: Why do you stay at that lousy job?
Answer: Didn't I tell you about what my boss did for me when my car wouldn't start or what the other associates did when my baby got sick?

Question: O.K., what's so great about Yuma?
Answer: I'm glad you asked—this is what is so great: the beauty of the desert, the abundance and variety of the wildlife, and, particularly, the friendliness and sincerity of the people.

All of these answers are either examples themselves or points that can be supported by examples.

Note: *Reasons* are also *examples.*

✓ Assignment

Whether your purpose is to clarify or to convince, to refute or to support, good examples will help to get your message across. For this assignment, write a paragraph using three to five well-developed examples to support your controlling idea. The basic organization of this paragraph should be the same as that for all other expository paragraphs covered in this text:

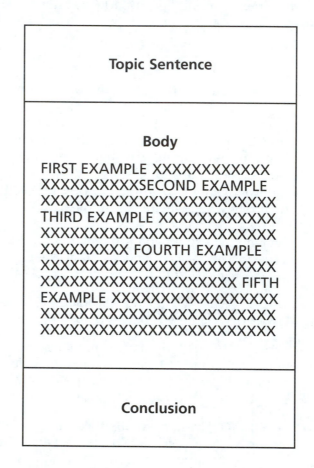

1. Topic sentence
2. Body
3. Conclusion

CHOOSING A TOPIC

Choosing a topic for a paragraph that explains with examples is not too difficult. On any day, listen to your own remarks, or those of your friends, and you will quickly see how often examples are used:

> Carol walks into her class that follows Spanish I, slams her books down on a desk, and says, "That teacher makes me crazy!"

> Their curiosity aroused, everyone now asks Carol for examples of *how* Señor Lopez, the Spanish professor, is causing her distress.

Bob, ecstatic over getting his mother's car for a week while his is in the shop, says, "My mom's a saint, a real Mother Theresa; this is only one of the ways she puts herself out so that I can make it to all of my classes."

If asked, Bob could easily give several more examples of how his mother has made personal sacrifices for him.

Think of the many uses of examples. Use the following list to find a familiar application of examples that you can write about:

> Examples of different kinds of things or people
>
> Examples of how different types of people would react to the same situation
>
> Examples of personality traits or habits of someone you have observed
>
> Examples that explain why you either like or don't like something or someone
>
> Examples of various ways to accomplish something, to achieve a goal, to solve a problem
>
> Examples of how to do something better, more efficiently, more cheaply, more enjoyably
>
> Examples of how something is better or worse than something else
>
> Examples of why someone should
>
> > change his/her attitude or behavior
> >
> > *or*
> >
> > do something differently
> >
> > *or*
> >
> > not do something at all

There are certainly many more uses of examples, but these situations should suggest some ideas for a topic.

✓ Topic Sentence

Writing a topic sentence for your "examples" paragraph follows the process that you should now be familiar with:

1. Choose a subject.
2. Express an attitude toward that subject.
3. Write a clear, specific topic sentence that fully expresses your controlling idea: Subject + attitude = controlling idea.

Note the following topic sentences:

1. Working at Sharkey's Tavern certainly was different.
2. My work experience at Sharkey's Tavern was a real education.
3. After bartending at Sharkey's Tavern for six months, I observed enough examples of abnormal social behavior to complete my Psychology II research paper.
   a. Which of these topic sentences are the most specific?
   b. What is wrong with sentences 1 and 2?
   c. Which key words in sentence 3 determine the focus of the controlling idea?
   d. With sentence 3 as your topic sentence, what would you expect the paragraph to explain?
   e. What kind of examples would support this controlling idea?

Now suppose the writer had chosen different wording:

Some of the regulars at Sharkey's Tavern where I tended bar were unforgettable characters.

a. Which key words in this topic sentence determine the focus of the controlling idea?
b. How would this topic sentence alter the emphasis of the paragraph?
c. What kind of examples would support this topic sentence?

If the writer changed the wording again, what kind of examples would support the following revision?

Working as a bartender at Sharkey's Tavern taught me more about people than did all my psychology books put together.

Even though the preceding sentences deal with the same basic topic, each new wording alters the focus of the controlling idea. As a result, each sentence requires different kinds of examples:

After bartending at Sharkey's Tavern for six months, I observed enough examples of abnormal social behavior to complete my Psychology II research paper.

Logical development: examples of abnormal behavior

Some of the regulars at Sharkey's Tavern where I tended bar were unforgettable characters.

Logical development: examples of unforgettable characters

Working as a bartender at Sharkey's Tavern taught me more about people than did all my psychology books put together.

Logical development: textbook examples contrasted to examples observed from personal experience

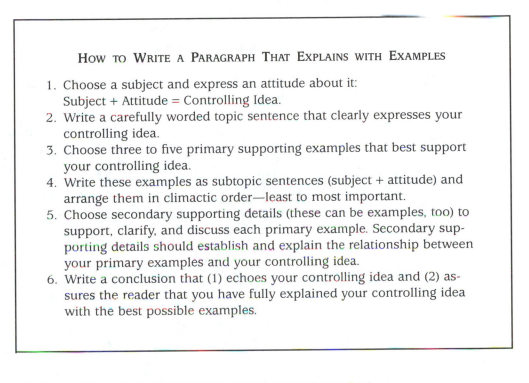

How to Write a Paragraph That Explains with Examples

1. Choose a subject and express an attitude about it:
   Subject + Attitude = Controlling Idea.
2. Write a carefully worded topic sentence that clearly expresses your controlling idea.
3. Choose three to five primary supporting examples that best support your controlling idea.
4. Write these examples as subtopic sentences (subject + attitude) and arrange them in climactic order—least to most important.
5. Choose secondary supporting details (these can be examples, too) to support, clarify, and discuss each primary example. Secondary supporting details should establish and explain the relationship between your primary examples and your controlling idea.
6. Write a conclusion that (1) echoes your controlling idea and (2) assures the reader that you have fully explained your controlling idea with the best possible examples.

EXERCISE 5A: CHOOSING EFFECTIVE CONTROLLING IDEAS

Put a check mark in front of each sentence that contains a controlling idea that could be developed with examples. Explain why the others cannot be effectively developed with examples.

_____ 1. The Trail of Tears, the forced removal of the Cherokee Indians from their homeland, is one of the most tragic stories in American history.

_____ 2. Some of the most profitable gambling casinos in the United States today can be found on Indian reservations.

_____ 3. Crazy Horse, the enigmatic leader of the Oglala Sioux, never allowed himself to be photographed.

_____ 4. In dealing with Geronimo, many American history texts
              dwell on myths, not facts.

_____ 5. Most North American Indian societies were very democratic
              in structure.

_____ 6. The first person to publicly propose the idea that the Ameri-
              can colonies should unite was the Iroquois leader Canassat-
              ego (at the Indian-British assembly in 1744).

_____ 7. The six-nation Iroquois Confederacy had a remarkably de-
              tailed constitution.

_____ 8. Many of the ideas incorporated into the U.S. Constitution
              may have come directly from the Iroquois Constitution.

_____ 9. Benjamin Franklin was so impressed with the Iroquois Con-
              stitution that he wanted to call our elected officials the
              "Grand Council" (the name of the Iroquois governing body)
              instead of the "Congress" of the United States.

_____ 10. The notion of the "barbaric" lifestyle led by Native Ameri-
              cans' societies is negated by numerous instances of whites
              captured by Indian tribes who never wanted to go back to
              white society.

✓ Body

After writing your topic sentence, you must gather and evaluate the information that will develop your controlling idea.

1. Choose the best examples to support your controlling idea.
2. Organize them in a pattern that will develop your controlling idea most
   convincingly.

CHOOSING YOUR EXAMPLES

First, you must search for the best examples to support your controlling idea.
Brainstorming is one way to find examples. (See Chapter 1, page 1.)

Do you remember Carol, the student whose Spanish professor was driving her crazy? When asked by classmates how this happened, she immediately blurted out several examples of his annoying characteristics:

> Jingles change and keys constantly
> Can't stay on the subject

Ignores student questions

Clears his throat incessantly

Always comes to class late

Speaks to only the brightest students

Dresses sloppily

Talks in a monotone

Returns homework and tests late

Paces continuously

Avoids eye contact

Seldom finishes the lesson

Has no compassion for the slow learner

Explains concepts too quickly

Your *first* list of examples should be similar to Carol's list.

Here are some guidelines for choosing examples to support your controlling idea:

1. CHOOSE THE CORRECT NUMBER OF EXAMPLES.

Review your list of examples: Choose the three to five examples from your list that most accurately and specifically support your controlling idea. These examples will be the primary (main) supporting details for your controlling idea. Fewer than three primary examples won't provide enough support for your controlling idea. More than five primary examples will turn your paragraph into nothing more than a list of examples, leaving little or no room to discuss or elaborate on your main points.

2. CHOOSE TYPICAL EXAMPLES.

A **typical example** is one that accurately represents and portrays the class, qualities, or characteristics of the point that you want it to illustrate or clarify.

You express the following controlling idea:

Novice golfers can eventually become proficient at the sport if they play regularly.

You give two examples to support it:

Dan Marino, a professional football player, and Mario Lemieux, a professional hockey player, mastered golf quickly once they began to play regularly.

Are these individuals well-chosen *typical* examples? Absolutely not! Neither Dan nor Mario represent typical examples that could support this controlling idea. Both are gifted natural athletes who have a decided advantage over most average persons who take up golf. Typical examples would be average persons with average ability who become proficient by playing regularly. This would include most of the world's golfers.

In the following paragraph, the student writer provides several well-chosen typical examples of inappropriate children's names. As you read, underline the examples that are *primary* support for her controlling idea. How many does she use?

Before prospective parents decide on the new baby's name, they should consider several important factors that could have an impact on their child as he or she grows older. For instance, names without specific gender, such as Robin, Kelly, and Chris create confusion for teachers who are trying to schedule boys' and girls' gym classes. Master Robin is likely to find himself in the girls' gymnastic program, and Miss Kelly is likely to be named monitor for the boys' restroom. Another problem for the growing child is the fine old family name that other children can distort in name-calling or teasing: Cosmos, Angel, or Nulcan that would seem perfectly suitable for a newborn child are ludicrous when the child is fifty years old. Bambi may seem to be a darling name for a newborn, but Grandma Bambi is an incongruous image. Names usually associated with notorious or outrageous persons should be avoided; Adolph Hitler Smith would spend most of his life defending himself from the abuse of his peers and the disapproval of society. A child who was given a common name

that is spelled differently will spend countless hours throughout life correcting report cards, registration forms, and anyone who asks his or her name for official forms. Mari, Alyce, Jonn, and Tym are examples of common names spelled uncommonly. Prospective parents should remember that of all the things they give their children, the only thing they will keep all their lives is a first name. Accordingly, the greatest care should be taken when choosing a name for a baby.

Cathy Windon

3. *CHOOSE* SPECIFIC *EXAMPLES.*

A **specific example** is one that provides exact, precise support for a controlling idea.

Specific examples aid understanding. What if this textbook did not provide specific examples of different kinds of paragraphs? How would you know how to write a narrative or descriptive paragraph if you had never seen an example of one? Or how many times have you heard a confused student (perhaps even you) ask the teacher to clarify a point with a specific example? Consider the following situation in which Betty has considered going out with George. Jan, who already knows George's style, uses clear, specific examples to enlighten Betty:

Jan: I've known some cheap people in my life, but I've never met anyone as tight as George.

Betty: What do you mean?

Jan: Well, for example, I have never once seen George leave a tip in a restaurant. Also, Burger King is his idea of high-end dining. Whenever George eats out with friends, he always heads for the rest room just before the server brings the check. If the check appears while he is still at the table, he simply waits patiently until someone else picks it up. Betty, you had better take some cash just in case.

Betty gets a clearer picture of George from each new example that Jan provides, and she is probably having second thoughts about going out with him. Jan continues to give specific examples of George's miserly habits.

Jan: Also, Betty, wear your Nikes and not heels; George won't spend money on gas if he doesn't have to. If any destination is within walking distance (for George, this means anything within a five-mile radius), plan on hiking, rain or shine—and bring your own umbrella. If George has to drive, he refuses to pay for parking. Even if there's a parking garage next to the theater, he'll drive for blocks until he finds a free lot or a space on some dark, deserted side street.

With each new example, Betty gets a clearer understanding of Jan's first remark about George. You can use precise examples, just as Jan did:

> To narrow *general knowledge (George is cheap)* down to *specific knowledge* (precise examples that prove George *is* cheap)

4. CHOOSE RELEVANT EXAMPLES.

A **relevant example** supports a point *precisely*. It must be appropriate and suitable for that point; it must pertain to that point.

Avoid irrelevant examples; they destroy paragraph unity.

a. If you are discussing easy and difficult professors, an example of a middle-of-the-road grader is *not* relevant.

b. If you are criticizing the overly complex explanations in a particular technical manual, a clearly explained concept from the same manual is *not* relevant to your controlling idea.

c. If you are discussing the poor food served in school cafeterias, all of the examples that you use should relate only to school cafeterias—not to hospital, office building, or department store cafeterias. These other cafeterias are *not* relevant examples.

If you want to make a point effectively, you must choose examples that are both relevant and specific. Suppose, for example, you were writing a paragraph to prove that some of the laws that have been passed in Massachusetts seem ridiculously funny in today's world. Examples such as the following are effective:

> According to an old law of Truro, Massachusetts, a young man could not get married until he had killed either six blackbirds or three crows.
>
> It is illegal to eat peanuts in church in Massachusetts.
>
> In Massachusetts, it is an infraction of the law to lounge around on bakery shelves.
>
> To take a bath in Boston, you must have a doctor's written prescription.

The following two examples, however, are *not* effective:

> Massachusetts has a ridiculous law about church.
>
> Massachusetts passed some funny laws about getting married and taking a bath.

These are not effective because they are not specific. They may be relevant—pertaining to the controlling idea—but they are still vague and unclear.

To take a bath in Boston, you must have a doctor's written prescription.

Now look at the following examples:

> Singing out of tune in North Carolina is against the law.
>
> In Gary, Indiana, it is illegal to attend the theater within four hours of eating garlic.
>
> Salt Lake City, Utah, has a law against carrying an unwrapped ukelele on the street.
>
> Florida's Sarasota still carries an old law that makes it illegal for anyone in a bathing suit to sing in a public place.

Barbara Seuling, *You Can't Eat Peanuts in Church and Other Little-Known Laws*

These examples would not be effective either because, although they are quite specific, they are completely irrelevant. Not one of these examples relates to a Massachusetts law.

EXERCISE 5B: CHOOSING RELEVANT EXAMPLES

Suppose, for a paper on Native Americans, you are writing a paragraph about their advanced state of medical knowledge compared to that of the early settlers. Put a check mark before the sentences that would be relevant to your paper.

_____ 1. Did you know that American Indians were taking aspirin for headaches and sore muscles for hundreds of years before Europeans discovered it?

_____ 2. The main ingredient in aspirin is salicin, which the Indians found in the bark of the willow tree.

———————— 3. Although a white settler, James Lind, is credited with "discovering" the cure for scurvy in 1795, American Indians had actually discovered the only cure for scurvy about 300 years earlier—large doses of vitamin C, which they found in the bark of the hemlock tree.

———————— 4. Native Americans also get no recognition for what may have been a very significant influence on our form of government.

———————— 5. Many of the ideas adopted in our Constitution may have come directly from Benjamin Franklin's and Charles Thompson's knowledge of the detailed constitution of the Iroquois Confederacy.

———————— 6. In the 1600s, European doctors were still trying (unsuccessfully) to cure malaria with leeches and strange potions, but the Quechua Indians in Peru had long before discovered the only effective remedy, quinine, in a bitter-tasting bark of a tree growing in the Amazon Basin.

———————— 7. Millions of Europeans were dying every year from malaria epidemics, still thinking that their knowledge of medicine was far superior to that of the "savages."

———————— 8. While the London College of Physicians was banning the use of the ipecocuana root because they thought it was poisonous, American Indians were using it to induce vomiting in cases of snakebite.

———————— 9. Syrup of ipecac is now recognized as one of the most critical drugs on hand in emergency rooms and poison centers throughout the country.

———————— 10. Native American mothers were lining their babies' diapers with sphagnum moss (a naturally sterile plant species) to absorb moisture long before modern technology finally came up with the idea of an absorbent diaper—Pampers.

ORGANIZING YOUR EXAMPLES

As stated at the beginning of this chapter, the examples in the body of your paragraph that support your controlling idea can function in two ways: as *primary support* and as *secondary support*.

Primary Supporting Examples

1. Directly support your controlling idea.
2. Express the major points of your controlling idea.
3. Are written as subtopic sentences, each with its own subject and attitude.

Secondary Supporting Examples

1. Directly support your primary examples.
2. Discuss and clarify your primary examples.
3. Indirectly support your controlling idea.

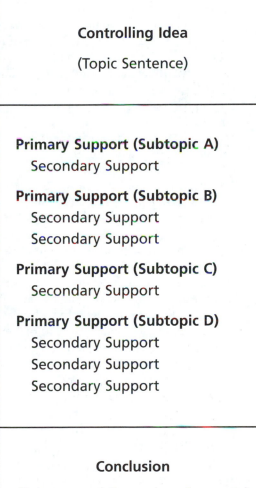

In the following example, a student has written a paragraph about Dr. Spooner, a Victorian scholar who was known for his riotous mistakes in speaking. Notice how the writer uses examples for both primary and secondary support as he describes some of Spooner's funniest blunders.

Topic sentence	**William A. Spooner (1844–1930), the Victorian scholar, was so prestigious that he became the Master of New College, Oxford, but he delighted his students because of the marvelously funny mistakes that he made in speaking.**
Primary support #1	In his personal life, his most frequent error was transposing the initial letters of words.
Secondary support for #1	Reporting a "crushing blow," he called it a "blushing crow." Once, he remarked to a delighted friend that he "had in his heart a half-warmed fish." [had in his heart a half-formed wish] To another friend he confided that he had never fully appreciated "Sheets and Kelly." [Keats and Shelley were famous British Romantic poets.]
Primary support #2	In his professional life, in both pulpit and lectern, he was equally tangled.
Secondary support for #2	Trying to help some parishioners be seated, he kindly offered, "Please let me sew you to your sheets." [show you to your seats] He also reproached a student for "hissing my mystery lessons." [missing my history lesson] He even threatened him with expulsion "on the next town drain." [on the next train out of town]
Primary support #3	Sometimes his mistakes with words led to physical mistakes.
Extended secondary support for #3	Mr. Spooner was found one evening wandering disconsolately about the streets of Greenwich. "I've been here for an hour," he complained. "I had an important appointment to meet someone at 'The Dull Man,' Greenwich, and I can't find it anywhere. The really odd thing is that no one seems to have heard of it." Late that night, he went home to Oxford. "You idiot," exclaimed his long-suffering wife, "it was 'The Green Man,' Dulwich, you had to go to.
Conclusion	**Not because of his considerable academic achievements, but because of his errors, "Spoonerisms," Dr. Spooner remains a legendary hero of amusement.**

Meanwhile, Carol, our frustrated Spanish student, remembered that her next assignment for English Composition I was the "Explaining with Examples" paragraph. She decided that Señor Lopez, her least favorite teacher, would be an ideal subject. Naturally, she didn't use his name and instead identified her subject as a fictitious former high school Spanish teacher, Señor Xerxes.

She then made a list of Señor Lopez' annoying characteristics for use as possible examples—the same traits that she had previously complained to her classmates about. Now, having subject, attitude, and potential examples, Carol wrote her topic sentence:

> Although most teachers care about their students and try to create a positive learning atmosphere in class, my high school Spanish teacher, Señor Xerxes, alienated almost every student who took his course.

Next, Carol reviewed her list of examples:

Can't stay on the subject	Ignores student questions
Clears his throat incessantly	Always comes to class late
Has no compassion for the slow learner	Talks in a monotone
Jingles change and keys constantly	Dresses sloppily
Speaks to only the brightest students	Paces continuously
Avoids eye contact	Seldom finishes the lesson
Explains concepts too quickly	Returns homework and tests late

After reviewing her list, Carol discovered that these examples could be grouped under one of three subject headings:

> his personal habits
>
> his teaching methods
>
> his attitude toward his students

She also realized that these headings alone said nothing; they had to make a statement—*express an attitude that would support her controlling idea*. By asking herself the following questions, she developed an attitude for each subject heading:

> **Question:** How did his personal habits turn students off?
> **Answer:** They were *distracting*.
> **Statement:** His personal habits were distracting.
>
> **Question:** How did his teaching methods turn students off?
> **Answer:** They were *ineffective*.
> **Statement:** His teaching methods were ineffective.
>
> **Question:** How did his attitude turn students off?
> **Answer:** It was *indifferent*.
> **Statement:** His attitude toward his students was indifferent.

Carol then made these statements—now *subtopic* sentences—the **primary supporting examples** for her controlling idea. She arranged them in climactic order, from least to most important.

I. His personal habits were distracting.

> (1st primary supporting detail)

II. His teaching methods were ineffective.

>   (2nd primary supporting detail)

III. His attitude toward his students was indifferent.

>   (3rd primary supporting detail)

Next, Carol used the examples from her list as **secondary supporting details,** placing each one under the appropriate primary example. She again used climactic order, from least to most important.

Topic sentence: Although most teachers care about their students and try to create a positive learning atmosphere in class, my high school Spanish teacher, Señor Xerxes, alienated almost every student who took his course.

I. His personal habits were distracting.

>   (1st primary supporting detail)

A. He dressed sloppily.   (least important)

>   (secondary supporting detail)

B. He jingled his change and keys constantly.
C. He cleared his throat incessantly.
D. He paced continuously.   (most important)

II. His teaching methods were ineffective.

>   (2nd primary supporting detail)

A. He avoided eye contact.   (least important)

>   (secondary supporting detail)

B. He talked in a monotone.
C. He couldn't stay on the subject.
D. He seldom finished the lesson.
E. He explained concepts too quickly.   (most important)

III. His attitude toward his students was indifferent.

>   (3rd primary supporting detail)

A. He always came to class late.   (least important)

>   (secondary supporting detail)

B. He returned homework and tests late.
C. He spoke to only the brightest students.
D. He had no compassion for the slow learner.
E. He ignored student questions.   (most important)

Carol then used this outline of primary and secondary supporting details to write her first rough draft. After several revisions, she wrote her final copy:

Although most teachers care about their students and try to create a positive learning atmosphere in class, my high school Spanish teacher, Señor Xerxes, alienated almost every student who took his course. First, his personal habits and mannerisms were very distracting and unprofessional. Some teachers have a trendy rumpled look, but Señor's clothes looked as if he had slept in them for a week. His teaching wardrobe consisted of a faded once-white dress shirt, baggy tan gabardine slacks (frayed and shiny), and an Aztec sunburst tie which had suffered many a leaky nacho. Most annoying, however, was his endless pacing, back and forth: hands in pockets, change jingling with every step, and clearing his throat to punctuate each thought. These habits only complemented his equally uninspiring teaching methods. He looked at the wall or the floor, but never at us—except when some underdressed bimbo batted her eyes and tossed him a question "en Español." His droning monotone floated whimsically from verb conjugations to the bullfights, as we fought to stay awake. He never did finish a lesson, and if it wasn't for the textbook, no one would have passed. When he did attempt to explain something, it was for "the quick," and not for us, "the dead." Señor's worst fault, however, was his attitude toward us, his unfortunate students. He couldn't have cared less if we passed or failed. He came to class (usually late), put in his uninspiring forty-five minutes, and immediately bolted for the teachers' lounge. Homework and tests were returned two to three weeks after being given, with grades only, and no comments. We were just another list of names in his grade book, except for the chosen few—straight A's and semifluent in Spanish. He never had time for slow learners or those of us who needed extra help, nor would he respond to questions from the class—unless someone would feed his ego. Fortunately, I passed Spanish I, and my other teachers, without exception, compensated for the time that I wasted with Señor Xerxes.

Although this version of Carol's paragraph has not yet been graded by her English instructor, you can see how she effectively organized her primary and secondary supporting details to support her controlling idea.

EXERCISE 5C: ORGANIZING IDEAS USING SUBTOPICS

Try writing subtopics for each of the following sentences:

1. The kinds of peer pressure one usually experiences as a college freshman can have a dramatic impact on a student's life.
2. My brother's generosity knows no bounds.
3. Few of today's athletes can be described as good role models.
4. Ryan is forever coming up with ingenious excuses for why he never has time to study.
5. Sometimes I think my dog is really a human in disguise.

✓ The Extended Example

Although your assignment was to write a paragraph using three to five well-developed examples to support your controlling idea, there are other creative ways to organize and to present examples. An **extended example**

> is usually used as primary support.
>
> is supported by a detailed narrative that discusses and clarifies its relationship to the controlling idea.
>
> can be used in combination with other types of examples.

In the following paragraph, the writer uses two short hypothetical examples followed by an extended example (a true experience) to support his controlling idea:

Topic Sentence	**A reputation that took years to build can be destroyed in minutes.**
Short example	A man has devoted forty years of his life to his job in a bank. He has given faithful and loyal service. One day he takes two hundred dollars of the bank's money home. The man is branded a crook, an embezzler. He is fired from his job; he is forever disgraced and possibly threatened with prison. Who remembers the forty years of good service?
Short example	Again, a man who is a loving husband and a kind and provident father for twenty-five years becomes infatuated with a girl. He takes her out. When his wife and children learn of this, he becomes an outcast. The twenty-five good years are forgotten.
Extended example	A spectacular case of more than sixty years ago proves that one misstep can ruin forever a carefully built reputation. In the years following World War I, the national craze for baseball grew progressively wilder. Fans crowded into stadiums. Stars swelled into heroes. Of all the teams, the Chicago White Sox were the best, with the best pitchers, runners, and teamwork. Then, in 1919, the Sox threw the World Series. People took their baseball very seriously in those days, so this crookedness gave them an ugly shock. After the scandal hearings, the guilty players were too frightened of mobs to leave the courtrooms. One of the guilty players, considered the best before Babe Ruth, was Shoeless Joe Jackson. As Jackson left the hearing, a youngster called out to him, "Say it ain't so, Joe." Even though the remark has remained as a wistful part of the American language, the scandal was, unfortunately, true. The Sox were wiped out as a team and the individual members barred from organized baseball and the baseball Hall of Fame. Baseball itself came perilously close to extinction.
Conclusion	**Reputation is, indeed, a fragile thing. It takes years to build, but only a moment to lose.**

CONCLUSION

A paragraph that explains with examples needs an effective **conclusion,** but it should *not* end with one of your examples. You expressed a controlling idea, you explained and clarified with good examples. Now write a conclusion that further reinforces the reader's confidence in your knowledge of the subject. This is your final opportunity to assure the reader that you have successfully explained, informed, convinced, persuaded, or clarified.

Avoid closing too strongly; conclude with a measure of subtlety and finesse so that the reader cannot detect your overwhelming enthusiasm for having done such a good job. An effective conclusion should provide

1. A solid, creative restatement (not verbatim) of your controlling idea.
2. A final reminder to the reader that your supporting examples successfully explained/clarified your controlling idea.

Notice how the conclusion of the following paragraph repeats and reinforces the attitude expressed in the controlling idea:

> **Russian cuisine today is much more than fare for a daily meal; it is an expression of a cultural history one thousand years old.** The Russian peasants were poor; they were used to a meager existence and had generations of practice making the most of it. Primarily a rural people, they lived off their land and developed a rich cultural and gastronomic tradition based on religious observance and the celebration of life, family, and friendship. The traditional staples of simple Russian peasant fare—bread, potatoes, noodles, cabbage, mushrooms, and cheese—all washed down with liberal quantities of vodka, remain the same today, with some refinements. Bread, the foremost staple of Russian food, is served with all meals, no matter how large or small, and is also the "chaser" for the many obligatory glasses of vodka that are consumed for all occasions, minor or significant. Potatoes, once eaten only boiled, are now baked into delicious dough envelopes (pagach) or served as potato pancakes fried in batter. Cabbage and noodles accompany any good meal, usually with beef in a Stroganoff, or in soup, such as borscht. Wild mushrooms, a national delicacy made immortal by Chekhov and Tolstoy, are still a great favorite, prepared separately or as an ingredient to enhance other dishes. Russians savor mushrooms sauteed, mixed with scrambled eggs or gravy, in mushroom sauerkraut soup, or in stuffed cabbage. Also, other alcoholic beverages, such as cognac, wine, and brandy, now accompany the ever-present vodka. These are consumed throughout the meal, inspiring loud toasts to everyone's health, followed with bites of bread, lunch meats, and cheese. During holidays, and especially at Easter, these foods are at their best; the eating and drinking does not even begin until after midnight mass. **The Russian meal is history, tradition, a celebration of everything good in life—it is much more than just food and a time to satisfy hunger.**

Tony Pieta

✓ Some Do's . . .

1. *Do* choose examples that are both specific and relevant. Remember that the quantity of your examples means nothing if the *quality* of your examples is poor.
2. *Do* provide enough examples to prove your point. One or two short examples will never satisfy the curiosity of an intelligent reader.
3. *Do* understand the purpose of your examples before you write your paragraph. Are you using examples to inform, to persuade, to clarify—or for all of these reasons?

✓ . . . and Don'ts About Explaining with Examples

1. *Don't* use a series of slanted examples that may distort the truth. Use unbiased, objective, representative examples.
2. *Don't* give a brief example and then move right on to the next example without explaining the first one. Clarify and discuss each example so that your readers will understand how it relates to the point that it supports.
3. *Don't* rely on a single extended example unless that example is comprehensive enough to illustrate your point.

SUGGESTED ACTIVITIES AND ASSIGNMENTS

Nothing clarifies meaning more consistently than the use of good examples. Without examples, teachers couldn't teach and students couldn't learn. Since examples are so useful in aiding understanding, writers call on them frequently. They are most often used to inform readers—to define a term, illustrate a generalization, clarify a comparison, and so on—but they can also be used to help the writer persuade the reader.

The philosopher, Will Durant, used examples to *clarify* his definition of education: "Education is a progressive discovery of our ignorance." Oscar Wilde, on the other hand, employed examples to *persuade* us that "nothing that is worth knowing can be taught." Examples helped Mark Twain *explain* what he meant when he said: "I have never let my schooling interfere with my education," and they also helped Will Rogers convince his audience that "there is nothing so stupid as an educated man, if you get off the subject he was educated in."

Will Rogers as the quintessential "common man" disapproved of the supposed superiority of the educated class. For example, newspaper mogul William Randolph Hearst once invited Rogers to his famous ranch for the weekend. Hearst encouraged Rogers to joke with and generally amuse his friends. After the weekend, Rogers sent Hearst a large bill. When Hearst responded that

Rogers was asked as a guest, not an entertainer, Rogers said that he only considered himself a guest when Mrs. Rogers was invited with him.

As a representative of the common man, Rogers highly rated honesty. A piano company once urged him to endorse their instruments even though he couldn't play. For their ad, he wrote, "Your pianos are the best I have ever leaned against." It was the man himself Will Rogers admired, not the polish his education gave to him.

1. Using the required textbook from your favorite class, select a chapter that you have not yet read. Then remove all of the examples from one section of the chapter. Tape strips of paper over those lines containing examples, and read that section aloud to your class. See if they understand the concepts being discussed. Ask them to explain those concepts in their own words. Then read the section aloud again, complete with the author's examples, and see if the examples enhance the students' understanding of the concepts. Ask the students to explain their concepts again in their own words, once they have heard the concepts explained with examples. How much did the examples contribute to the students' understanding?

2. The sentences following are *aphorisms,* brief assertions of general truths about human nature in wise and witty form. Using one of these as a topic sentence, develop a paragraph with specific examples.
   a. Man is the only animal that laughs and weeps; for he is the only animal that is struck by the difference between what things are and what they might have been. (William Hazlitt)
   b. One can bear grief, but it takes two to be glad. (E. Hubbard)
   c. Socrates said, "Know thyself." If I knew myself, I'd run away. (Johann Wolfgang von Goethe)
   d. It is impossible for a man to be cheated by anyone but himself. (Ralph Waldo Emerson)
   e. Make me chaste, o God, but not quite yet. (St. Augustine)
   f. You can give without loving, but you cannot love without giving. (William Faulkner)
   g. Swans have an air of being proud, stupid, and mischievous—three qualities that go well together. (Denis Diderot)
   h. Certainly, the dog is loyal. But why, on that account, should we take him as an example? He is loyal to men, not to other dogs. (Karl Kraus)
   i. Home is the place, where, if you have to go there, they have to take you in. (Robert Frost)
   j. From what we get, we can make a living; what we give, however, makes a life. (Arthur Ashe)

3. Think of someone you know well. Select a particular habit or characteristic—recklessness, absentmindedness, chronic lateness, wearing mismatched clothes—and develop a paragraph describing that person through the use of examples.

SENTENCES

Using subtopic sentences is a natural for the paragraph developed by examples, but subtopic sentences can be used in almost any type of development. In narrating about a mountain climbing trip, you might well divide your paragraph into three steps—the trip up, the moments on top of the mountain, and the trip down—announcing each step in a subtopic sentence. In describing someone, you might use subtopics such as

A. His face reminded you of a bulldog's.
B. His body was heavy, but it didn't seem to be fat.
C. His movements were graceful, like those of an athlete.

Subtopics are an effective way to develop paragraphs of comparison/contrast, division and classification, process, definition, and persuasion. But subtopics alone are not usually enough.

The well-developed paragraph generally requires both *primary* and *secondary support*. Subtopic sentences that directly support the controlling idea provide the primary support. Other sentences, however, are needed to provide the secondary support to illustrate or clarify your main supporting points. It is this secondary support that puts flesh on the bare bones of your paragraph and develops it fully enough to show your readers exactly what you mean. Notice how the author of the following paragraph clarifies each main supporting point with secondary details:

Watching television, you'd think we lived at bay, in total jeopardy, surrounded on all sides by human-seeking germs, shielded against infection and death by a chemical technology that enables us to keep killing them off. *We are instructed to spray disinfectants everywhere,* into the air of our bedrooms and kitchens and with special energy into our bathrooms, since it is our very own germs that seem the worst kind. We explode clouds of aerosol, mixed for good luck with deodorants, into our noses, mouths, underarms, privileged crannies—even into the intimate insides of our telephones. *We apply potent antibiotics to minor scratches and seal them with plastic.* Plastic is the new protector: we wrap the already plastic tumblers of hotels in more plastic, and seal the toilet seats like state secrets after irradiating them with ultraviolet light. We live in a world where the microbes are always trying to get at us, to tear us cell from cell, and we only stay alive and whole through diligence and fear.

Lewis Thomas, *The Lives of a Cell,*
Notes of a Biology Watcher

✓ The Underdeveloped Paragraph

The following paragraph is underdeveloped because, although there are three subtopic sentences, there is no secondary support for any of the three.

> A couple of years ago, a woman wrote an essay called "I Want a Wife" because, she maintained, wives were servants to their husbands. They were high-class servants, she said, but they were servants all the same, and she wanted one. There was much in what she said, but she did not say more than half of it. Husbands are equally servants to wives. A husband is expected to do the most unpleasant household chores or those that are in any way dangerous. In times of family difficulty, the family turns to him for practical solutions, even when such solutions seem impossible. In usual circumstances, the heavier financial responsibility rests on his shoulders. Rather than quarreling about who contributes more to the marriage, I think both husbands and wives would be happier if they concentrated on supporting each other.

EXERCISE 5D: DEVELOPING SUPPORTING DETAILS

Develop each of the writer's subtopics with two or three examples of specific supporting detail.

Topic sentence: Husbands are equally servants to wives.

Subtopic A: He is expected to do the most unpleasant chores or those that are in any way dangerous.

_____

_____

Subtopic B: In times of family difficulty, the family turns to him for practical solutions, even when such solutions seem impossible.

_____

_____

Subtopic C: In usual circumstances, the greater financial responsibility rests on his shoulders.

_____

_____

Concluding Sentence: Rather than quarreling about who contributes more to the marriage, I think both husbands and wives would be happier if they concentrated on supporting each other.

EXERCISE 5E: DEVELOPING SUPPORTING DETAILS

The following paragraph is underdeveloped because, although there are three subtopic sentences, there are no secondary supports for any of the three.

Playing on my high school basketball team taught me much more than I had ever expected to learn. Coach Reilly taught me far more than the fine arts of dribbling and guarding and making good hook shots: he taught me some of life's most valuable lessons. I learned, for example, that I am capable of almost anything *if* I am willing to work hard enough to achieve my goals. I also learned how to accept constructive criticism. But the most important lesson I learned from my coach is that winning isn't everything. After three years with Coach Reilly, I was not just a better basketball player: I was a better person.

Pick out each subtopic sentence and make up details to support each subtopic.

Subtopic A:

_____

Supporting details:

_____

_____

_____

Subtopic B:

_____

Supporting details:

_____

_____

_____

Subtopic C:

_____

Supporting details:

_____

_____

_____

✓ Restrictive and Nonrestrictive Clauses

As you attempt to make your paragraph clear to your reader by showing which points are major by making them your primary supports and which are minor, by making them secondary supports, you must do the same thing in your sentences. You have already learned to subordinate less important ideas in your sentences. In this section, you will learn to show your reader what clauses in your sentences are necessary to its meaning and which clauses provide added but not necessary information.

Whether clauses are necessary (restrictive) or unnecessary (nonrestrictive) is shown by punctuation. Later in this chapter, we include a review of punctuation.

Recognizing the distinction between restrictive and nonrestrictive modifiers is important not only for sentence structure but also for punctuation. The basic distinction is that a **restrictive modifier** is essential to the meaning of the sentence, whereas a **nonrestrictive modifier** merely adds information to a sentence that would already be clear without it.

> *Restrictive:* The man *who is wearing a gray pin-striped suit* is his father.

The modifying clause here, *who is wearing a gray pin-striped suit,* is essential to the meaning of the sentence. It designates or points out the subject. Without it, we would not know which man was being referred to.

> *Nonrestrictive:* His father, *who was wearing a gray pin-striped suit,* met him at the airport.

The modifying clause here merely adds information to a sentence that would already be clear without it. Although it gives additional information, it is not essential to the core sentence, "His father met him at the airport."

The restrictive modifier, being an essential part of the sentence, is *not* set off by commas. The nonrestrictive modifier, however, *is* set off by commas because you can take it out of the sentence without changing the sentence's meaning.

> *Restrictive:*   The elm trees *which are diseased* will be cut down.

The writer does not mean "all elm trees will be cut down." Only the trees "which are diseased" will be cut down.

Note how punctuation could alter the meaning completely:

> *Nonrestrictive:*   The elm trees, which are diseased, will be cut down.

Here, *which are diseased* is nonrestrictive. The core sentence is "the elm trees will be cut down" meaning all the elm trees. The modifying clause, *which are diseased,* merely adds additional explanatory information.

Whether or not a modifying phrase or clause is restrictive or nonrestrictive may depend on content and the writer's intention. **You must signal your intention clearly by the punctuation you use.**

The elm trees which are diseased
will be cut down.

> The student radicals who are disrupting classes should be expelled.

Here the writer does not mean that all student radicals should be expelled, only that those student radicals *who are disrupting* classes should be expelled.

> The student radicals, who are disrupting classes, should be expelled.

The punctuation changes the meaning here; clearly the writer does mean that *all* student radicals should be expelled.

Although many fine distinctions can be made among nonrestrictive elements, the general rule for punctuation is this: **Any modifying word, phrase, or clause not essential to the meaning of the sentence should be set off by commas. (If such a modifier comes at the beginning or end of the sentence, only one comma is needed.)**

Note the punctuation in the following sentences:

The suit that I bought at Taylor's is hanging in George's closet.

My suit, the blue checkered one that I bought at Taylor's, is hanging in George's closet.

Long before sunrise, at 3:00 A.M., the men were aroused for patrol duty.

During the summer of 1969, after his freshman year at Edinboro, he made his first trip to Wyoming.

The only thing to do in a case like that is to get the best lawyer you can find.

MODIFIERS AND PUNCTUATION

RESTRICTIVE MODIFIER:	Provides information that is **essential** to the sentence, so it should not be set off with commas:
	The girl *who asked me to marry her* is now the Assistant Director of the FBI.
	(If you remove this clause, the sentence doesn't identify the girl: "The girl is now the Assistant Director of the FBI.")
NONRESTRICTIVE MODIFIER:	Provides only secondary detail that is not essential to the meaning of the main clause. Since it interrupts the main flow of thought, it should be set off with commas:
	My old girlfriend, *who is now working for the FBI,* was a real whiz in math.
	(If you remove this clause, the main idea is still clear: "My old girlfriend was a real whiz in math.")

EXERCISE 5F: PUNCTUATING RESTRICTIVE AND NONRESTRICTIVE CLAUSES

Punctuate the following sentences to show whether the clauses are restrictive (necessary—no punctuation) or nonrestrictive (not necessary to meaning of sentence—set off by commas).

1. The man who had been badly cheated hired a lawyer.

    _____

2. The cheater a well-known businessman expected to get away with it.

    _____

3. The lawyer who had dealt with the cheater before ignored his reputation.

    _____

4. The man who had been cheated was irate.

    _____

5. The man who cheated expected to get away with his scam.

    _____

6. The grades of the papers which are late will be lowered.

    _____

7. The children who were naughty won't be asked to the picnic.

    _____

8. The women's club which was most creative won an award.

    _____

9. The women's club which was most creative enjoyed their meetings.

    _____

10. Anyone who likes drama will love *Emma*.

    _____

✓ Parenthetical Expressions and Other Interrupters

Parenthetical expressions are sentence interrupters not directly connected to the sentence in which they occur. They are set off by commas before and after the interruption.

The Senate will, *of course,* have to act on the bill if it is to become law.

The mere possession of marijuana, *I believe,* should not be a criminal offense.

The nature of our society, *according to the author,* has changed irreversibly since World War II.

Interrupters that create a sharp break in thought or in grammatical structure should be set off by dashes.

He then asked the motley crowd—*beggars, drunks, prostitutes, and the permanently unemployed*—if they were prepared for the Second Coming.

He wrote this brilliant novel—*completely broke at the time*—in just sixty-four days.

A dash may also be used to set off a final word or phrase that summarizes or emphasizes the idea that precedes it.

She had everything in the world she could want except one thing—love.

Sometimes the dash can be used for a final twist or striking afterthought.

He cursed and flayed them, drove them day and night, worked them until they dropped—turning raw recruits into fighting men.

Use a dash following an initial list when it is followed by *that, this, these,* or a similar pronoun as the subject of a summarizing statement.

Hot dogs, potato chips, mustard, onions, cherry pie, ice cream—*those* were things she ate while watching television.

The waste, the callousness, the inefficiency, the mindless routine—*that* is what I hate about military service.

The dash should be used *sparingly.* It should never be used carelessly as a substitute for the comma or the semicolon.

✓ A Punctuation Review

Throughout this book, you have been learning about the importance of being clear. You cannot be clear without correct punctuation. Notice how punctuation alone can change the meaning of a sentence.

Turn the heat on Rocky.

Turn the heat on, Rocky.

Study for the test; on Wednesday, the tutor will be here to answer your questions.

Study for the test on Wednesday; the tutor will be here to answer your questions.

Does it make any difference where you put the punctuation mark? It could make a great deal of difference to Rocky or to a student who wants to pass the test.

You should be familiar with several basic rules of punctuation.

1. **Use a comma when you put a dependent clause before an independent or main clause.**

   When I have to take a test, I get nervous.

2. **Use a comma before the coordinating conjunctions when you connect two main clauses.**

   I used to hate movies, but now I'm a fan.

3. **Use a semicolon between two main clauses when you do not use a coordinating conjunction.**

   I never eat breakfast; I never have time.

4. **Use a comma between words, phrases, or clauses in a series.**

   Words, phrases, and clauses in a series must be separated by commas.

5. **Use a semicolon before and a comma after a conjunctive adverb.**

   I never have any money; therefore, I can never go on vacation.

6. **Use a comma both before and after an adverb not used as a conjunction.**

   The engine, then, will need a complete overhaul.

7. **Use a comma before and after a nonrestrictive modifier.**

   My brother, who is a cowboy, lives in Arizona.

8. **Use a comma before and after parenthetical expressions and other interrupters.**

   The book, in my opinion, is an exciting story of the West.

9. **Use a dash to set off interrupters that create a sharp break in thought.**

   His excuse—if you could call it that—was miserable.

10. **Use a comma after words of enumeration, between elements of month-day-year dates, and between elements of addresses.**

    One, two, button your shoe.

    On October 31, 1997, she moved.

    Her new address is 909 Maple Lane, Oxford, MS 38655.

✓ Additional Points on Punctuation

1. **Avoid the comma splice.**

Incorrect:	The program was quite exciting, it had many scenes from combat films.
	You will have to decide what you want to do however, you should get Mr. Fields' advice.
Correct:	The program was quite exciting; it had many scenes from combat films.
	You will have to decide what you want to do; however, you should get Mr. Field's advice.

2. **Don't separate subordinate elements from the main clause.**

Incorrect:	I met him in Albany. Coming around the corner from the bus depot.
	The air show was a big thrill for me. Because I had never seen one before.
Correct:	I met him in Albany, coming around the corner from the bus depot.
	The air show was a big thrill for me because I had never seen one before.

3. **Don't put commas around restrictive modifiers.**

   The man *who owns the apartment building* is a retired railroad engineer.

   The groups *that complain the loudest about government regulations* are also the first to call for protection from the big corporations.

4. **Use a comma to separate coordinate adjectives.** Adjectives are coordinate if the comma could be replaced by *and*. You could say, "tall and slender and graceful" or "bright and energetic and young," but you would never say "little and old man."

5. **In most cases, separate introductory words, phrases, or clauses from the main clauses of the sentence.** Notice how confusing the following sentences are if you read them without a pause.

> Underneath, the planks were all rotted.
>
> Beneath the surface, hot springs bubbled and percolated.
>
> As we drove by, the old mansion looked like the perfect setting for a horror movie.

6. **In a series of three or more items, put the comma before the *and*.** You are never wrong in including the comma before *and*. Leaving it out could sometimes cause doubt. For example, suppose you described a series of flags as "blue, green, purple, orange and black." Your reader might well wonder whether there were four flags or five.

> We met Fred, Bill, and Tony.
>
> An attack was launched by land, by sea, and by air.
>
> He knew that the car was expensive, that he didn't need such a big car, and that he was foolish for buying it.

EXERCISE 5G: PUNCTUATION REVIEW

Correct the punctuation in the following sentences. You may want to make two sentences. If the sentence needs no punctuation, put a *C* at the end.

1. Jack said to his mother will you please feed the dog.
2. There are three things to consider before going on an overnight hike shoes food and medications.
3. College expenses are high now and are getting higher every year.
4. My mother asked if the prom was worth all the work it required.
5. Tony and Millie smiled at each other and said certainly.
6. To play golf gets more and more popular and more and more expensive.
7. It's been said the more money a person makes the longer hours he chooses to work do you think that is true.
8. As a branch of literature science fiction is of course not new.
9. As early as the second century Lucian a Greek writer wrote a story of a journey to the moon.
10. Many writers famous for other kinds of literature wrote science fiction. Swift did and so did Aldous Huxley and H. G. Wells and it was Jules Verne's major theme.
11. Usually however earlier writers thought of science fiction as only entertainment and less important than the bulk of their writings.

12. Contemporary science fiction writers take science fiction seriously and so do modern critics of science fiction.

13. The critics insist that the writers must observe certain rules such as using inventions or gadgets or machines that are logical extensions of real discoveries.

14. There is a general agreement among these writers that they must not create anything in their books that goes against the laws of nature.

15. To make sure that every detail is correct film and television industries hire doctors physicists and biologists.

16. When children's books are not clearly imaginary the critics are especially careful to assure scientific correctness.

17. In America some of the best known science fiction writers are actually scientists several of international stature who write under pen names.

18. Some critics and sociologists believe that science fiction is the only literature for the future because life in the future will really extend to other planets.

19. Arthur Koestler distinguished journalist and novelist disagrees with this opinion of science fiction because he says our imagination is limited.

20. Even good readers Koestler says cannot project themselves into the distant future any more than they can project themselves into the distant past.

21. The historical novel is almost dead today he believes because the figures of the past like the figures of the future are visible only dimly.

22. Every culture is an island Koestler sums up communicating with other islands but it is only familiar with itself.

23. Art means seeing the familiar in a new light it also means seeing tragedy in the trivial event.

24. The novels of Swift Huxley and Orwell are great works of literature because the gadgets of the future and the strangeness of alien worlds serve merely as a background.

25. They are literature to the extent that they are not science fiction but are works of disciplined imagination.

WORDS

The Glaring—and Not-So-Glaring—Errors

The **glaring error** is the phrase used by English teachers and others to signify an error that marks one as unobservant or uneducated, or even stupid or as having some other egregious failing. It simply identifies a mistake that is immediately apparent to the perpetrator's reader or listener, and the reader or listener, recognizing the error, jumps to the conclusion that the writer or speaker is a dunce.

Actually, glaring errors are often caused by bad habits of speech. We all hear people using incorrect words, and we often pick them up. You can get away with using some of them in speech because they sound like the correct usage; for example, if you say, "I *should of* gotten an A on that test," your listener may have heard it as, "I *should've* gotten an A on that test," which is correct. However, in writing, the error is there for all to see.

Most of the glaring errors, the ones you want to avoid at all costs, come from using nonstandard English, incorrect subject-verb agreement, or some dialects, such as *dees* and *dose* for *these* and *those*.

The following lists include some widely used nonstandard words and phrases. Although you may hear them often, to use them in college writing is a glaring error.

NONSTANDARD WORDS

you'uns/yuns	nowheres	was you
theirselfs	we was	themself
that there	hisself	this here
youse	y'all	them there
cain't	these here	so's you can

MORE NONSTANDARD WORDS AND EXPRESSIONS

Here are some more nonstandard words, phrases, and expressions that may have slipped into your vocabulary. Eliminate these errors before turning in your paragraphs.

COULD OF/WOULD OF/SHOULD OF/HAD OF

Incorrect: I wish I *had of* gone.
Correct: I wish I *had* gone.

Incorrect: I *could of* gone swimming.
Correct: I could *have* gone swimming.

OFF OF/IN BACK OF

Incorrect: He fell *off of* the horse.
Correct: He fell *off* the horse.

Incorrect: The garage is *in back of* the house.
Correct: The garage is *behind* the house.

HAD OUGHT/HADN'T OUGHT

Incorrect: He *hadn't ought* to have said that to me.
Correct: He *ought not* to have said that to me.
           He *should not* have said that to me.

AT   *At* is usually unnecessary at the end of a question.

Incorrect: Where is she *at?*
Correct: Where is she?

In the following example, *at* is necessary at the end of the question: "What on earth are you staring at?"

THEM/THEM THERE   Do not use *them* or *them there* before a noun.

Incorrect:	*Them* apples will make great cider.
Correct:	*Those* apples will make great cider.

WENT AND/GO AND/TRY AND   Do not use *went and, go and,* or *try and* when you mean *went to, go to, try to.*

Incorrect:	We *went and* saw the movie.
	I will *go and* see who is at the door.
	You could *try and* do it alone.
Correct:	We went *to see* the movie.
	I will go *to see* who is at the door.
	I will *see* who is at the door.
	You could try *to do* it alone.

The following example is correct because two separate actions are intended:

We will go to the fire and do our best to help the victims.

WE WAS/YOU WAS/THEY WAS

Incorrect:	We *was* eating our dinner when the phone rang.
Correct:	We *were* eating our dinner when the phone rang.

HE DON'T/SHE DON'T/IT DON'T   Do not use *don't* when *he, she,* or *it* is the subject.

Incorrect:	She *don't* look like a heavy drinker to me.
Correct:	She *doesn't* look like a heavy drinker to me.
	She *does not* look like a heavy drinker to me.

GOOD/WELL   Do not use *good* as an adverb; use *well.*

Incorrect:	She drives the car real *good.*
	The engine ran *good* after the tune-up.
Correct:	She drives the car quite *well.*
	The engine ran *well* after the tune-up.

Well can be used as an adjective meaning "in good health." "He was not *well* this morning; in fact, he had to leave work early." *Good* is used correctly as an adjective in the following examples: "I feel *good.*" "The lawn looks *good* to me." "The steak is *good.*" "His health is *good.*"

BAD/BADLY   Do not use *bad* as an adverb; use *badly.*

Incorrect:	The engine runs *bad.*
	He scored *bad* on his test.
Correct:	The engine runs *badly.*
	He scored *badly* on his test.

Bad is used correctly as an adjective in the following examples: "I feel *bad*." "The fish smells *bad*." "It looks *bad* for our team."

> **LEARN/TEACH**   Do not use *learn* when you mean *teach*.
>
> *Incorrect:*   No one in the family could *learn* him any English.
> *Correct:*   No one in the family could *teach* him any English.
>   He could not *learn* English from anyone in the family.

Finally, be alert to words that change according to their use in the sentence. For instance, some words change their form when they change from singular (*man, mouse*) to plural (*men, mice*). Pronouns change their forms for gender (*he, she, it*). Those are obvious. Less obvious are changes in form to indicate whether the pronoun is a subject or an object. Note the following examples:

> *Nonstandard:*   *John and me* are team captains. (subject)
> *Standard:*   *John and I* are team captains. (subject)
>
> *Nonstandard:*   *Him and me* are winners. (subject)
> *Standard:*   *He and I* are winners. (subject)
>
> *Nonstandard:*   The teacher told *he and I*. (object)
> *Standard:*   The teacher told *him and me*. (object)
>
> *Nonstandard:*   Between *he and I* . . . (object of preposition)
>   Between *him and I* . . . (object of preposition)
> *Standard:*   Between *him and me* . . . (object of preposition)
>
> *Nonstandard:*   Send the memo to *he and I*. (object of preposition)
> *Standard:*   Send the memo to *him and me*. (object of preposition)

Who changes its form, too, depending on its use in the sentence.

> *Nonstandard:*   *Who* do you mean?
> *Standard:*   *Who* is at my window? (subject)
>   *Whom* do you mean? (object)
>
> *Nonstandard:*   *Who* are you writing to? (object of preposition)
> *Standard:*   To *whom* are you writing? (object of preposition)
>   *Whom* are you writing to? (object of preposition)

Never use the *double negative*. Two no's make a yes. Never use two negatives in one clause. One *no, not, none,* or *nothing* is sufficient to make the sentence negative. Using two negatives in one clause not only gives the impression of poor knowledge but also makes the sentence say the opposite of what you meant to say.

> *Incorrect:*   I don't got none. (This means you do have some.)
> *Correct:*   I don't have any.
>   I have none.

Incorrect:	My teacher doesn't know nothing. (This means he does know something.)
Correct:	My teacher doesn't know anything.
	My teacher knows nothing.
Incorrect:	I don't have no time for games. (This means you do have some.)
Correct:	I don't have any time for games.
	I have no time for games.

Don't confuse *it's* with *its*. *It's* = it is. *It's* is a contraction like *don't* ("do not") or *didn't* ("did not"). The apostrophe replaces a letter that is omitted. You may use many of these contractions in your speech every day: "*Let's* go to the movies" obviously means "Let us go to the movies." "I *shouldn't* go" obviously means "I should not go."

Its = belonging to it (possessive). Like other possessives, such as *his, hers,* and *theirs, its* does not use the apostrophe to show ownership: "The dog ate *its* bone," "The ship lost *its* rudder."

Incorrect:	Its time to go to class.
Correct:	It's time to go to class.
Incorrect:	My car lost it's wheel.
Correct:	My car lost its wheel.

✓ Misused Words

The following words are often misused, and while they do not qualify as glaring errors, their improper use implies that you do not know the rules of standard usage that are established by the majority of educated people. Learn the proper usage of these often misused words

affect/effect

Affect is a verb meaning "to produce an effect or change in." "How will this test *affect* my average?"

Affect also means "to pretend." "He *affected* a British accent."

Effect is a noun meaning "a result or consequence." "What *effect* will this test have on my average?"

Effect is also a verb meaning "to accomplish or make happen." "We must soon *effect* a solution to this problem."

alike/unlike/not alike/unalike

Alike means "in the same way or manner." "All persons should be treated *alike* under the law."

Unlike means "different or dissimilar." "The United States, *unlike* England, does not have a royal family."

Not *alike* also means "different or dissimilar." "Sally and Jane are *not alike* in the ways they dress."

Unalike is nonstandard and should not be used.

all right/alright

All right means "acceptable, correct, satisfactory." "The tax experts said it was *all right* to take the deduction."

Alright is not standard English and should not be used.

allot/alot/a lot

Allot is a verb that means "divide, distribute." "The state will *allot* the funds for our new park."

Alot is nonstandard and should not be used. "I liked her *alot,*" for example, should be "I liked her very much."

A lot is most commonly a piece of land. "There is *a lot* near us that we would like to buy." Colloquially, it means much. "*A lot* of time was wasted." This usage should be avoided in college writing, however.

almost/most

Almost means "close to, nearly." "He *almost* lost the election; *almost* half the voters stayed home."

Most means "the majority of nearly all of a group." "*Most* of the workers refused to cross the picket line."

(Do not use most in place of almost. "He went to look for work *most* every morning" is incorrect.)

already/all ready

Already means "by this time, before the time mentioned." "The sun had *already* begun to set."

All ready means "all prepared, completely ready." "The fans were *all ready* to cheer for the home team."

altogether/all together

Altogether means "wholly, completely." "We are not *altogether* satisfied with his explanation of how the money was spent."

All together means "all in one place." "They were *all together* in one room."

amount/number

Amount refers to bulk items or a quantity that cannot be counted. "The *amount* of grain India received was not enough to prevent widespread starvation."

Number refers to something that can be counted. "There is a large *number* of people at the banquet this year."

awhile/while (both in the sense of a period of time)

Awhile is an adverb. "If you will wait *awhile,* I'll go with you."

While is a noun. "We were invited to sit down for a *while.*"

(*While* is also used as a subordinate conjunction, but it should be used this way only in the sense of time. "*While* the music played, they danced together" is correct, but "*While* I like sushi, Harry likes sukiyaki" is not. In this case, the correct sentence would be "Although I like sushi, Harry likes sukiyaki.")

foul/fowl

Foul is an adjective meaning "offensive to the senses; disgusting, unfavorable." "Don't use such *foul* language!" "This is a *foul* day." "Sewage has a *foul* odor."

Foul is also a noun meaning "an act contrary to established rules." "He earned a *foul* for slashing." It can also be used as an adjective. "She hit a *foul* ball to left field."

Foul can also be used as a verb meaning "to tangle." "The anchor line was *fouled* in the propeller."

Fowl is a noun meaning "a domestic bird used for food." "The chicken is a barnyard *fowl.*"

from/than

From, instead of *than,* should be used to indicate discrimination or distinction.

"Carl's ten-speed is different *than* mine" is incorrect. Correct usages are "Carl's ten-speed is different *from* mine" or "Carl's ten-speed differs *from* mine."

infer/imply

To *imply* is to hint or suggest; you *imply* something to someone. "The newspaper articles *imply* that the mayor is a crook."

To *infer* is to arrive at a conclusion, to conclude; you *infer* something from evidence. "We can *infer* from the testimony of the witness that the mayor is a crook."

knew/new

Knew is a verb, the past tense of *to know;* "a past or previous awareness of something." "I *knew* that I had always loved her."

New is an adjective meaning "of recent production." "This is a *new* car."

Also, it means unfamiliar or strange: "This is a *new* experience for me."

know/no/now

Know is a verb meaning "to perceive; understand; be aware of; to have knowledge of." "I *know* how to fish."

It also means "to be acquainted with." "I *know* John well."

No is an adverb meaning "denial or refusal." "*No,* I'm not going."

No also means "Not in any degree." "We have *no* more milk."

Now is an adverb meaning "at the present time." "You must do it *now.*"

less/fewer

Less is used with items you can weigh or measure. "*Less* grain than was needed was sent to India."

Fewer is used with items you can count. "There are *fewer* people at the banquet this year than there were last year."

real/really

Real means "actual, in existence." "The danger was not imaginary; it was all too *real.*"

Really is an adverb (often overused) meaning "extremely." "We were *really* exhausted from the hike."

(Never use *real* in place of *really* as in "The party was *real* nice.")

shear/shears/sheer

Shear is a verb meaning to cut with a sharp instrument. "He *sheared* the sheep."

Shears is a noun meaning a large scissor-like cutting instrument. "My garden *shears* are dull."

Sheer is an adjective meaning "transparently thin." "She hung *sheer* drapes on her windows."

Sheer also means "unmixed with anything else." "This martini is *sheer* gin."

Sheer also means "utter or absolute." "Her dreams of winning the lottery are *sheer* fantasy."

And finally, *sheer* means "extending down or up very steeply." "It was a *sheer* drop of five hundred feet from the ledge."

then/than

Then is usually an adverb meaning "a particular time." "It was *then* that he decided to change his job." "The cow *then* took a huge mouthful of grass."

Than is a conjunction generally used to introduce the second member of a comparison. "My brother is three years older *than* I." "I like nothing better *than* a bowl of warm grits on a chilly winter morning."

through/threw/thru

Through is a preposition that indicates passage from one side to another, indicates between parts of, or is a synonym for finished. "The bird flew *through* the window." "Tarzan swung *through* the trees." "He was *through* with his work." "This is not a *through* street." "This is a *through* train."

Threw is the past tense of to throw. "The President *threw* the first baseball of the season."

"He *threw* a party;" "The baby *threw* a tantrum" are slang. "He gave a party" and "the baby had a tantrum" are correct.

Thru is a nonstandard variation of through and should not be used in college writing.

(Do not confuse *through* with *thorough,* which means "fully, completely, or perfectly done." "The painters did a *thorough* job on our house."

who/that/which

Who is a relative pronoun used to refer to a person. "The boy *who* lives next door is my best friend."

That and *which* are relative pronouns referring to animals or things. "The horse *that* won the race was a two-to-one favorite." "This jacket, *which* is my favorite, is beginning to show some wear."

EXERCISE 5H: ELIMINATING ERRORS IN WORD USAGE

Cross out the incorrect words or phrases and write the correct form on the line below each sentence.

1. Happiness don't come from alot of things but from a few friends.

   _____

2. Only a human being has the power to change hisself into what he wants to be.

   _____

3. Their ain't nobody who doesn't have someone who looks up to him, who thinks he's perfect.

   _____

4. Everyone, in his lifetime, has had someone treat him real bad.

   _____

5. You don't have to try and win every game; just have fun.

   _____

6. Most all men think being a father is hard, but they should just follow their own instincts.

   _____

7. Some dads all ready know that there kids just need them to be there.

   _____

8. The president hisself likes junk food.

   _____

9. Some of them fast-food restaurants make alot of money for their owners.

   _____

10. I could of made the team if the coach would of learned me to hit the curve ball.

    _____

11. Me and Danny were real good fielders.

_____

12. The coach thru us off of the team for awhile.

_____

13. Its alright to laugh at jokes, but you hadn't ought to make jokes out of people.

_____

14. He inferred that the amount of tickets sold was inadequate.

_____

15. Wherever the prom is held at, it will be a better place then they chose last year.

_____

EXERCISE 5I: ELIMINATING NONSTANDARD USAGE

In the following passage, cross out each error and replace it with the correct form of the word or phrase.

The dominant image of the American Indian, seen in everything from cigar boxes to textbooks to Hollywood movie ads, is the Plains Indian chief in full headdress, but now that I am older and wiser, I realize that Native Americans hadn't ought to be portrayed in such a stereotypical manner. My textbooks should of pointed out, for example, that the Plains Indians constituted only one segment of the Indian population on one part of North America. In a book that my Dad bought for my brother and me, I learned that there were hundreds of different Indian nations and tribes in this country who spoke different languages, practiced different religions, lived in different kinds of homes, dressed in different kinds of clothes, told different kinds of stories, sang different songs, ate different foods, created different forms of art and held vastly different beliefs regarding dating, marriage, childrearing, divorce, and death, Native Americans, theirselfs, of course, are well aware of this cultural diversity, but most of the kids that I went to school with grew up thinking of "the Indians" as one single ethnic group. Some of these kids loved American history and scored real good on all of their tests, but they never realized how many of the "facts" that they learned about the Indians were not true at all. Most Indian tribes, for example, were not even led by a "chief." Rarely was one person officially designated as "THE" leader of a tribe. Most North American Indian societies were much more democratic in structure: they were more commonly ruled by councils. The word "chief," in fact, is not even an Indian word: it is an English word forced on Indians by British officials who wanted an easy way to negotiate treaties with the Indians. Geronimo, hisself, was never "chief" of the Apaches: he was a shaman—a medicine man.

chapter 6

Comparing

or Contrasting

ORGANIZATION

One of the best ways to make your writing interesting and informative is to develop a controlling idea by **comparing** or **contrasting**.

> A **comparison** shows **similarities** between persons, places, things, ideas, or situations.
>
> A **contrast** points out **differences** between persons, places, things, ideas, or situations.

We compare and contrast so often that we aren't even aware of it. We do it in many ways and for a wide variety of reasons.

> "Class, do not consider this exam to be retribution for your inattention; instead, seize it as an opportunity to convince me that you deserve a passing grade for this course." (formal English)
>
> "You should see this girl in my sociology class; she could be Demi Moore's twin sister!" (conversational English)
>
> "Show up late for work one more time and you're toast." (colloquial English/slang)

✓ Uses of Comparisons and Contrasts

COMPARISONS AND CONTRASTS ARE POWERFUL INSTRUCTIONAL TOOLS:

They stimulate thinking: analytical, imaginative, and creative.

They generate proof to support arguments.

They provide understanding of complex concepts.

They provide an efficient way to examine alternative courses of action.

COMPARISONS AND CONTRASTS HELP US TO MAINTAIN OUR PERSPECTIVE IN A COMPLEX, DIVERSE, AND CONTRADICTORY WORLD:

They allow us to examine a particular situation, problem, or individual from different viewpoints.

They enable us to avoid superficial judgments—to see things as they actually are—not as they appear to be.

They enable us to rely on reason rather than emotion in decision making.

They make us more sensitive to cultural and ethnic diversity.

They help us to evaluate so that we can choose wisely:

"What will I major in?"

"Is this the person for me?"

"Which computer is best for my needs?"

"Which applicant should I hire?"

✓ Assignment

Write a paragraph that develops your controlling idea by stating either the *similarities* between two things (comparing) or by stating the *differences* between two things (contrasting). **Remember:** Compare *or* contrast, but do not compare *and* contrast in your paragraph.

WHAT CAN I WRITE ABOUT?

1. **Choose a subject that you are interested in,** but *avoid* oversimplified topics, such as the following:

"My dog is different from my cat."

"College is different from high school."

"The processes for baking a cake and making cookies are quite similar."

2. Choose a topic that will also interest your reader. The following subjects are always popular and relevant:

Love and esteem	Health and wellness
Personal success	Financial security
Self-improvement	Physical and mental fitness

3. Draw ideas from personal experiences and preferences, family experiences, and job experiences, such as the following:

"Although my parents came from vastly different ethnic backgrounds, they were a formidable team because their methods of disciplining children were remarkably similar."

"Unless you have worked under both systems, it is difficult to realize the difference between union and nonunion."

4. Choose a topic that you want to learn more about and can research. (Always give sources of borrowed material; see Chapter 10.) Note the following examples:

"The standards of sexual conduct imposed upon women in the military differ from those applied to men."

"The chaos in today's schools is at least partially due to the switch from teacher authority to parental authority."

In the following paragraph, the student writer contrasts family life with young children and with teenagers:

Living with teenagers today has drastically changed my once quiet home life, but I remember a time when my house was my own. That was several years ago, a time when these so-called young adults were much younger. I long for the days when eight o'clock meant that the table was cleared and the children were in bed. It was so quiet and peaceful back then, unlike today. Now, the only peace that can be found is outside the house far away from the noise emanating from the stereo and the latest dancing ritual. Yes, eight o'clock was the time to find my best girl and me snuggling up on the couch, with popcorn in hand, watching our favorite shows. Whereas today, this time is lost, for my couch is now monopolized by a teenage boy and his newest blond-haired attraction, hypnotized by the current episode of *Beavis and Butthead*. Back in the good old days, during a long day at work, I could hear my loving wife's voice just by picking up the phone, unlike today, when all I can hear is a busy signal. At one time, the ringing phone would bring pleasurable feelings of anticipation. "Who could it be?" I would wonder. Often, it was a friend wanting to make plans for the evening. Presently, I relate the ring more closely to the bell that one might hear at a boxing match as I watch two teenagers battling for control over the phone. I also remember buying groceries for my family, taking special care to pick out all of our favorite foods, packing the cart until it overflowed. I purchased enough food to last us for weeks. Now, two days after a bountiful trip to the market, I come home to find that half the football team has emptied my refrigerator and is headed for the nearest Pizza Hut. These examples make it seem that any semblance of order or peace in the household is lost when teenagers dominate the family; however, the mystery and excitement that accompanies them adds an element of joy that makes parenting a teenager well worthwhile.

Greg Rea

Look over the following list of sample topics. You may select a subject from the list, or you might choose an original subject.

Possible Contrasts

two close friends
two methods for accomplishing a task
two pets
two boy/girlfriends
two churches you have attended
two particular (or individual)
    teachers' styles
two types of parenting
two types of relationships
two management styles
contrasting male-female behavior
two different states/countries you
    have lived in
two cars, trucks, or sport utility
    vehicles: same type but
    different manufacturer

two types of nightclubs, bars, brewpubs,
    discos
two methods of fishing or hunting
two aircraft: same type but different
    manufacturer
two wives/husbands
two teaching styles
two types of marriage
two types of exercise/workouts
two quarterbacks
two styles of cooking
two sets of behavioral standards
two different types of schools you
    attended
Freddy Krueger and Jason Voorhes

Possible Similarities

monkeys/dolphins and humans
behaviors of twins
pets and their owners
Marilyn Monroe and Madonna
your supervisor and a boot camp drill
    instructor
mothers and sons
Cindy Crawford and Elle Macpherson
Bruce Lee and Jean-Claude Van Damme
Mother Teresa and Princess Diana

two religions/denominations
two cultures
Tiger Woods and Jack Nicklaus
Harrison Ford and Mel Gibson
the very old/very young
Jay Leno and David Letterman
Denzel Washington and Will Smith
Selena and Jennifer Lopez
readers and movie-goers
players and spectators

Note: The personalities listed here were deliberately paired because of the *similarities* they share. You may have to do some research to complement your personal observations. Remember, if you choose from this group, *compare—*don't contrast.

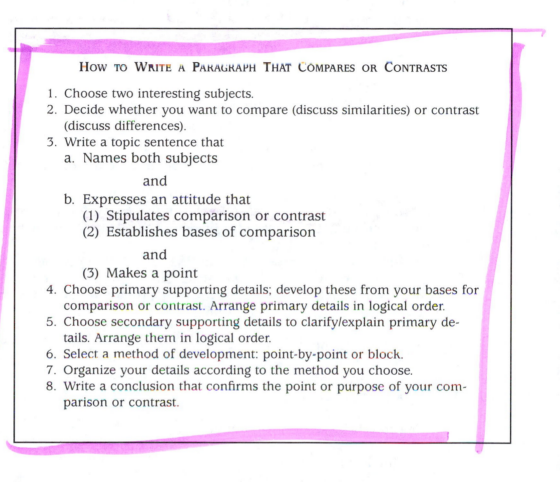

How to Write a Paragraph That Compares or Contrasts

1. Choose two interesting subjects.
2. Decide whether you want to compare (discuss similarities) or contrast (discuss differences).
3. Write a topic sentence that
   a. Names both subjects

      and

   b. Expresses an attitude that
      (1) Stipulates comparison or contrast
      (2) Establishes bases of comparison

      and

      (3) Makes a point
4. Choose primary supporting details; develop these from your bases for comparison or contrast. Arrange primary details in logical order.
5. Choose secondary supporting details to clarify/explain primary details. Arrange them in logical order.
6. Select a method of development: point-by-point or block.
7. Organize your details according to the method you choose.
8. Write a conclusion that confirms the point or purpose of your comparison or contrast.

✓ **Topic Sentence**

Choose the two subjects that you want to compare or contrast. For example, suppose you see yourself as an expert on football history; therefore, you decide to contrast two of America's most famous football coaches

Your *broad/general* subjects = two legendary coaches

Narrow your subjects so that you can

develop your controlling idea in a single paragraph
choose *specific* primary and secondary details to support your controlling idea.

Your *narrowed* subjects: "Bear" Bryant and Knute Rockne

Express your attitude, which tells the reader how you intend to discuss your subjects—your method of development.

1. Your attitude must tell whether you intend to compare or contrast. In the following example, the word *differed* indicates a *contrast* of your subjects:

(subjects)

"Bear" Bryant and Knute Rockne

and

(attitude stating *contrast*)

"Bear" Bryant's coaching methods *differed* from those of Knute Rockne.

2. Your attitude should also establish the bases for your contrast. *Bases* are the criteria or standards of judgment that you will use when contrasting one subject with the other.

To determine your bases, ask yourself, "How do the coaches differ? In which areas or categories do these coaches differ?" Based on your memory and on some research, list four bases as your primary criteria for contrast, from least to most important. For example:

1. Approach to discipline
2. Training methods
3. Respect for players
4. Attitude toward winning

Now add the bases to your attitude:

(subjects)

"Bear" Bryant and Knute Rockne

and

(attitude stating *contrast* and *bases*)

Although both were highly successful, "Bear" Bryant's approach to coaching was much more relaxed than Knute Rockne's in his discipline, his training methods, his respect for players, and his attitude toward winning.

Note: **Your bases must be identical for both subjects in your comparison or contrast.** For example, if, when discussing two movies, movie A and movie B, you talk about the script, the acting, and the cinematography of movie A, then you must also talk about the script, the acting, and the cinematography of movie B *and,* in the same sequence.

3. Finally, your attitude must state or strongly imply a purpose—make a point—that tells what your comparison or contrast intends to prove or demonstrate.

This point is the heart of your controlling idea. If you do not make a point, your paragraph is no more than a list of obvious similarities or differences. The following example expresses the point of the Rockne/Bryant essay.

> That *there is no one way to coach a successful football team* is proved by the records of two of America's greatest coaches, Knute Rockne and "Bear" Bryant, whose methods of preparing teams were vastly different.

Avoid the temptation to take the easy way out, as this student tried to do:

A pointless topic sentence:	"There are several differences between ducks and chickens." [No kidding!]
+	
Superficial primary supporting details, badly organized, with no secondary support:	Ducks have bills, but chickens have beaks.
	Ducks have webbed feet, but chickens have claws.
	Ducks can swim, but chickens sink.
	Ducks quack, but chickens cluck.
	Ducks can survive in the wild, but chickens can't.
	Ducks can fly long distances, but chickens can't.
	Ducklings imprint, but chicks meander.
	Ducks, when cooked, don't have white meat, but chickens do.
+	
A redundant conclusion:	"As you can see, ducks are indeed different from chickens."
=	
A contrast that proves nothing.	

EXERCISE 6A: CHOOSING EFFECTIVE CONTROLLING IDEAS

Put a check mark before any of the following sentences that would be suitable for a comparison or contrast paragraph.

_____ 1. The two teachers who taught me the most have much in common.

_____ 2. Solitaire has several advantages over other card games.

_____ 3. Playing third base is more difficult than playing any other infield position.

_____ 4. My girlfriend Christine has a special beauty.

_____ 5. Learning to write is like learning any other skill.

_____ 6. My dad was a wit, but my mother was a humorist.

_____ 7. There are three reasons why I enjoy spelunking.

_____ 8. The memories that lingered in the old house almost brought me to tears.

_____ 9. Everyone should visit Paris at least once.

_____ 10. You wouldn't recognize the city park now that the high school seniors took it on as their project.

EXERCISE 6B: ACCEPTABLE CONTROLLING IDEAS

Reread the sentences not checked as suitable for a comparison/contrast paragraph. Explain which sentences would be acceptable topic sentences for other types of development and which would not work as a topic sentence at all.

BODY

✓ Types of Development

There are two basic methods of developing a paragraph that compares or contrasts: the *point-by-point method* and *the block method.*

To learn these methods, allow the letter *A* to represent one of your subjects and the letter *B* the other.

THE POINT-BY-POINT METHOD

The **point-by-point** method alternates *A* with *B* in the body of your paragraph: *A/B   A/B   A/B.* For example, in a paragraph that states and discusses important differences between two subjects, *A* and *B,* use the following configuration:

A	B
Make your first point about *A* . . . then explain how *B* differs *A/B*	
Make a second point about *A* . . . then explain how *B* differs *A/B*	
Make a third point about *A* . . . then explain how *B* differs *A/B*	
Make a fourth point about *A* . . . then explain how *B* differs *A/B*	
Make a fifth point about *A* . . . then explain how *B* differs *A/B*	

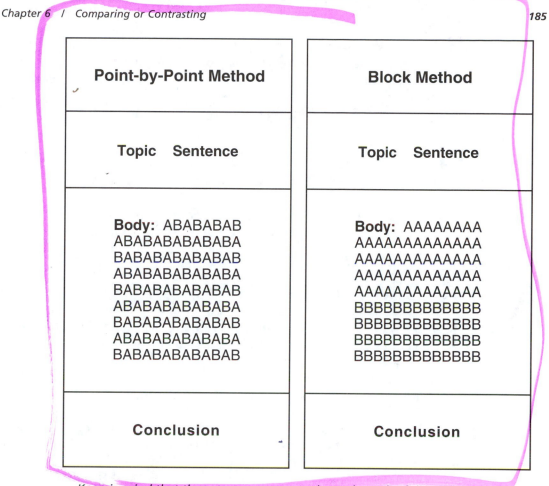

Point-by-Point Method	Block Method
Topic Sentence	Topic Sentence
Body: ABABABAB ABABABABABABA BABABABABABAB ABABABABABABA BABABABABABAB ABABABABABABA BABABABABABAB ABABABABABABA BABABABABABAB	**Body:** AAAAAAAA AAAAAAAAAAAAA AAAAAAAAAAAAA AAAAAAAAAAAAA AAAAAAAAAAAAA BBBBBBBBBBBBB BBBBBBBBBBBBB BBBBBBBBBBBBB BBBBBBBBBBBBB
Conclusion	Conclusion

Keep in mind that these two patterns need not always be followed rigidly, but they do provide the clearest ways to develop a comparison or contrast.

Think of each *A/B* grouping as one *primary* supporting detail for your controlling idea: *A/B   A/B   A/B   A/B   A/B.* Then, if you need more contrasting details, simply continue this *A/B* progression until you have enough primary details to develop fully your controlling idea. Four to six primary supporting details are usually sufficient for a single compare/contrast paragraph.

The main advantage of the point-by-point method is that it provides immediate feedback to the reader. Because point *B immediately* follows point *A,* your reader can quickly grasp the meaning and/or intent of your comparison or contrast.

Most Effective Uses of the Point-by-Point Method
1. For comparisons or contrasts using *brief, specific details*
2. For comparisons or contrasts containing *numerous, difficult to remember details*

THE BLOCK METHOD

In the **block method, first, discuss point** *A* **fully.** The details in *A* should support your controlling idea and follow the most logical sequence based on your purpose.

Second, **discuss point** *B* **fully.** Follow a sequence in point *B* that corresponds to the sequence of details in point *A*. Each detail in *B* should pair in sequence with its similar or differing counterpart in *A*.

The main advantage of the Block Method is that it enables you to explore a point in depth, **to develop it fully without intrusions:**

1. You can concentrate and focus on one aspect at a time, presenting a concept or building an impression through descriptive imagery.
2. You have many opportunities to experiment with style and creativity when using the block method.

Most Effective Uses of the Block Method
1. For comparisons or contrasts that discuss *fewer, less specialized details*
2. For comparisons or contrasts requiring some *in-depth* development and/or *focused* concentration on individual concepts or impressions

In the following paragraph, the student writer selected the block method to discuss differences between the mountain bike and the racing bike.

Although mountain bikes and racing bikes are both bicycles, their construction differs in many ways because of the purposes for which they are intended. For example, a mountain bike has thick, knobby tires and reinforced wheel rims which are designed for off-road or rough road riding; these thick tires hold very little air pressure, making them extremely flexible and able to withstand the impact of hard and/or sharp objects in their path. The mountain bike also has a very thick, durable frame that is able to withstand much punishment without cracking, breaking, or chipping. The mountain bike's straight handlebars, which provide better control over rough terrain, also improve rider comfort because the rider remains in an upright position at all times. Mountain bikes also have a wide seat, which provides excellent cushioning and a relatively comfortable ride under all conditions. In contrast, the racing bike has very thin, smooth tires, mounted on light alloy rims, which allow greater speed due to less friction with the road; however, the bike must be ridden only on smooth pavement and not on rough or uneven surfaces. Also, the frame is extremely thin and lightweight, allowing greater speed and less wind resistance. The downward curving handle bars on the racing bike force the rider to remain in the tucked position at all times, drastically reducing wind resistance while increasing speed. Although the racing bike has a very narrow, uncomfortable seat, it, too, reduces the bike's weight and wind resistance. When deciding whether to buy a mountain bike or a racing bike, one must consider his or her purpose for using the bike. For off-road or rough road riding, the heavier, sturdier mountain bike is the logical choice, exchanging speed for durability. However, for smooth surface touring or competition, the lighter, faster racing bike is much more efficient.

Tim Denny

WHICH METHOD TO USE: POINT-BY-POINT OR BLOCK?   Your topic and your purpose (the aim of your comparison or contrast) should point you toward one method or the other, based on the recommended uses of each. In general:

1. Use the point-by-point method when you have numerous specialized or technical or hard to remember details to discuss.
2. Use the block method when you have fewer, less specialized details and must deal with each aspect in some depth.

In the following paragraphs, both of which focus on two contrasting perceptions of the same scene, a woman who is trying to refinance her home writes of her experience with the appraiser who came to evaluate her property. As she escorted the appraiser around her property, she could not help but notice how his perspective differed from hers. *Note:* Paragraph A is printed the way the author wrote it. Paragraph B, however, has been rearranged to follow the block method.

Paragraph A (Point-by-Point Method)

The whole inspection went like this. I saw one thing; the appraiser saw another. By my garage, I saw a charming old windmill, a welcome sight when I would round the corner from the east, but he saw a rusty piece of junk that should be torn down. I saw fields of wildflowers; he saw unmowed weeds. I saw valuable timber and firewood, but he saw brush that should be cleared. I saw quantities of free fertilizer from the horses renting my pasture, yet he saw filth. I saw a handy source of free lumber for projects; he saw a shed badly in need of repair. Furthermore, I saw a rare species of vireo safely nesting in a corner of the front porch. He, however, looked at me in horror, appalled that I would allow birds to nest on my porch. I was not surprised to get a letter a few days later denying me the loan.

Patricia Westfall

Paragraph B (Block Method)

The whole inspection went like this. I saw one thing; the appraiser saw another. By my garage, I saw a charming old windmill, a welcome sight when I would round the corner from the east. I also saw fields of wildflowers, valuable timber and firewood, quantities of free fertilizer from the horses renting my pasture, and a handy source of free lumber for projects. I saw a rare species of vireo safely nesting in a corner of the front porch. He, on the other hand, saw a rusty piece of junk that should be torn down. He saw unmowed weeds and brush that should be cleared. He saw filth and a shed badly in need of repair. Finally, he looked at me in horror, appalled that I would allow birds to nest on my porch. I was not surprised to get a letter a few days later denying me the loan.

Note: For some topics, either method can be effective. For example, in the Rockne/Bryant contrast, you may use either of the two methods. Which one is better, however, is a matter of personal judgment.

Point-by-Point Method

If you use the point-by-point method, every time you say something about Rockne, you must say something about Bryant. You might, for example, emphasize the contrast at the beginning by telling your reader that although both coaches were highly successful, their methods of coaching were quite different:

> Topic sentence: *Subjects* (Rockne and Bryant) + *attitude* (different approaches to coaching).

Every time you say something about Rockne, say something about Bryant, either in the same sentence *or* in the sentence immediately following:

> Topic sentence
> Point on Rockne/Point on Bryant
> Point on Rockne/Point on Bryant
> Point on Rockne/Point on Bryant
> Point on Rockne/Point on Bryant
> Conclusion

The conclusion reinforces the controlling idea of distinct differences between the two.

With the point-by-point method, your comparison (pointing out similarities) or contrast (pointing out differences) is made immediately. You state point A and then the contrasting point B. Thus, the basic organization of your paragraph looks like this:

I. Topic Sentence
II. Development
   A transition B
      A transition B
   A transition B
      A transition B
III. Conclusion

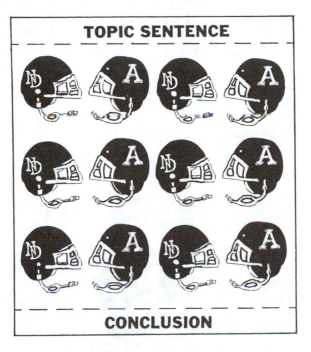

Point-by-point method.

Note: A *transitional word* or *phrase* is usually necessary between each *A/B* combination of the point-by-point method: *A* transition *B*.

Block Method

If you use the block method, (1) put all of your material about Rockne in the first part of your comparison/contrast, and (2) put all of your material about Bryant in the second half of your paragraph.

Topic sentence (same as first)

All about Rockne

   (transition)

All about Bryant

Conclusion

The block method also requires an *explicit transition*, a *linking word or phrase*, to join the two parts of the discussion. Here are examples of transitions you might use:

"Bryant, on the other hand, . . ."

"As for Bryant, . . ."

"Unlike Rockne, Bryant . . ."

"Bryant, in contrast, . . ."

"While Rockne . . . , Bryant . . ."

In this method, your basic organization will look like this:

   I. Topic Sentence
  II. Development
     (subtopic 1)
     AAAAAAAAAAAA
     (transition)
     (subtopic 2)
     BBBBBBBBBBBB
 III. Conclusion

Block method.

Again, when deciding whether to use the point-by-point or the block method, consider your topic and purpose. The point-by-point method is better when you want to emphasize detailed similarities and differences; you show the comparison or contrast immediately to your reader by pairing one with the other.

In the following paragraph, the writer uses the point-by-point method to prove that children no longer use their imaginations to create playthings:

Toys made by today's high-tech companies rob children of the fun of making toys by using their imaginations. At one time, a little girl would take a cardboard box and, with the help of scissors, glue, and old magazines, would convert it into a doll house. A doll swimming pool would be improvised from a plastic dishpan "swiped" from mother's kitchen sink; a roller skate would make an ideal sports car. Today, however, little girls demand a Barbie Dream House with miniature furniture of intricate detail. There must be a Tropical Pool and Patio Set beside the house along with a radio-controlled plastic sports car that has motor sounds and working headlights. In the past, boys would take an orange crate, old lawn mower wheels, and scrap lumber to create their own Indy 500 racers. Now, it is, "Gentlemen, start your engines," on the authentic battery powered replica that goes up to speeds of five miles per hour. This has a price tag of only $300. Playing army was once easy to do; any stick found in the yard could immediately become a toy rifle. Dirt clumps and fallen apples made great hand grenades. However, futuristic laser toys or paint guns with sensors are the fad today. Both boys and girls liked to "rough it" by camping in the backyard. Dad's old army blanket strung over the clothesline made a serviceable tent at one time. Also, an old comforter provided both warmth and grand padding. Today's young people want dome tents and insulated sleeping bags decorated with their favorite characters, from Batman, the Tasmanian Devil, or Jurassic Park/Lost World. Somehow, over the years, children have drifted away from devising their own toys. Instead of rushing to purchase the latest trendy supertoy, parents should take the time to help their children rediscover the pleasures of inventing toys through their imaginations.

Karen Miller

The block method, on the other hand, allows you to concentrate on one aspect at a time, giving the reader a full picture before crossing over to the other aspect of the comparison or contrast. In the following essay, this student writer decided that the block method was the more effective way to discuss her two contrasting pregnancies:

My moods and behavior when pregnant at twenty-five differed substantially from those I displayed when pregnant at forty. At twenty-five, I was extremely happy and eagerly looked forward to the birth of my first child. Most of my free time was spent trying to choose a perfect name for the baby who I felt was surely going to be a girl. While embroidering baby clothes and decorating the baby's room, I daydreamed about watching my child grow, doing things for her, doing things with her. When I learned of my pregnancy, I quit smoking immediately; however, I gained fifty pounds, suffered constant backaches, endured severe headaches, and felt generally miserable. Each day, I became more impatient waiting for my baby to be born. My discomforts were soon forgotten after the birth of my beautiful little girl. On the other hand, learning that I was pregnant at forty was a shock that filled me with fear and concern—fear that, at my age, there would be something wrong with the baby. Even though I constantly thought about the baby being born deformed or born with Down's syndrome, I decided that abortion was not for me. During this pregnancy, I did not stop smoking, gained very little weight, and never felt better in my whole life; however, I was embarrassed whenever I had to go out in public. Very little time was spent choosing a name or preparing for the baby's arrival, but I did spend much time thinking about starting over again with piano lessons, Scouts, 4-H Club, and school activities. As I approached the end of my term, I added an additional fear. Would the actual delivery of the baby be complicated because of my age? One, two, three, my daughter jumped into this world feet first, and she is an exceptionally bright child with no serious medical problems. Although my pregnancies contrasted dramatically, the results were the same, and I now have two beautiful daughters.

Doris Meany

✓ Choosing Your Details

PRIMARY SUPPORTING DETAILS. Remember, the heart of your controlling idea is the point that you want to make; therefore, all of your supporting details, primary and secondary, must support this point.

SECONDARY SUPPORTING DETAILS. Secondary supporting details provide direct support for each primary supporting detail. To prove the point expressed in the controlling idea, you must contrast the secondary details about the first subject with the secondary details about the second subject. *Note:* (1) Arrange secondary details in a logical sequence, and (2) use only relevant details.

Follow these steps to list your secondary supporting details:

1. Write each primary supporting detail.
2. Write both subjects under each primary detail.
3. List secondary supporting details under each primary detail.
   a. Each primary supporting detail has either two or three secondary supporting details, which is a good balance. *Do not* have six secondary details under one primary detail but only two under another. This destroys the symmetry of your paragraph.
   b. Continue to improve the wording of your primary and supporting details as you progress from outlining to rough drafts.

EXERCISE 6C: ELIMINATING IRRELEVANT DETAILS

Eliminate the irrelevant sentences from the following paragraph. Underline the irrelevant sentences and list their numbers on the line below the paragraph.

(1) It's easy to understand the difference between optimism and pessimism when you look at my two sisters. (2) Faced with exactly the same circumstances, they have completely opposite reactions. (3) One sister is pretty, the other plain. (4) One is fairly tall, the other short. (5) While going shopping

one day, Jane, the optimist, said, "Isn't it beautiful today!" (6) Connie replied, "It's nice now, but in a few months, it'll be snowing." (7) In the store, Connie complained about the slow service, while Jane thought it was great that they had more time together. (8) Connie told me about the lousy lunch they had; Jane remarked that she felt fortunate that they were able to eat out. (9) They both used to be quite poor, but both had jobs now. (10) When it rained as they were going home, Connie complained that nothing went right for her. (11) Jane said walking in the rain exhilarated her—she felt like a kid again. (12) Jane had a great time on the trip; Connie was miserable.

✓ Conclusion

An effective conclusion for a comparison/contrast paragraph is usually a *judgment* (a perception or opinion) that the writer *derives* as a result of contrast or comparison. In a paragraph contrasting Knute Rockne to Bear Bryant, for example, you might reach this conclusion:

> The fact that these contrasting personalities were two of the most successful coaches in football history proves that there is more than one way to inspire a football team.

Although conclusions confirm the point or purpose of your comparison or contrast, they can vary according to the writer's purpose. For example:

1. *Purpose:* to illustrate that although two competing items have substantial differences, both can still do the same job.

   > Even though the Jeep Cherokee and the Ford Explorer sport utility vehicles differ in body construction, cargo space, and engine options, they are both well engineered and excellent performers for this class of vehicle.

2. *Purpose:* to illustrate that although two mechanisms perform the same function, one is safer and easier to work with than the other.

   > Although the fuse box and the breaker panel accomplish the same purpose, it is much safer and easier to flip a switch to reset a tripped breaker than to search for a bad fuse and replace it with a new one.

3. *Purpose:* to illustrate that differences are sometimes more advantageous than similarities.

   > Therefore, because of differences in gender, ethnic origin, and socioeconomic background in public elementary school classrooms, today's publicly educated children embrace diversity more willingly than their privately educated counterparts.

4. *Purpose:* To illustrate through contrast that specific measures are bringing desired results.

   Fishermen on the Ohio River, who are now catching bass, walleye pike,
   pickerel, and perch, instead of just carp and catfish, demonstrate that
   our antipollution standards are working.

5. *Purpose:* To illustrate that exterior appearances are not accurate indica-
   tors of inner qualities.

   Although the characters portrayed in *Frankenstein, The Elephant Man,
   The Hunchback of Notre Dame,* and *The Phantom of the Opera* are
   grotesque misfits who are shunned by society, they still can express love,
   feel sympathy, and show compassion.

This student writer uses the block method to portray her hometown as
it once was in contrast to what it has now become. With the Christmas season as her basis, she establishes fully developed contrasting pictures and
moods through vivid descriptive imagery. Note how her concluding sentence
reinforces the point she makes in the controlling idea:

> **When I was a child, downtown Aliquippa at Christmastime was a won-
> derful, exciting, magical place to be, but today, it cries in anguish over
> events which have left it desolate and forgotten.** The holiday season always
> began the day after Thanksgiving. Hundreds of excited people lined the av-
> enue, anxiously awaiting the arrival of the traditional parade of marching
> bands, majorettes, drill teams, pompom girls, elves, and Santa's helpers dressed
> in holiday apparel. The highlight of the parade was a huge float that was fash-
> ioned to look like Santa's sleigh and reindeer. Upon the sleigh sat Santa and
> Mrs. Claus, tossing Christmas gifts of stockings, candy, toys, trinkets, and gift
> certificates to the eager spectators. As I walked along the avenue, I stared in
> awe. All the stores had unveiled windows that displayed beautifully created
> Christmas scenes. Lights twinkled and garlands glistened while the animated
> figurines winked and blinked, waved and bowed against a snow-filled back-
> drop. Nativity scenes and nearby carolers declared "Joy to the world . . ." as
> the sound of "Merry Christmas, Merry Christmas!" echoed in my ears. It was
> wonderful, it was exciting, it was breathtaking. *Today, however,* the holiday sea-
> son is not greeted by crowds of people anxiously awaiting its arrival. The pa-
> rade consists of derelicts wandering from one dimly lit bar to the next. The
> highlight of the evening consists of a pathetic group of street people gathered
> in front of the local liquor store, waiting for a handout. As I walk among the
> array of vacant buildings, I see the store windows either boarded up or heavily
> laden with dirt and grime. The old, faded Christmas decorations, hanging drea-
> rily along the avenue, make a feeble attempt to remind the few passing mo-
> torists that the holiday season has arrived. The once familiar sounds of "Merry

Christmas, Merry Christmas" are now echoes of silence. *Although Christmas in downtown Aliquippa was once enchanting, today, at Christmas, it is deserted, it is abandoned—it is forgotten.*

Beatrice Perry

✓ Some Do's . . .

1. *Do* make a point with your comparison or contrast. Let your reader learn something from your paragraph. Is one way of doing something better or worse than another? Is one teaching style more effective than another?
2. *Do* compare or contrast two items on the same bases. If you discuss speech content, energy, and the use of visual aids of speaker A, then you have to discuss speech content, energy, and the use of visual aids of speaker B.
3. *Do* use transitional words or phrases to let your reader know when you are introducing a new point of comparison or contrast. Your reader has to see where one point of comparison or contrast ends and another begins.
4. *Do* understand the difference between a comparison or contrast and an analogy. An *analogy* is a special form of comparison that points out significant similarities between two things that don't normally fall into the same general category. For example, comparing two ways of running a business is a simple comparison—comparing management style A with management style B. However, showing how running a business is like running a war is an analogy between business and war—two separate, distinct entities. Good analogies often provide the most effective means of communicating a point, but they have to be constructed with great care in order to be effective.

✓ . . . and Don'ts About Comparing or Contrasting

1. *Don't* bore your reader by stating the obvious: "Living in the country is different from living in the city," "My mother is different from my father."
2. *Don't* try to compare *and* contrast two items in the same paragraph. Focus either on similarities or differences, but *not* both.
3. *Don't* shift back and forth from the point-by-point method to the block method. Decide which method of arrangement is more suitable for your topic and then stick to it.
4. *Don't* write an unbalanced comparison or contrast. Give each item equal weight. Don't write three sentences about topic A and then twelve sentences about topic B.

SUGGESTED ACTIVITIES AND ASSIGNMENTS

1. Interview your grandparents or any friend or family member over 65 and find out what they were like when they were your age. Prepare a series of questions ahead of time and take along a tape recorder and a notebook. Find out what kind of social forces affected their lives as young adults. What sorts of things did they worry about most when they were your age? What was it like to be young in the 1930s? In the 1940s? What did they do for fun? How long did they date each other before they got married? How did they feel about school? What were the teachers like in those days? Which classes did they enjoy most? What did they want to do with their lives when they were your age? Were they able to fulfill any of their dreams? Were they happy?

   After the interview, play back the tape and think about what you learned from the conversation. See if you find any interesting comparisons or contrasts between

   a. You and your grandparents at your age
   b. Society then and society now
   c. Your image of your grandparents before the interview and your image of your grandparents after the interview.

2. Choose two sports or games that you like to play. Think about them carefully, then make a list of all the things they have in common. From this list, determine what it is about these games or sports that appeals to you.

3. Sometimes an interesting contrast can be drawn from two things that are normally considered alike. Following is a list of synonyms. Use your imagination to point out your own subtle distinctions between the two terms in each pair. Form a small group and choose five pairs of words that interest you. Discuss the differences in the meanings of the words. How do you use these words in your everyday conversations? Can you use them interchangeably? How do you think these words differ? See if the other members of the group interpret these words as you do. If necessary, use a dictionary to help determine subtle distinctions between these synonyms.

   a coward/a wimp   eating out/dining out
   a borrower/a sponger   working/earning a living
   a dog/a mutt   learning/acquiring information
   a brawl/a knock-down-drag-out   preparing for a test/getting psyched up
       fight   for a test
   a schnook/a schlemiel   teaching/presenting information
   being married/being MARRIED   nervous/uptight
   a bluff/a real snow job

SENTENCES

✓ Agreement of Subject and Verb

The comparison/contrast paragraph differs from the other methods of development in that it has two subjects, the two things you are comparing or contrasting. You must move the reader from one subject to the other as clearly and easily as possible. An incorrect verb or an inaccurate or missing antecedent could misdirect your reader.

As you learned in Chapter 1, the most important part of any sentence is the actor-action team—the *subject* and *verb*—but a subject and verb cannot work well as a team unless they are coordinated properly. In order to write good sentences, you must first understand that subjects and verbs have to agree in *number*.

Read the following sentences aloud:

> The whole house smell like dead fish.
>
> Bob are handsome.
>
> Three blue spruce trees grows in her backyard.
>
> Tom and his wife seldom speaks to strangers.

Just reading these sentences aloud will probably alert you that something is wrong, for these sentences contain a serious error: The subject and verb do not agree in number. Verbs, like subjects, are singular or plural. If you use a singular subject, then you must use a singular verb; if you use a plural subject, then you must use a plural verb.

What do singular verbs look like? When the subject is *one* place, *one* thing, or *one* person other than *I* or *you,* add an *s* to a verb in the present tense to get a singular verb—one that you can use with a singular subject.

> Jim *plays* football.
>
> The engine *sputters.*
>
> Dodge City *looks* like a tourist trap.
>
> Mark *studies* every night. (If a verb ends in *y,* drop the *y* and add *ies.*)

If the subject of a sentence is plural (refers to two or more), do not add an *s* to the verb.

> Jim and Ed *play* football.
>
> The engines *sputter.*
>
> These places *look* like tourist traps.
>
> Mark, Beth, and John *study* every night.

As these examples illustrate, you can refer to two or more things with one plural word (*they, engines, places*) or with two or more singular words (*Jim and Ed*).

The form of the verb changes when the number and the person of the subject changes.

Singular Number	**Plural Number**
1st person—I am eating pies.	We are eating pie.
2nd person—You are eating pie.	You are eating pie.
3rd person—He, she, it is eating pie.	They are eating pie.

Note: Only a change in the subject has any effect on the form of the verb.

> My dog (she) chases squirrels.
>
> Not all dogs (they) chase squirrels.
>
> The keys (they) of the old piano were a dirty yellow.
>
> An elaborate dinner (it) with three fine wines was John's idea of a perfect evening.
>
> The child, the cat, and the dog (they) go down the street together.
>
> Neither Sean (he) nor Judy (she) is going to the picnic.
>
> The class (it, as a single unit) agrees with the professor.

PROBLEMS IN SUBJECT-VERB AGREEMENT

PROBLEMS IN SUBJECT-VERB AGREEMENT

1. Identifying the true subject
2. Using a plural verb with compound subjects
3. Using the correct form with (a) collective nouns, (b) correlative conjunctions, (c) indefinite pronouns, (d) inverted sentences, and (e) with here/there/where.
4. Using nouns of measurement, weight, time, or money
5. Using singular nouns that are plural in form

---

1. Identifying the true subject.   Since the verb form depends on the subject, you must:

1. Identify the true subject.
2. See that the verb agrees.

Singular subjects call for singular verbs, and plural subjects call for plural verbs. Don't be confused by nouns or pronouns that come between the subject and the verb.

       subject   verb

The worst *feature* of these roads *is* the potholes.

  subject   verb

A *line* of ragged and hungry children *waits* at the gate.

  subject   verb

The *risk* to the workers *seems* unreasonably high.

   subject   verb

The *repetition* of similar sounds *stirs* the emotions.

The words *roads, children, workers,* and *sounds* are plural, but they do not affect the verb form because they are not the subjects of the sentences.

    2. Using a plural verb with compound subjects. When two or more subjects are joined by *and,* they form a plural subject and require a plural verb.

My *cousin* **and** *one* of her classmates *are* going to Los Angeles.

The company *president* **and** his *secretary were* on the plane.

The exception to this rule occurs when the two subjects joined by *and* form a single unit.

Macaroni and cheese is nutritious.

White tie and tails is the correct dress.

    Using the correct form with false compounds. When the subject is followed by a phrase like *in addition to, as well as, accompanied by,* or *together with,* these expressions do not take the place of *and.* They do not form a compound subject.

The *mayor,* as well as all the council members, *is* going to attend the ceremony.

The *president,* accompanied by his aides and advisors, *is* scheduled to arrive tomorrow.

The *players,* as well as the *coach, are* elated by the victory over the Saints.

The phrase between the subject and the verb, often set off by commas, does not affect the verb form.

    3a. Using the correct form with collective nouns. Some of the more common collective nouns are *team, jury, class, committee, crew, gang, flock,* *family.* These collective nouns take singular verbs when the group acts as a unit.

> The jury *is* ready to bring in its verdict.
>
> The class *is* working on a practice test.
>
> The family *is* gathered around the Christmas tree.

A plural verb should be used only when the sense of the sentence is plural—when it is clear that you mean the individual members and not the group.

> A flock of geese *were* landing, one by one, on the still surface of the pond.
>
> The committee *were* taking their seats. (Logically, they cannot all take the same seat.)

3b. Using the correct form with correlative conjunctions.   Following are the commonly used correlative conjunctions: *either . . . or, neither . . . nor, not only . . . but also, not . . . but, . . . or. . . .* When compound subjects are joined by correlative conjunctions, the verb agrees with the nearer of the two subjects.

> Either the patrolmen or the *sergeant is* responsible.
>
> Neither the warden nor the *guards were* prepared for a riot.
>
> Not only the scouts but also the *scoutmaster was* completely confused.
>
> The parents or the *child is* sure to suffer.

3c. Using the correct form with indefinite pronouns.   The following pronouns take singular verbs:

one	anyone	everyone	another	many a one
each	anybody	everybody	each one	anything
either	someone	nobody	another one	everything

Each of the *girls has* a good job.

Somebody has left the lights on.

Everybody in the whole class *has* a different opinion.

The indefinite pronouns *some* and *none* may be singular or plural, depending on the sense of the sentence.

None of the fathers *were* as tall as their sons.

None of the young workers *was* ready to take that job.

Some of the fish *were* bullheads.

Some of the meat *was* quite tender.

3d. Using the correct form with other inverted sentences.   There are other types of sentences in which the subject follows the verb.

Standing on the shelf *were* a model *plane* and a toy control *tower.*

Somewhere under the eaves *is* a giant hornets' *nest.*

3e. Using the correct form in sentences beginning with here, there, and where.   In sentences beginning with *here, there,* and *where,* the verb must agree with the subject that follows it.

Here *are* the *papers* Jim completed.

There *goes one* of Fleigel's trucks.

Where *are* those three *welders?*

4. Using nouns of measurement, weight, time, or money.   Plural nouns that indicate a unit of measurement, weight, time, or money usually take a singular verb.

A thousand *bushels is* a poor yield.

Ninety-seven *dollars is* too much to pay.

Three hundred and sixty *pounds is* a mighty big man.

5. Using singular nouns that are plural in form.   The following nouns, though they look plural, always take singular verbs:

mathematics	politics	statistics
physics	civics	measles
economics	news	molasses

The following nouns always take plural verbs:

pants	glasses	riches
scissors	trousers	binoculars

EXERCISE 6D: CHOOSING THE CORRECT VERB

Cross out the incorrect verb in the following sentences.

1. The feelings of the majority of the American people (is, are) at odds with the ruling of the Supreme Court on school prayer.

2. Where (has, have) moral values been taught in the past?
3. There (is, are) some people who believe schools should not teach about sex.
4. Standing against the Supreme Court ruling (is, are) most conservatives and many liberals.
5. Eighty percent of Americans (disapproves, disapprove) of the ruling that (bans, ban) prayers at graduation ceremonies.
6. Politics (invades, invade) almost every aspect of our lives, critics say.
7. Now the members of the Supreme Court (has, have) ruled when and where we can pray, said one critic.
8. Seventy-six percent of Americans (says, say) that it's right for a school to put up a manger scene or a menorah during the holidays.
9. Over half, 53 percent, (agrees, agree) that it's right for a school to post the Ten Commandments.
10. The opinion of American citizens (reflects, reflect) a sharp contrast to this decision of the highest court in the land.

EXERCISE 6E: CORRECTING AGREEMENT OF SUBJECTS AND VERBS

Correct all errors in subject-verb agreement by drawing a line through the incorrect verb forms.

1. *Sixty Minutes* (is, are) a news magazine show.
2. The staff (take, takes) on controversial subjects.
3. One of their programs (shows, show) the atrocities of the Serbs against a Croatian woman who survived the terror.
4. She (tells, tell) of being raped by six or seven soldiers, along with their commander, on three consecutive nights.
5. One of her tormentors (has, have) literally gotten away with murder, she says.
6. On a huge bonfire made hotter by the addition of burning tires, scores of village men, some wounded, some sick, (was, were) thrown to be burned to death.
7. One correspondent said that Bosnia (has, have) turned into a slaughter-house.
8. American peace keeping forces (has, have) made no arrests of these war criminals.
9. Another of their programs (contrasts, contrast) two views of welfare and affirmative action by opposing black leaders.
10. There (is, are) differing opinions in the black community about how these programs affect black Americans.
11. One of the black men, who has his own radio talk show in Los Angeles, (insists, insist) that affirmative action (is, are) insulting to blacks.

12. It (suggests, suggest) that the only way blacks can succeed is by preferential treatment.
13. Working hard, working long hours, getting an education and staying free of drugs and crime (is, are) how people get ahead, he (maintains, maintain).
14. The whole welfare system (hurts, hurt) the black community.
15. *Sixty Minutes* (prides, pride) itself on presenting contrasting views.

✓ Agreement of Pronouns and Antecedents

If pronouns could talk, they would probably have a lot to complain about. People constantly misuse them. Even after proofreading, many writers (and speakers) overlook errors in pronoun usage, but using pronouns correctly is not difficult if you just keep this guideline in mind:

> **A pronoun must agree in number, gender, and person with the word that it refers to (its antecedent).**

Here are some examples:

Number: My *sisters,* Marie and Antoinette, said that *they* hated pumpkin pie, so Mom said, "Let *them* eat cake."

Gender: *Alan* said that *he* had just read a good definition of a class reunion: an excuse to get together to see who's falling apart.

Person: As soon as *it* spotted the hunter, the *deer* vanished.

In the third example, the pronoun *it* comes before *deer,* the noun that it refers to. You can place a pronoun before its antecedent, *as long as the antecedent is clear.*

✓ Problems in Pronoun-Antecedent Agreement

THE INDEFINITE ANTECEDENT. If your antecedent is indefinite—*anybody, anyone, somebody, someone, everybody, everyone, nobody, no one, each, either, neither, a doctor, a steelworker, the average businessperson,* and so on—then you need a singular pronoun. For example:

Everyone should have the right to live *his* life the way *he* sees fit.

This particular rule of pronoun-antecedent agreement (the use of the singular male pronoun to refer to an indefinite third person) needs to be refined, however. Obviously, a mother, a daughter, a sister, a girlfriend, a grandmother, or a great aunt also has the right to live her life the way she sees fit, so women, as well as men, are included in the term everyone, Yet the sentence refers to living his life the way *he* sees fit. To many people, using a male pronoun to refer to persons in general seems illogical. Unfortunately, however, the alternative of using both the male and female pronoun forms every time you want to refer to an indefinite third party can weaken your writing. For example, an otherwise simple textbook explanation could become quite cumbersome and confusing:

> When writing a narrative paragraph, the student should arrange the details of *his* or *her* narrative in chronological order. *He* or *she* should also narrow *his* or *her* subject to a single significant event and use the simple past tense to relate *his* or *her* story to *his* or *her* reader. The student should also make sure that *his* or *her* narrative is unified. *He* or *she* should not include details that do not relate to *his* or *her* main point.

Can you imagine reading a whole book like this?

If, on the other hand, you are making a brief statement, or if you are using an indefinite antecedent only a few times in your paragraph, then there is nothing wrong with using both the masculine and feminine pronouns. For example, you might begin a paragraph with the following topic sentence:

> When I was a child, my father taught me that everyone has the right to express his or her opinions, but now that I am older, I realize, sadly, that my father himself never had the courage to express his own convictions.

Sometimes you can avoid the indefinite antecedent problem altogether by using a plural antecedent ("All citizens have the right to express their opinions"), but this alternative will not always work. You can't simply eliminate indefinite antecedents from your vocabulary. Traditionally, the pronouns *he, him,* and *his* have included both male and female, all humankind. Keep in mind, though, that one of the most important ideas in this book is that specific, vivid language helps to create interesting, worthwhile writing. If you have many problems with indefinite antecedents, you are probably using too many pronouns and altogether too many general, nonspecific words.

THE MISSING ANTECEDENT.   Unless the antecedent is clear, a pronoun is meaningless. For example, "She witnessed the murder" means nothing to the sheriff until he knows who she is, so watch out for sentences such as the following:

> *Wrong:*   The whole softball team apologized, but *she* was too
>   angry to listen.

Who was too angry to listen? The sentence should include a specific antecedent for *she*.

> *Correct:* The whole softball team apologized to *Mrs. Nelson,* but *she* was too angry to listen.
>
> *Correct:* The whole softball team apologized to the *coach,* but *she* was too angry to listen.
>
> *Wrong:* In Ireland, *they* say that Dingle Bay is a piece of heaven on earth.
>
> *Correct:* *The Irish* say that Dingle Bay is a piece of heaven on earth.

The pronoun *it* is the most likely to have the missing antecedent. Some students use *it* so frequently that they forget they are using a pronoun. Consequently, they make errors like the following:

He got sick and died of it. (Of what? Pneumonia? Jungle rot?)

He got shot, and it is in him yet. (What is in him yet?)

In some commonly accepted sentences, such as "It is raining" or "it's late," *it* has no antecedent and needs none.

THE VAGUE ANTECEDENT.   Another problem is the use of *this, that, these,* and *those* without a specific antecedent.

> *Wrong:* Steven would never deceive anyone about anything, and *this* is one of his most appealing qualities.
>
> *Correct:* Steven would never deceive anyone about anything, and *this uncompromising honesty* is one of his most appealing qualities.

THE AMBIGUOUS REFERENCE.   Ambiguous means capable of being interpreted in more than one way. Thus, if you use a pronoun that could logically refer to more than one noun, you have an ambiguous reference.

> *Ambiguous:* Bert told Ernie that he should marry Miss Piggy.
> (*Who* should marry Miss Piggy? Bert or Ernie?)
>
> *Clear:* Bert said to Ernie, "You should marry Miss Piggy."
> Bert suggested that Ernie marry Miss Piggy.
> Bert said to Ernie, "I should marry Miss Piggy."

If you make a practice of placing a pronoun as close as possible to the word it refers to, you can decrease the chances of having an ambiguous reference.

> *Ambiguous:* Adam was arguing with the gardener about what type of snake *he* found under Eve's apple tree.
> (The reader doesn't know whether *he* refers to Adam or to the gardener.)

Clear: *Adam* argued that the snake *he* found under Eve's apple
         tree was a copperhead, but the gardener insisted that it
         was a water moccasin.

Clear: Adam and Eve's gardener said that he found a copper-
         head under the apple tree, but Adam insisted that it was
         a water moccasin.

Clear: Adam was arguing with the gardener, Lucifer Temp-
         towski, about what type of snake Mr. Temptowski found
         under Eve's apple tree.

EXERCISE 6F: CORRECTING AGREEMENT OF PRONOUNS AND ANTECEDENTS

Correct the errors in pronoun-antecedent agreement in the following sentences. If the sentence is correct, put a C at the end of the sentence. Remember, you may have to change the verb if the pronoun is the subject.

1. The American taxpayer is being fleeced by their own government agencies.
2. Taxpayers are becoming increasingly tired of this.
3. Many agencies are being investigated for its spending.
4. The agency that supplies rooms for the homeless currently pays about
   $3,000 a month for a place for some of their clients.
5. That would pay for an apartment in a nice hotel.
6. One shelter, Angels by the Sea, charges $100.00 per night for their rooms.
7. They have ninety-five rooms.
8. It is supposedly owned by the Mafia.
9. The landlord told the reporter that he wasn't sure of the facts.
10. This is an outrage.
11. The student disagreed with the teacher. He said the capital of Pennsyl-
    vania was Pittsburgh.
12. Carla made it a habit to disagree with everyone; this made her unpopular.
13. In sports, they say that winning is the only important thing.
14. Although the fight was hopelessly one-sided, he refused to stop it.
15. Someone has been calling me late at night, and if I find out who it is,
    they will be in serious trouble.

✓ Incomplete and Illogical Comparisons

In everyday conversation, you frequently hear such statements as these:

It is just too hot.
Suzy is such a pretty girl.
The Ewings are so wealthy.

These are incomplete comparisons.

1. In writing, avoid the words *so, such,* and *too* unless you complete the comparison.

Incomplete:	We had such a big dinner.
Complete:	We had such a big dinner *that I didn't even want break-fast the next morning.*
Incomplete:	It is such a pretty little cottage.
Complete:	It is such a pretty little cottage *that I have often dreamed of living there.*

If no comparison is intended, replace the *so, such,* or *too* with *very, extremely,* or *exceedingly.*

Incomplete:	Suzy is so pretty.
Complete:	Suzy is extremely pretty.

2. Do not omit words necessary to make a comparison clear and exact.

Incomplete:	Ruth works as hard, if not harder, than her husband.
Complete:	Ruth works *as* hard *as* her husband, if not harder.

3. Avoid thoughtless or illogical comparisons.

Illogical:	His salary was lower than a janitor.
Complete:	His salary was lower than a janitor's salary.
Complete:	His salary was lower than a janitor's.
Complete:	His salary was lower than that of a janitor.
Illogical:	The Sahara is larger than any desert in the world.
Complete:	The Sahara is larger than any other desert in the world.
Complete:	The Sahara is the largest desert in the world.

EXERCISE 6G: MAKING COMPARISONS CLEAR AND COMPLETE

Rewrite the following sentences to make them clear and complete. If the sentence is correct, circle the number.

1. Reading the fine print is so much better.

_____

_____

2. It is so time-consuming.

   _____

   _____

3. Some people feel it is harder than any reading.

   _____

   _____

4. Education is what you get from reading the fine print.

   _____

   _____

5. Experience is what you get if you don't.

   _____

   _____

6. Learning from experience is tougher.

   _____

   _____

7. My experience was worse than my wife.

   _____

   _____

8. The car I bought was so cheap.

   _____

   _____

9. Like many other used cars, its guarantee was limited.

_____

_____

10. My repair bill is larger than any bill I owe.

_____

_____

WORDS

✓ Metaphors and Similes

Metaphors and Similes

METAPHOR—A comparison that says that one thing *is* another.

Her words were weapons.

SIMILE—A comparison that says one thing is *like* another.

The old oak tree stood there like a sentinel, guarding the little one-room school.

He was as dangerous as a loaded gun.

One of the important ways in which we are able to understand new things or new ideas is to compare these new and unknown things to other things and ideas that we do know. Language helps us to do this through figures of speech called *metaphors* and *similes*. These are comparisons, usually made in very few words, which increase our understanding. The characteristics of good metaphors and similes are that they create imaginative images (note the similarity of the previous two words), which are not worn out by overuse.

A **metaphor** says that one thing *is* another—"A is B":

Knowledge is power.

War is hell.

A **simile** says that one thing is like another—"A is like B" using words such as *like, as,* and *than:*

> Her hair hung down her pallid cheeks like seaweed on a clam.
>
> At the party, he was as dangerous as a loaded gun.
>
> Donna is as stable as Jello.
>
> She absorbs knowledge as a sponge absorbs water.

Not every comparison is a simile. For example, if you say that the city of São Paulo is like New York City, you have made a comparison, but no simile is involved. On the other hand, when the poet says, "My love is like a red, red rose," he isn't making a literal comparison. He certainly doesn't mean that his sweetheart has long, prickly stems.

Remember: To be a simile, a comparison must make an *image;* it must not merely attempt to convey information but must aim to deepen understanding through imagination.

In a metaphor, the comparison is *implied* rather than expressly stated. The metaphor, in effect, goes one step farther than the simile. Instead of saying that something is *like* something else, it *implies* that something *is* something else.

> Yesterday *is* but a dream.
>
> Our doubts *are* traitors.

When Snoopy climbs on top of his doghouse and proclaims, "Happiness is a warm puppy," he is using a metaphor. A metaphor is a comparison of two things in a nonliteral sense. The literal meaning of a word is its strict dictionary meaning—exactly what the word denotes. For example, Snoopy could have used the literal meaning of happiness and said, "Happiness is the quality or state of being delighted, pleased, content, or glad," but it wouldn't have had the same effect as "Happiness is a warm puppy." By using the positive *connotation* of a "warm puppy" instead of the *denotation* of happiness, Snoopy creates a feeling of happiness. Who could feel anything but happy when he pictures himself snuggling up with a cute, little, soft, warm puppy?

Metaphors can add vividness to your writing. They can conjure up an image in a very few words. (That's why poets use them so much.) However, there are several things that you must be wary about when using the metaphor:

1. Don't use unclear metaphors.   There will be little chance for error in the simile "She was quick as a cat"; but if you use the metaphor "She was a cat," your readers may get a different image than quickness. One may think of sleekness or gracefulness. Another may get the image of a gossip whose tongue is sharp, or of a hissing, clawing monster.

2. Don't mix your metaphors. Although often amusing, mixed metaphors do not give a clear picture to the reader. If, for example, on describing a solitary and desolate wilderness, you use ". . . where the hands of man never set foot," the reader will respond—but with laughter. If you say, "Like a cougar stalking its prey, he ran around like a chicken with its head cut off," you have certainly given the reader a confused picture.

3. But don't be afraid to try the extended metaphor. The comparison does not have to be completed in a few words. Perhaps your whole paragraph will be based on the metaphor. For example, you might have as your topic sentence, "From his throne high in the loftiest tree in the forest, the eagle surveys his realm." Then you can write your entire paragraph by comparing the eagle to a king.

✓ Clichés

A simile that has been used too often is called a **cliché.** You will want to use similes in your paragraphs, but the surest way to bore your audience is to fill up your writing or your speech with *clichés.* These worn-out phrases no longer create an image or carry meaning.

Notice also that clichés are phrases, not single words. Although a single word may be ill chosen for a particular use (because it is inaccurate or vague or too general), a single word at least escapes the curse of being a cliché. The word *snow,* for example, always creates an image, but *white as snow* has been used so many times that it no longer stimulates the imagination.

Clichés generally fall into one of the following three categories:

1. **Worn-out quotations,** like *home sweet home, birds of a feather, you can't keep a good man down.*
2. **Overused combinations of words,** like *at this point in time, last but not least, blushing bride, have a nice day.*
3. **Worn-out similes,** like *pretty as a picture, good as gold, sly as a fox.*

Since these threadbare metaphors are the most boring of all clichés, you must make every effort to avoid them in your writing. This isn't difficult to do once you become aware of them. Here are some examples:

Similes

clean as a whistle	swims like a fish
sick as a dog	so quiet that you can hear a pin drop
avoid like the plague	hard as a rock
like a bat out of hell	like a bull in a china shop
like a pot calling the kettle black	quick as a wink
spread like wildfire	sly as a fox
pure as the driven snow	hell has no fury like a woman scorned

busy as a beaver
cool as a cucumber
blind as a bat
loose as a goose
smart as a whip
drunk as a skunk (or a fish or a hoot owl)

white as snow
clear as a bell
snug as a bug in a rug
light as a feather
like a fish out of water

Sick as a dog.

Overworked Expressions

gone but not forgotten
wet behind the ears
to the bitter end
it's the thought that counts
down but not out
with his back against the wall
burn your bridges behind you
turn over a new leaf
home free
rack your brain
it goes without saying
give me a break
burned out
time and time again
at the present time
too little, too late
you can't have your cake and eat it too

take a turn for the worse
hard to come by
treading on thin ice
at the crack of dawn
in this day and age
out of the frying pan into the fire
caught up in the rat race
too many irons in the fire
at the drop of a hat
turn a cold shoulder
few and far between
get a grip (or a handle) on things
in a bind
up against it
go for it
washed up
last but not least

pouring money down the drain (or a rat hole)

don't count your chickens before they are hatched

this is going to hurt me more than it hurts you.

between a rock and a hard place

a few bricks shy of a full load

robbing the cradle

See how many you can add to the list.

EXERCISE 6H: IDENTIFYING EFFECTIVE METAPHORS

Read the following metaphors and similes. Tell which are effective and which are not. Explain your choices.

1. He was as busy as Santa Claus on Christmas Eve.
2. My dog is a complete security system with a bark for a siren and a bite for a gun.
3. Reading the book was a roller-coaster ride.
4. The boat I bought needed more repairs than the *Titanic*.
5. My boyfriend is a mixture of Tom Cruise and Danny DeVito.
6. Eating at that diner is like sampling dishes at the cholesterol factory.
7. My private beach is like a place where the hands of man have never trod.
8. A visit from him is as welcome as a hospital stay.
9. His boss was a bottleneck he had to graduate from.
10. Giving her a drink is like playing Russian roulette.

EXERCISE 6I: WRITING YOUR OWN METAPHORS

Use a dictionary to find the literal meanings of the italicized examples. Then write your own explanation of each by using a metaphor.

war

> **Literal:** War is a major armed conflict between nations or between organized parties within a state.
>
> **Metaphor:** War is hell.

frustration

> **Literal:** Frustration is the feeling that one has been "prevented from achieving a goal or gratifying a desire."
>
> **Metaphor:** Frustration is knowing the answer to the last essay question but having only five minutes left to finish the test.

1. *marriage*

   Literal: _____

   Metaphor: _____

2. *loneliness* _____

   Literal: _____

   Metaphor: _____

3. *love*

   Literal: _____

   Metaphor: _____

4. *jealousy*

   Literal: _____

   Metaphor: _____

5. *freedom*

   Literal: _____

   Metaphor: _____

EXERCISE 6J: ELIMINATING CLICHÉS

Improve the following sentences by rewriting them to eliminate all the overused word combinations and clichés. If you can think of a more original comparison, by all means use it. Otherwise, just omit the clichés.

1. Juan was proud as a peacock when he got an *A* in Physics I.
2. I can't help it if you're mad; I'm just telling it like it is.
3. You calling me a liar is like the pot calling the kettle black.
4. Franco was pleading, "Look, that incident took place over a year ago; it's water over the dam; let's go back to square one and start all over again."
5. Avoid him like the plague; he shoots from the hip.

6. When my wife caught me out with my girlfriend, I was between a rock and a hard place.
7. Daffodils are Spring.
8. Opening a new book is like starting a new adventure.
9. When I complained about the rain, my wife told me to get a life.
10. Telling my girlfriend that I thought she had gained a few pounds was burning the bridges behind me.
11. I decided to turn over a new leaf—quit procrastinating, study more, watch TV less, and lay off the beer.
12. Tuition is hard to come by in this day and age, and I'm treading on thin ice with a 2.0 QPA.

Drunk as a skunk.

EXERCISE 6K: ELIMINATING CLICHÉS AND SLANG

Underline the clichés and/or slang in the following paragraph. Then rewrite the paragraph without using clichés or slang expressions.

Variety is the spice of life, and my husband, Gene, is living proof. Gene is as strong as a horse and as brave as a lion. You ought to see him when he gets mad; his face turns as red as a beet, and he acts as fierce as a tiger. Sometimes though, he can be as gentle as a dove, but trying to get him to help me with the housework is like pulling teeth. He's always as hungry as a bear, yet he refuses to help me with the dishes. He gets as stubborn as a mule and finds more excuses than Doan's has back pills. He claims that he is as busy as a beaver, is spread too thin, or has a million and one things to do. I suppose he does have his fingers in too many pies, but he still turns a deaf ear. Talking to him is like talking to a brick wall; he gets mad as a hatter and tries to make me feel as dumb as an ox. Then, quick as a wink, before I know it, he'll start purring like a kitten and tell me that I'm his one and only, the apple of his eye. All of a sudden, I see him as the true-blue one-in-a-million husband, and there I am, sitting on top of the world looking at things through rose-colored glasses. So, what I'm saying is that married life may not be a bowl of cherries, but don't ever sell it short, and don't knock it until you've tried it.

chapter 7

Classifying

ORGANIZATION

In this chapter, you will learn another method of exposition—**classification:** the procedure of dividing items into classes, groups, or categories for specific purposes.

Classification is essential as you attempt to make sense of the world around you and the people in it. By the time you get to college, classification affects many areas of your life. For example, you may be classified as

Buddhist, Christian, Hindu, Jew, Muslim, etc.

Democrat, Independent, Libertarian, Republican, etc.

Business major, Criminal Justice major, Liberal Arts major, Nursing major, etc.

All areas of study from grade school through college are classified. Arithmetic is classified according to addition, subtraction, multiplication, and division. Art and literature courses are classified according to historical periods: classical, medieval, renaissance, neoclassical, romantic, and modern.

All of us, sooner or later, are classified by many others according to the following categories and many others:

sex	marital status
educational level	annual income
homeownership	credit rating
number of dependents	age group

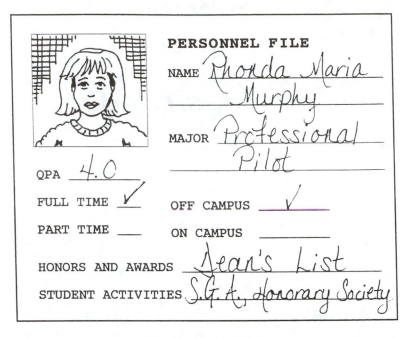

PERSONNEL FILE

NAME *Rhonda Maria Murphy*

MAJOR *Professional Pilot*

QPA *4.0*

FULL TIME *✓*   OFF CAMPUS *✓*

PART TIME ___   ON CAMPUS ___

HONORS AND AWARDS *Dean's List*

STUDENT ACTIVITIES *S.G.A., Honorary Society*

We are all classified.

Our status according to these classifications determines how we are perceived by government, by employers, by business, and by service agencies. The only secrets about ourselves that remain are those that are locked deep within our minds.

Large organizations cannot function without classifying their governing personnel:

Federal leadership:	legislative, executive, judicial
Military leadership:	executive (commander in chief), department of defense, officer ranks, enlisted ranks
Corporate leadership:	stockholders, board of directors, upper or top management, middle management, first-line or top management
Community college leadership:	county commissioners, board of trustees, college administration

We classify each day of our lives without even realizing that we are doing it. How could you tell someone what kind of books you enjoyed if they were not classified?

science fiction	horror
biography	frontier documentary
romance	international intrigue
mystery	military history

Even a simple question such as "Where do you want to eat?" can involve several types of classification based on various considerations:

Considerations	Classification
Budget status:	inexpensive, moderate, expensive
Occasion:	family outing, dining with friends, special occasion
Food preference:	Chinese, Italian, Mexican, American, gourmet, deli
Atmosphere:	family style, intimate, upscale elegant
Type of restaurant:	private club, tavern, buffet, ethnic, fast food
Beverage specialties:	beers, mixed drinks, wines, specialty coffees/teas
Dress:	casual, tastefully moderate, formal

Your mind whips through these categories in microseconds, dividing and classifying even more. Finally, your stressed brain now totally declassified, you decide: "Let's order a pizza!"

By using classification, you can create order out of confusion by breaking down a general subject area into its component parts. You can then discuss and/or clarify the function of these parts as they relate to the whole. Think of classification as the intellectual parallel to sorting clothes after removing them from the dryer. By sorting out the individual pieces from the entire load and arranging them in various piles, you create a logical arrangement that is (1) easier to understand, and (2) easier to work with.

As a writer, you can use classification

to analyze	to inform
to interpret	to persuade
to explain	to introduce concepts

✓ Assignment

Write a paragraph that explains and/or informs by classifying.

1. Choose a subject that interests you, and divide it into its primary components—at least three, no more than five.
2. Arrange the components in the most logical order for presentation to your reader.
3. Write a topic sentence that
   a. states your subject
   b. names its components
   c. expresses your point or purpose

Note: Your point or purpose may be repeated in your conclusion or appear only in your conclusion.

4. Discuss the significance and/or characteristics of each component as it relates to the whole (your subject).

5. Write a conclusion that focuses on the importance of your topic as a whole—subjects *and* components.

The following lists represent three different approaches to classifying. You may choose one of these topics or a variation as your subject.

Different Categories of	The Organization of	Spatial Division of
sports fans	a family budget	a favorite room
customers/patrons	a preventive maintenance	a county fair
coaches	program	a tactical formation
teachers	a collection: coins, stamps,	a floor plan
professional athletes	books, dolls, trains	a kitchen
wines/beers	the Sunday paper	a train layout
dates (social)	a chain of command	a school building
pets	an athletic team	a garden
aircraft	a workshop	an outlet mall
sales associates	a VFD, police department,	a yacht or ship
bosses	or EMS team	a laboratory
drivers	a wardrobe	a hospital wing/operating
students	a management team	room/ICU
excuses		a health club
shoppers		a working barn (dairy
politicians		or other)
friendships/relationships		an airport
		a prison
		a supermarket
		a department store
		a library

In the following paragraph, the student writer classifies monsters that have thrilled generations of moviegoers:

For years, moviegoers have enjoyed being frightened by every type of monster that Hollywood has managed to invent, whether it be natural, artificial, or extraterrestrial. The monsters which are products of nature may be exaggerated versions of real creatures, such as the single-minded shark in *Jaws,* the revenge seeking killer whale in *Orca,* the exploited gorilla in *King Kong,* or Ahab's nemesis in *Moby Dick.* They may be extinct animals, such as dinosaurs that return to destroy entire cities or run amuck in a Jurassic zoo park which attempts to put them on display. The artificial monster may be the cursed product of misguided human creativity. The most famous is Dr. Frankenstein's monster, the grotesque imitation of a human, composed of cadaver parts and activated by a jolt of electricity. The monster's pathos and anguish contrasts with its creator's monomani-

---

HOW TO WRITE A PARAGRAPH THAT CLASSIFIES

1. Choose a subject that interests you.
2. Divide the subject into component parts: classes, categories, or groups. Include *all* significant components.
3. Arrange these components in a logical sequence.
4. Determine the purpose of or point to be made by your classification.
5. Write a topic sentence that states
   a. the subject
   b. the number of subject of divisions
   Note: You may state your point or purpose in the topic sentence, in the conclusion, or both.
6. Discuss each category fully, showing how each relates to your subject. Provide equal coverage of each.
7. Write a conclusion that gives the reader a sense of closure, one that focuses on your topic as a whole as opposed to the last category that you discussed.

---

acal pride and madness. Artificial monsters can also combine human and animal features, such as Dr. Jekyll's Mr. Hyde, the teenage werewolf, Count Dracula's alter ego bat, the Fly, and gentle Bigfoot Harry, sheltered by the Hendersons. A medieval favorite, the dragon, is a malevolent killer and social scourge in *Dragonslayer,* yet is sensitive and self-sacrificing in *Dragonheart.* A fascinating variation of the artificial monster category is the rogue android gunfighter in *Westworld,* who stalks the tourists whom he was programmed to interact with. The extraterrestrial movie monster comes from outer space. He may be an invader as in *War of the Worlds* and *Independence Day,* or he may simply seek and destroy unsuspecting intergalactic transport drivers, as in *Alien.* Now, thanks to special effects, these creatures can terrorize the bravest moviegoers. Films like *Alien* play to our deepest fears of the unknown. The best and worst of these monsters sneak around the edges of our imaginations long after the cinema's lights come on, playing on fears that lurk just beneath the surface of our subconscious minds.

Bill Littler

Note the following situations using classification:

Purpose: to explain the operation of an internal combustion engine

1. Classify—divide the operation into its four phases: intake, compression, power, exhaust.

2. Arrange the phases according to the sequence in which they occur: (1) intake, (2) compression, (3) power, (4) exhaust.
3. Explain, using sufficient details, the role of each phase as it relates to the engine's operation.

Purpose: to explain a pretrial process chronologically

1. Classify—divide the process into its five steps: arrest, booking, detention or release, formal accusation, preliminary hearing.
2. Arrange the steps into a logical sequence: (1) arrest, (2) booking, (3) detention or release, (4) formal hearing, (5) preliminary hearing.
3. Explain, using sufficient details, the role of each step as it relates to the pretrial process.

Classification is very closely related to **outlining,** which is also a process of making order out of confusion. Here is a basic classification of a professional football team, using the outline format:

A professional football team is composed of three separate teams: Offense, Defense, and Special Teams.

I. Offense	II. Defense	III. Special Teams
A. Quarterback	A. Linemen	A. Kick-off
B. Receivers	1. Up linemen	1. Placekicker
1. Inside receivers	2. Down linemen	2. Ballmen
2. Ends	B. Linebackers	B. Kick return
C. Running backs	1. Inside	1. Deep returners
1. Halfbacks	2. Outside	2. Linemen
2. Fullbacks	C. Defensive Backfield	C. Punts
D. Linemen	1. Safeties	1. Punter
1. Center	2. Cornerbacks	2. Hatchet men
2. Guards		
3. Tackles		
4. Tight ends		

Nic Clare

To clarify your possibilities, classify as follows:

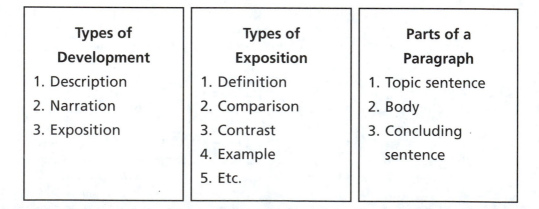

Types of Development	**Types of Exposition**	**Parts of a Paragraph**
1. Description	1. Definition	1. Topic sentence
2. Narration	2. Comparison	2. Body
3. Exposition	3. Contrast	3. Concluding sentence
	4. Example	
	5. Etc.	

This student writer, a fan of alternative music, expertly classifies his favorite types of music and related performers:

I classify my favorite music and artists into three categories, each with sub-divisions. The first category is Metal. It combines distorted, "choppy" guitar playing with lyrics of violence and evil. There are three main sub-divisions: (1) Speed Metal, (2) Death Metal, and (3) Heavy Metal. Speed Metal acts include Slayer, Megadeth, and Anthrax. Death Metal, my personal favorite, features the bands Immolation, Autopsy, and Morbid Angel. The last sub-division is Heavy Metal: the various acts include Ozzy Osbourne, Metallica, and AC/DC. The second category, Crossover, is exactly what its name implies. It mixes the guitar rhythms of metal with the speed and aggression of Punk Rock. The two sub-divisions are Hardcore and Grindcore. Uniform Choice, The Gorilla Biscuits, and Shelter are three of the more popular hardcore bands. The second sub-division is Grindcore. Bands falling in this division include Napalm Death, Carcass, and Sore Throat. The final category is Punk Rock. Punk Rock's trademark style is slow, anthem-type guitar rhythms with socially conscious lyrics. The two sub-divisions are original Punk and New Wave Punk. Original Punk launched this form of music with the Sex Pistols, G. B. H., and Broker Bores. New Wave Punk resulted from the original form; Bands like Fugatie, R. E. M., and Love and Rockets characterize this style. Almost every band playing alternative music falls into one of the categories and sub-divisions; furthermore, all of my records, compact discs, and tapes are arranged in this order.

Neal Henry

✓ Topic Sentence

The topic sentence for a classification paragraph should achieve the following:

A. Identify the subject to be classified
B. State an attitude that
   1. gives the number of categories in the classification
   2. names the categories
Note: All categories do not necessarily have to be named in the topic sentence for every classification. For example:

> There are three types of teachers at my college who make learning a pleasure. First is the intellectual, who also knows how to communicate to his students. . . . Second is the competent pragmatist, who cares little for research but relishes the classroom. . . . Third is the. . . .

C. Have a useful and/or informative purpose

Which of the following sentences could be used to introduce a classification paragraph?

> I am convinced that the Toyota Land Cruiser is more rugged than the Lincoln Navigator.
>
> My boyfriend's definition of love is sincere—but unrealistic.
>
> Public speakers fall into three categories: the assured, the anxious, and the indifferent.

It is the last one, of course. Note its components:

Subject: "Public speakers"
Attitude: 1. number of categories: "fall into three categories"
              2. names of categories: "the assured, the anxious, and the indifferent"

Write your topic sentence.

1. *Choose a subject* of interest to both you and your reader. It should be one that
   a. you are very familiar with
   b. one that you can research
2. *Narrow your subject* so that you can discuss it fully in a single paragraph.
   Broad: Sailboats
   Narrowed: My friend Larry's 42-foot Morgan Out Island ketch
3. *Determine the purpose* for your classification or the point that it will make. Purpose: to inform the reader that there are U.S. military commands trained specifically for covert operations. You may state or imply this purpose
   a. In your topic sentence:
      To perform "stealth" operations worldwide, the U.S. Armed Forces relies on four commands trained specifically to accomplish covert missions: Air Force Special Operations Command, Army Special Forces, Marine Force Reconnaissance, and Navy Seals.
   b. In your conclusion:
      Although these four special use commands routinely provide support for conventional operations, they are specifically trained to carry out highly precise covert missions.
4. *Select at least three, but no more than five, categories* of classification for your subject.
   a. Your categories should be *logical divisions* of your subject area.

      Illogical: A formal education requires the completion of five levels of schooling: elementary, middle, high school, college undergraduate, and the doctoral program.

Logical: A formal education requires the completion of five levels of schooling: elementary, middle, high school, college undergraduate, and postgraduate.

b. Your categories should *represent all members* of the group or subject area.

Not representative: There are three primary types of drive trains in American passenger and sport utility vehicles: rear-wheel drive, front-wheel drive, and on-demand four-wheel drive.

Representative: There are four primary types of drive trains in American passenger cars and sport utility vehicles: rear-wheel drive, front-wheel drive, on-demand four-wheel drive, and all-wheel drive.

c. Your categories should be consistent as to type. *Do not switch categories.*

Inconsistent: The average community college class contains three types of students: the dean's list student, the ambivalent student, and the bored student.

Consistent: The average community college class contains three types of students: the interested student, the ambivalent student, and the bored student.

5. *Combine narrowed subject and categories* that are logical, consistent, and representative to form your topic sentence.

1. In the following example, this Early Childhood Education major's assignment was to write a paragraph on an aspect of childhood behavior and to be prepared to read it aloud to her Observation and Guidance class. The subject, children's behavior patterns, had always intrigued her, so she decided to research the topic.

Broad topic: children's behavior patterns

2. Because her topic was so broad, she limited it to a particular aspect of children's behavior patterns.

Narrowed topic: frequently observed negative behavior patterns in children

3. Purpose

4. Based on her research, she identified three common categories of negative childhood behavior and arranged them in a logical order:

1. Exercising control
2. Seeking revenge
3. Withdrawal

Next, she wrote a topic sentence stating her subject and dividing it into the three categories:

> Children usually prefer to gain attention in positive ways, but when their efforts go unrecognized, they tend to solicit attention in negative ways, such as exercising control, seeking revenge, or withdrawing from their social communities.

Rather than stating her purpose in the topic sentence, she decided that it would be more effective as part of her conclusion.

> *Purpose:* to identify frequently observed negative behaviors in children, along with their causes, which will enable caregivers to help these children to modify their behaviors
>
> *Purpose stated in conclusion:* knowing why a child exhibits one of these negative behavior patterns can help the caregiver to better understand the child and help him to modify his behavior.

EXERCISE 7A: CHOOSING EFFECTIVE CONTROLLING IDEAS

Put a check mark before each of the following sentences that would make appropriate topic sentences for a division and classification paragraph.

_____ 1. I am thinking of joining one of the armed services so I have investigated the advantages and disadvantages of each.

_____ 2. My mother started lifting weights at age 64, and you won't believe the difference it has made in her life.

_____ 3. All recreation can be divided into four categories.

_____ 4. Horror movies, the kind that make you scream, come in four distinct types.

_____ 5. Luck plays a part in all sports, but you can isolate the factors that enable any team to win consistently.

_____ 6. Physical health is immensely important, but there are other types of health that are needed for happiness.

_____ 7. My girlfriend is gorgeous; in fact, the boys call her Gorgeous Georgia.

_____ 8. Last Thursday I had the scariest moment of my life.

_____ 9. There are four varieties of dirty clothes.

_____ 10. Five skills must be mastered before a person can play a decent game of golf.

EXERCISE 7B: CLASSIFYING TOPIC SENTENCES

Look at the sentences not checked as suitable for a paragraph of division and classification. Discuss which of those would be acceptable as topic sentences for development by another method.

✓ Body

The function of the body in a classification paragraph is to demonstrate or explain how each division relates to the whole. In other words, you must explain how each category relates to the subject in your topic sentence.

CHOOSING DETAILS

Topic sentence: Children usually prefer to gain attention in positive ways, but when their efforts go unrecognized, they tend to demand attention in negative ways, such as exercising control, seeking revenge, or withdrawing from their social communities.

I. **Primary Support**   In a paragraph that classifies, *each* division, category, or grouping provides the subject for *one* primary supporting detail.

First Division: exercising control

First Primary Supporting Detail: Power-seeking children feel important only when they are in complete control; being the boss in every situation becomes their sole objective and gratification.

Second Division: seeking revenge

Second Primary Supporting Detail: Vengeful children are convinced that they are not loved, thus their goal is to hurt others because they feel that they have been hurt.

Third Division: withdrawing from their social communities

Third Primary Supporting Detail: Some attention-starved children substitute withdrawal for aggression.

II. **Secondary Support**   As in other paragraphs, the secondary supporting details reinforce, clarify, and explain each primary supporting detail.
   A. They should be *relevant*
   B. They should be relatively *balanced* as to amount of content. Don't discuss one category in great detail and then say almost nothing about another. Each division should have its fair share of development.

ORDERING DETAILS

 I. **Arrange your divisions in a logical sequence.**   The purpose of classification is to give the reader a better understanding of the process, concept, or object that is being examined. Just dividing a concept into its component parts is not enough. For the reader to understand the concept clearly, you must arrange your divisions in the order that most logically demonstrates how they relate to the whole concept.
   A. *To explain a procedure,* take the reader sequentially from the first step to the last step. Don't omit steps, or present the first step, then the last step, then all the steps in between. *Don't put the cart before the horse.*

Don't put the cart before the horse.

   B. *To explain requirements or criteria;* begin with the least important requirement and proceed to the most important.
   C. *To explain structure of an object;* classify the different parts in an understandable and predictable sequence, such as
      1. *According to function;* from the least important to the most important
      2. *According to location;* moving from front to rear, moving from top to bottom, moving from side to side, by quadrants/sections.
II. **Ensure Adequate Development of Your Subject**
   A. First, as previously discussed, divide your subject into its most significant and representative categories. Your classification must include all members of the group.

B. Second, do not discuss categories or groupings superficially. Be sure to include all important components or aspects of a division or category when you explain it.

CONCLUSION

I. Remember, in a classification paragraph, purpose can be expressed in the conclusion as well as in the topic sentence.

II. The conclusion should leave the reader's mind focused on the topic as a whole—not just on one aspect.

For example, if you are analyzing the different positions for driving a snowmobile—sitting, kneeling, standing—don't conclude with a sentence about the standing position: "The standing position is also good for traction." This sentence concludes only one classification—it could not conclude the entire paragraph. Conclude, instead, with a statement that pulls the paragraph together: "The position that you choose will depend on your expertise, the terrain, your speed, weather conditions, and the depth of the snow."

Now, let's put it all together, using our student paragraph as a model:

Topic Sentence	Children usually prefer to gain attention in positive ways, but when their efforts go unrecognized, they tend to demand attention in negative ways, such as exercising control, seeking revenge, or withdrawing from their social communities.
Primary support #1	Power-seeking children feel important only when they are in complete control; being the boss in every situation becomes their sole objective and gratification.
Secondary support for #1	When their dominance is challenged, these youngsters become even more defiant. If their struggle for power and authority expands, they may transfer that desire to the pursuit of revenge.
Primary support #2	Vengeful children are convinced that they are not loved, thus their goal is to hurt others because they feel that they have been hurt.
Secondary support for #2	They relish the role of being cruel and disliked, and any retaliation directed toward them only intensifies their need to seek revenge. For these children, castigatory attention is better than no attention at all.
Primary support #3	Some attention-starved children substitute withdrawal for aggression.
Secondary support for #3	Withdrawn children feel inadequate and unloved because they are repeatedly discouraged in their attempts to succeed and/or receive insufficient praise for their accomplishments. As a result, their gloomy personalities may alienate them from their families and also cause them to become outcasts among their peers.
Conclusion and statement of purpose	Although these behaviors are neither appropriate nor desirable, they are, nevertheless, pleas for love, attention, and recognition. Knowing why a child exhibits one of these negative behavior patterns can help the caregiver to understand the child better and help him to modify his behavior.

Jeanine Doffin

A master of the essay, E. B. White captures the essence of New York City through classification. Note how he identifies his categories in the paragraph body with emphasis on the last. His conclusion is an exemplary tribute to the "settlers" who give the city its true identity:

> **There are roughly three New Yorks.** There is, first, the New York of the man or woman who was born there, who takes the city for granted and accepts its size and its turbulence as natural and inevitable. Second, there is the New York of the commuter—the city that is devoured by locusts each day and spat out each night. Third, there is the New York of the person who was born somewhere else and came to New York in quest of something. Of these three trembling cities the great-est is the last—the city of final destination, the city that is a goal. It is this third city that accounts for New York's high-strung disposition, its poetical deportment, its dedication to the arts, and its incomparable achievements. Commuters give the city its tidal restlessness; natives give it solidity and continuity; but the settlers give it passion. And whether it is a farmer arriving from Italy to set up a small gro-cery store in a slum or a young girl arriving from a small town in Mississippi to es-cape the indignity of being observed by her neighbors, or a boy arriving from the Corn Belt with a manuscript in his suitcase and a pain in his heart, it makes no dif-ference: each embraces New York with the intense excitement of first love, each absorbs New York with the fresh eyes of an adventurer, each generates heat and light to dwarf the Consolidated Edison Company.
>
> E. B. White, "Here Is New York," *Collected Essays of E. B. White*

You can even have fun with classification, and this student paragraph is proof. Note how his creative conclusion echoes the controlling idea with a dramatic assertion.

> **Apples have always done the devil's work, and they spread evil in three ways: mind control, physical attacks, and metaphorical deception.** In the be-ginning, apples already controlled the minds of men and animals. Some think that the serpent beguiled Eve, but, in fact, it was the apple that put the serpent up to it. The hapless snake took the rap for man's fall while the apple just hung around, enjoying the fruits of Eden's demise. In order to spread its evil, the apple poisoned the mind of Johnny Appleseed, an American pioneer. As a re-sult, Johnny walked across the land, sowing seeds of evil all across North America. Transcending nature, the apple then embraced technology to control men's minds. Today, a fanatic core of Apple users is waging a sinister campaign to subvert divinely inspired "Big Blue." Apples have also asserted their domi-nation through violence, physically attacking unsuspecting victims. William Tell's son was attacked by an apple, but Tell's marksmanship saved the boy just as the apple was about to drain the lad's brain of knowledge. Sir Isaac Newton, while contemplating under the tree, had actually suspected the apple's dark side, and when one overeager apple bounced off his head, Newton quickly re-

alized the gravity of the situation. Had he not moved away instantly, the whole tree full would have finished him off, according to plan. Even Snow White, the personification of goodness and purity, could not withstand the apple's fatal attraction. It took a princely miracle to release her from the spell cast by Satan's pomaceous angel. A final insidious device of the deadly fruit is metaphorical deception. Think of the innocents from home and abroad who came to seek enlightenment, but who instead succumbed to sin in "The Big Apple." Consider, too, the lost souls in purgatory who opted for worldly salvation, blindly assuming that "an apple a day would keep the doctor away." Mistakenly, everyone thinks that "one bad apple can spoil the barrel." There is no such thing as one bad apple—they are *all* bad!

T. J. Higgs

✓ Some Do's . . .

1. *Do* provide a sensible, consistent pattern of organization for your reader. Choose a single, logical basis of division and classification, and then stay with it.
2. *Do* arrange your categories in an effective, logical order—first to last, least important to most important.
3. *Do* make sure that you have included all important members of a particular category in your division and classification. If, for example, you are analyzing the components of a good job interview, don't limit your discussion to poise and appearance. There are other factors far more important than a person's poise and appearance.

✓ . . . and Don'ts About Classifying

1. *Don't* break a concept down into its component parts without showing how each part relates to the whole. You need to provide your readers with more than an outline.
2. *Don't* discuss one category at length and then introduce the next category with only a single sentence of explanation. Explain each part of your analysis fully, so that you have an even, balanced discussion.
3. *Don't* end your classification with a final detail about the last part of your analysis. Add a conclusion that refers to the *whole* paragraph, not just to the last part of the paragraph.

SUGGESTED ACTIVITIES AND ASSIGNMENTS

1. Get together with several of your classmates and make a list of 20 to 25 board games. Classify these games in as many meaningful ways as you can. (What kinds of games are they? What skills do you need to play these games?) Then see if your group can devise a game that incorporates two or more of these skills.

2. You can classify any group of things, persons, facts, or ideas in different ways; but if your classification has no purpose, then it will provide useless information. For example, a college admissions director might usefully classify students as full-time, part-time, transfer, or nontransfer; but to classify students as short, medium, or tall would serve no useful purpose. You have to have some sensible guiding principle in mind in order for your reader to learn something from your analysis.

The following is a list of characteristics, each of which helps to identify a mother. Suppose this person were your mother. Help someone else understand what kind of person she is by viewing her from different perspectives. Classify your mother in different ways. For example, you might classify her on the basis of how she allocates her time, on the basis of the different facets of her personality, on the basis of the types of skills she possesses, or on the basis of who benefits from those skills. When you have finished, compare your classification with those of your classmates. See how your categories differ.

counselor	gardener
cook	member of school board
artist	nutritionist
friend	grievance committee chairperson
systems analyst	philosopher
interior decorator	aerobics instructor
union officer	Meals on Wheels volunteer
church organist	designer of computer software
problem solver	part-time student
chauffeur	collector of antiques
critic	free-lance writer
financial manager	math tutor
camper	peacemaker
movie buff	confidant
laundress	decision maker
president of local historical society	seamstress
wife	hostess
member of Hunger Action Coalition	Democratic committeewoman

SENTENCES

✓ Importance of Continuity

The sentences in a division/classification paragraph, as in any paragraph, are not separate islands of thought. They are parts of a whole that must be linked through various devices. This linking of parts is particularly important in division and classification, since the writer must move from one division (or classification) to another in developing the paragraph. The writer must take the reader along as she moves from one part to another by connecting the parts smoothly and clearly.

The most important unifying device is the topic sentence itself. Every sentence in the paragraph needs to be clearly related to the controlling idea. Furthermore, the sentences must be arranged in some sequence to provide the readers with an ongoing progression of thought. You need an orderly and sensible pattern of development to take your readers with you. It is your job to keep the readers from becoming distracted. You want them to devote full attention to the information you are trying to convey. This smoothness is called **continuity.**

A paragraph is said to have good continuity when ideas are smoothly linked together. The linking process is called **transition,** and the bridges between ideas are called **transitional devices.** The proper use of transitional devices can make you a better writer.

1. They help to clarify meaning by bridging the gap from one idea to the next.
2. They help to keep your readers from becoming distracted or disoriented; they are able to follow more clearly what you are saying.
3. They help achieve a smoother style.

✓ How to Make Your Paragraph Stick Together

Some of the devices that aid unity and continuity in the development of the paragraph are (1) enumeration, (2) reference of pronouns, (3) use of transitional words and phrases, (4) repetition of key words and phrases, and (5) parallel wording.

ENUMERATION. Using words such as *first, second, third, or then, later, finally* serves to guide the reader in step-by-step fashion through the development of the paragraph. Such devices are especially helpful in a paragraph providing specific information or giving explicit instructions to the reader.

UNIFYING DEVICES

1. Enumeration
2. Pronoun reference
3. Connecting words
4. Repetition
5. Parallel wording

The following passage illustrates how enumeration can aid paragraph unity and coherence.

> The truth is girls are not treated the same as boys in classrooms across America. *First,* teachers, men and women, call on boys more often than girls. . . . *Second,* boys receive more positive feedback than do girls. . . . *Third,* girls are more likely to be reprimanded when they call out answers though they do so eight times less often than boys. . . . *Fourth,* women get only two percent of the text-book space, even in the most modern history books. . . . *Fifth.* . . .

Note: You should never use *firstly, secondly, thirdly.* It is pretentious and grammatically unsound.

When one is writing on technical subjects or giving explicit instructions, numbers are frequently used to ensure clarity and precision, as in the following example.

> These, then, as every student pilot learns, are the four forces that act on an airplane in flight: (1) weight pulls it down, but (2) lift of its wings holds it up; (3) drag holds it back, but (4) pull of the propeller keeps it going.

Note that the numbers in parentheses do not change the other punctuation. Numbers, however, are not ordinarily used in the paragraphs you write in freshman composition class.

PRONOUN REFERENCE. Using pronouns such as *he, she, it, these, we, those,* or *they* to refer to a subject named in a previous sentence helps to unify the paragraph. The following passage shows how the repetition of the pronoun can unify a paragraph. *We* carries the idea of *us as a people* throughout the paragraph.

> Something will have gone out of *us as a people* if *we* ever let the remaining wilderness be destroyed; if *we* permit the last virgin forests to be turned into comic books and plastic cigarette cases; if *we* drive the few remaining members of the wild species into zoos or to extinction; if *we* pollute the last clean air and dirty the last clean streams and push our paved roads through the last of the silence, so that never again will Americans be free in their own country from the noise, the exhausts, the stinks of human and automotive waste, and so that never again can *we* have the chance to see ourselves single, separate, vertical, and individual in the world, part of the environment of trees, and rocks, and soil, brother to the other animals, part of the natural world and competent to belong it it.

> Wallace Stegner, *The Sound of Mountain Water*

Pronoun reference must be clear and consistent, as follows:

1. The noun that the pronoun represents must be given first. Do not start out with *this, that, they, it, he,* or *she;* the reader will not know to whom or to what the pronoun refers.

2. The pronoun must agree in number with the noun to which it refers. If the noun is *child,* then you must use a singular pronoun, *he* or *she*—not *they.* If the noun is *people,* you must use a plural pronoun, *they*—not *he* or *one.*

3. The pronoun must be consistent in number or person with the noun to which it refers. If the noun is *motorist,* the pronoun you must use is *he* or *she,* not *you* or *we.* If the noun is *company,* the pronoun you must use is *it,* not *he* or *they.* Be sure to avoid inconsistent shifts in pronoun reference.

Inconsistent:	Each student at this college must pass freshman English. They can't graduate if they don't.
Consistent:	Each *student* at this college must pass freshman English. *He* can't graduate if he doesn't.
Inconsistent:	A middle-income family cannot afford the tuition. They don't qualify for financial aid.
Consistent:	A middle-income *family* cannot afford tuition. *It* doesn't qualify for financial aid.
Inconsistent:	John has no one to support except himself. You don't need a big income.
Consistent:	John has no one to support except *himself. He* doesn't need a big income.

Do not use a pronoun until you have identified the subject.

TRANSITIONAL WORDS AND PHRASES. Transitional words and phrases serve as pointers to guide the reader in much the same way as road signs guide the motorist. Words and phrases such as *of course, as a result, on the other hand, nevertheless, however,* or *consequently* direct the reader along the course of development from topic sentence to conclusion.

Words and phrases like *in the morning, later, afterwards, next, in the evening, at last,* or *finally* show progression or changes in time. Leaving out such words can be very confusing to our reader. Consider the following:

The party was a real blast; it didn't break up until 3:00 A.M. I made some coffee and toast, but that didn't help my headache at work.

Unless you include some transition before the second sentence, the reader will not know when you made the coffee. However, if you insert *at daybreak,* the reader will stay with you:

> The party was a real blast; it didn't break up until 3:00 A.M. At daybreak, I made some coffee and toast, but that didn't help my headache at work.

Any contrast or shift in thought should be clearly marked for the reader. You do not say, "I like ham, and I hate eggs." You need a word that shows contrast here.

> I like ham, *but* I hate eggs.
> I like ham; *however,* I hate eggs.
> I like ham; *on the other hand,* I hate eggs.

You can also show a concession by use of transitional words.

> *Although* I failed the test, I passed the course.
> *Even though* I like dogs, I hate that terrier.

If you want to show simple addition, use *and, also, again,* or some similar word.

> She bought the car, *and* she paid for it in cash.

If you are going to illustrate a point, tell your reader what you are doing. Before you tell the story or give the illustration, use an expression like *for example.*

> He was a real delinquent. *For example,* he once was arrested for having broken forty-three street lights.

Read this paragraph. What is wrong with it?

> He was a delinquent in many ways. His mother loved him. He was a truant. He was arrested for breaking street lights. He stole a car. He was a bully in the school. He was intelligent. He make poor grades. His mother was worried and hurt. She never let him know. She was there. She believed in him. She let him know it. He never felt deserted. She stood behind him. He reformed. A mother's love saved her son.

Now see what happens when transitional words are included:

> *Although* he was a delinquent in many ways, his mother *still* loved him. *Even though* he *often* skipped school and was *once* arrested for breaking street lights, his mother kept right on loving him. *At one time,* he even stole a car. *In addition,* he was a bully at school, and *although* he was intelligent, he *still* made

poor grades. *Even though* his mother, *of course,* was worried and hurt, she never let him know. She was *always* there. She believed in him, *and* she let him know it. He never felt deserted *because* she always stood behind him. *Finally,* he reformed. A mother's love, *in this situation,* saved her son.

Isn't this clearer?

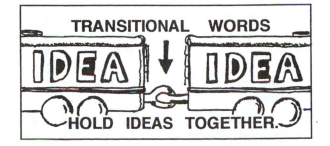

See what the addition of a few transitional words can do. If you learn to use the following transitional words effectively, your writing will be more precise and also more forceful.

To show addition:	and, moreover, furthermore, in addition, also, again
To show contrast:	but, on the other hand, however, yet, nevertheless, on the contrary, conversely
To show similarity:	likewise, in the same way, in like manner, similarly
To show emphasis:	in fact, indeed, certainly
To show concession:	granted, even though, although, though
To introduce an example:	for example, for instance, that is, in other words, in particular
To introduce a result:	thus, therefore, consequently, hence, then, so
To introduce a conclusion:	in summary, in conclusion, finally, in short

REPETITION OF KEY WORDS AND PHRASES.   Paragraph unity is often aided if you repeat key words and phrases that keep the central idea before the reader. In the following paragraph, notice how the key words are repeated throughout the paragraph.

The large *size* of the human *brain* evolved in response to the development of *cultural information.* A big *brain* is an advantage when dealing with such information. *Big-brained* individuals were able to deal more successfully with the *culture* of their group. They were thus more successful reproductively than their *smaller-brained* relatives. They passed on their genes for *big brains* to their numerous offspring. They also added to the accumulating store of *cultural information,* increasing slightly the premium placed on *brain size* in the next generation. A self-reinforcing selective trend developed—a trend toward increased *brain size.*

Paul R. Ehrlich, *The Population Bomb*

✓ Parallel Wording

> I came, I saw, I conquered.
>
> . . . of the people, by the people, for the people
>
> A penny saved is a penny earned.

These are examples of **parallel wording**—the use of the same word or sentence pattern several times. Parallelism is used for emphasis; it is a repetition used to make a strong point; it forces the reader to notice. Note the difference between the foregoing parallels and the following nonparallels:

> I came and saw the country, and then it was conquered by me and my men.
>
> . . . that came from the people and was designed by them for the purpose of the group itself
>
> If you save a penny, it is just as if you had earned it.

Notice that the second set does not have the impact of the first because parallel wording was not used; therefore, the second group does not have the strength, the emphasis, of the first. Repeating the sentence pattern, especially the verb form, may add both clarity and emphasis to the paragraph.

You may use parallelism in a series of words:

> Our flag is red, white, and blue.

or in a series of phrases:

> Harry was in trouble with his mother, with his teacher, and with his girl.

or in a series of clauses:

> John ran up the steps; Susan ran down the steps; Joe stood bewildered on the landing.

Do not overuse parallelism, however. If you do, your writing becomes tiresome. Emphasizing everything is the same as emphasizing nothing.

Do not try to make nonparallel things parallel.

> Jerry was a reader, a writer, a studier, and neat.

Neat does not fit the pattern and should not be included in the parallel structure. It is better to say:

> Jerry was a reader, a writer, and a studier. He was also neat.

(Notice the change in meaning if *also* is omitted.)

Study the parallel wording in the following paragraph.

> The teacher wanted the students to study the chapter, not skim it. He wanted them to understand the rules, not memorize them. He wanted them to discuss the issues, not talk around them. He wanted them to enjoy the class, not laugh at it. The students did not seem to be able to tell the difference.

Note the pattern that prevails throughout the paragraph: "He wanted them to _____, not _____." This parallelism makes the paragraph both clear and strong.

The two following paragraphs use parallel structure effectively to make their points clear.

> The policeman against environment deterioration must be the powerful Department of Population and Environment. . . . It must be carefully insulated against the forces that will quickly be aligned against it. *It is going to cost* industry money. *It is going to cost* municipalities money. *It is going to* hit a lot of us where it hurts. *We may have to* do without two gas-gulping monster cars per family. *We may have to* learn to get along with some insect damage in our produce. *We may have to* get along with much less fancy packaging of the goods we purchase. *We may have to* use cleaners that get our clothes something less than "whiter than white." *We may have to* be satisfied with slower coast-to-coast transportation. Such may be the cost of survival. Of course, *we may also have to* get along with *less* emphysema, *less* cancer, *less* heart disease, *less* noise, *less* filth, *less* crowding, *less* need to work long hours or "moonlight," *less* robbery, and *less* threat of war. The pace of life may slow down. *We may have more* fishing, *more* relaxing, *more* time to watch TV, *more* time to drink beer (served in bottles that MUST be returned).
>
> Paul R. Ehrlich, *The Population Bomb*,
> pp. 152–153

Note how the parallel grammatical structure, especially the *who* clauses, adds clarity and force to the following passage:

> It is not the critic *who* counts; nor the man *who* points out how the strong man stumbled, or where the doer of deeds could have done them better. The credit belongs to the man *who* is actually in the arena, *whose* face is marred by dust and sweat and blood; *who* strives valiantly; *who* errs and comes short again and again; *who* knows the great enthusiasms, the great devotions; *who* spends himself in a worthy cause, *who*, at the last, knows in the end the triumph of high achievement, and *who*, at the worst, if he fails, at least fails while daring greatly so that his place will never be with those timid souls *who* know neither victory nor defeat.
>
> Theodore Roosevelt

PARALLEL WORDING WITH CORRELATIVES.   Elements linked by **correla-tive conjunctions** *(either . . . or, neither . . . nor, not only . . . but also, both . . . and)* should be parallel in structure.

Faulty:	Either he will win an award for his photography or his sketches.
Parallel:	He will win an award *either* for his photography *or* for his sketches.
Faulty:	She neither has the time nor the inclination to go to card parties.
Parallel:	She has *neither* the time *nor* the inclination to go to card parties.
Faulty:	She is not only famous for her movie roles but also in working with orphans.
Parallel:	She is famous *not only* for her movie roles *but also* for her work with orphans.
Faulty:	They hoped both to gain new members and raising money for charity.
Parallel:	They hoped *both* to gain new members *and* to raise money for charity.

EXERCISE 7C: USING PARALLEL STRUCTURE

Make the following sentences parallel.

1. Walt Whitman was an admired poet, an innovative newspaper editor, and he volunteered as a nurse in the Civil War.

   _____

   _____

   _____

2. Our substitute minister is boring, dull, and doesn't have a good sense of humor.

   _____

   _____

   _____

3. Going to college stimulates your intellectual life, broadens your social life, and it also makes you feel as if you are no longer a kid.

_____

_____

_____

4. College life is simultaneously a challenge and a reward and a frustration when you have to work too hard.

_____

_____

_____

5. My girl is a set of contradictions: she's a party girl but shy; she's an excellent student but unsure of herself; sports are a piece of cake for her.

_____

_____

_____

6. Before my first college class, I was eager but anxious, hopeful but fearful, and I remembered my old high school classes wistfully.

_____

_____

_____

7. Harry was a great winter sports athlete, excelling in skiing, snowmobiling, and nifty on skates.

_____

_____

_____

8. Laura, who admired Harry a lot, went to all the meets, cheered all the events, and the parties appealed to her, too.

_____

_____

9. Joe was a snob and a bore, but he had one good quality—he was reliable.

_____

_____

10. On a field trip, the art class visited two museums, saw three nineteenth-century mansions, and had a great ball game in the park.

_____

_____

EXERCISE 7D: CORRECTING FAULTY PARALLELISM

Correct the following sentences by making the elements parallel with correlative conjunctions.

1. Jason will either go into the Marines but perhaps he may choose the Navy.

_____

2. He will be missed not only by his family and his girl friend will miss him a lot too.

_____

3. My math instructor is either absentminded or careless.

_____

4. My mother neither punishes my little brother or she doesn't notice when he misbehaves.

_____

5. My pal is both a good student but also a great musician.

   _____

6. The team wanted both to win tonight's debate and then sweeping the entire league.

   _____

7. Marianne is a champ not only in tennis but she wins at golf most of the time.

   _____

8. She neither skips practice and she takes as many lessons as she can afford.

   _____

9. Alfred is not only our baby sitter but he cuts our grass.

   _____

10. The children in the newsreels from Zaire are either crying from hunger or exhaustion.

   _____

EXERCISE 7E: PARALLEL CONSTRUCTION

Write original sentences using the following patterns:

1. Parallel words

   Example: Zak is shrewd, greedy, and unethical.

   a. _____

   b. _____

   c. _____

2. Parallel phrases

> *Example:*   People like Zak overestimate their own capabilities and
> underrate the skills of others.

a. _____

b. _____

c. _____

3. Parallel clauses

> *Example:*   People like Zak exasperate their colleagues, they alienate
> their friends, and they embarrass their family.

a. _____

b. _____

c. _____

EXERCISE 7F: TRANSITIONS

Identify all of the unifying devices used in the following essay.

What is Poverty? Listen.

You ask me what is poverty? Listen to me. Listen without pity. I cannot use your pity. Listen with understanding.

Poverty is living in a smell that never leaves. It is a smell of young children who cannot walk the long dark way in the night. It is the smell of milk which has gone sour because the refrigerator doesn't work, and it costs money to get it fixed. It is the smell of rotting garbage.

Poverty is being tired. I have always been tired. They told me at the hospital when the last baby came that I had chronic anemia and that I needed a corrective operation. I listened politely. The poor are always polite. The poor always listen. They don't say that there is no money for the iron pills or better food or worm medicine. Or that an operation is frightening and costs so much. Or that there is no one to take care of the children.

Poverty is dirt. You say, "Anyone can be clean." Let me explain about housekeeping with no money. Every night I wash every stitch my school-age child has on and hope her clothes dry by morning. What dishes there are, I wash in cold water with no soap. Even the cheapest soap has to be saved for the baby's diapers. Why not hot water? Hot water is a luxury. I do not have luxuries.

Poverty is asking for help. I will tell you how it feels. You find out where the office is that you are supposed to visit. You circle the block for four or five times, then you go in. Everyone is busy. Finally someone comes out and you tell her you need help. That is never the person you need to see. You go to see another person and, after spilling the whole shame of your life all over the desk between you, you find that this isn't the right office after all.

Poverty is looking into a black future. Your children won't play with my boys. My boys will turn to other boys who steal to get what they want. And for my daughter? At best there is for her a life like mine.

"But," you say to me, "there are schools." Yes, there are schools. But my children have no books, no magazines, no pencils, no crayons or paper.

And most important of all, they do not have health. They have worms. They have infections. They do not sleep well on the floor. They do not suffer from hunger, but they do suffer from malnutrition.

Poverty is cooking without food and cleaning without soap. Poverty is an acid that drips on pride until all pride is worn away. Some of you say that you would do something in my situation. And maybe you would—for the first week or month. But for year after year after year?

Curtis Ulmer, Teaching
the Disadvantaged Adult

EXERCISE 7G: PUTTING IDEAS IN LOGICAL ORDER

Arrange the following sentences to form a logical, coherent paragraph. On the line at the bottom, list what you consider to be the correct sequence. Could more than one be the first sentence? What's your opinion? _____ Yes _____ No

1. Sometimes just the presence of a dog deters criminals; one look at the animal, ready and willing to do his job, keeps the bad guys from causing mischief.
2. Finally, dogs routinely accompany their trainers to schools and civic functions where they generate good public relationships for police departments.
3. Because their sense of smell is estimated to be 150,000 times more acute than a human being's, the dogs far surpass man at any type of tracking.
4. Police dogs are a great asset to any police force because they have capabilities that their human counterparts do not.
5. Other dogs have been trained to sniff out drugs, even minute quantities in carefully concealed places; still others can find bodies even under heavy debris; and some are trained to find drowning victims, even under feet of water.

6. The criminal, knowing the dog bites, is afraid of it; therefore, the dog makes the dangerous job of the police officer a little safer.

7. K-9 dogs are certainly worth their cost to policemen; as one policeman said, "You have a partner who would lay down his life for you, and all he asks in return is a little food, a little water, and a pat on the head now and then."

8. Some dogs track fleeing felons; some seek out people who are lost or hurt in some catastrophe.

9. However, if the criminal is not stopped by the appearance of the dog and decides to flee, this canine officer is quite capable of chasing him, knocking him down, and holding him until his partner arrives.

10. Even in tracking, the jobs of the dogs can be classified into several types.

11. The four main categories in which the K-9 Corps can aid its officers are tracking, deterring suspects, apprehending criminals, and establishing good public relations.

EXERCISE 7H: USING TRANSITIONS

Rewrite the following paragraph, putting in the transitional words and phrases needed to improve the continuity. Be careful that you do not change the meaning of the paragraph.

> I am an amateur photographer. I am pretty good. I am often asked to take pictures for friends and relatives. They have birthdays and celebrations. My best friend Pete asked me to get a picture of his two-year-old blowing out his birthday candles. I agreed. The baby's name is Ryan. He is excitable. He was not used to a camera. I took many pictures. I was trying to relax Ryan. He blew out the candles. I didn't get the picture. I was out of film.

WORDS

As if we don't have enough trouble with one word meaning several different things (Chapter 1, page 20), or with the substandard English we hear all around us (Chapter 5, page 211), and the clichés that abound in our language Chapter 7, page 247), the English language also contains many words that look alike or sound alike. We often get away with using the wrong word in speech because we speak quickly and the listener is busy trying to interpret what we mean, or, perhaps, is preparing a reply.

In writing, however, the error stands out. The reader is usually alone, quiet, unhurried. Readers can read and reread the passage to find errors or weaknesses. They can edit and rewrite. They can get outside help—mainly the dictionary.

Make use of these advantages. Check every word that is not completely familiar before you submit work. Besides improving grades, the dictionary habit will enlarge your vocabulary, which is a real boost to your educational, social, and vocational potential. Researchers have shown that vocabulary and intelligence are closely related. It you want to test a person's intelligence but you don't have an IQ test to give, a vocabulary test will do.

Occasionally, an incorrect look-alike or sound-alike word will fit meaningfully into a sentence. This can cause real trouble. Suppose you wrote

We vote to adopt the amendment.

when you meant to write

We vote to adapt the amendment.

You could end up with a bad amendment.

Likewise, if you meant to write "my brother's wives" instead of "my brothers' wives," you might give a bad impression of your brother.

✓ Look-Alike or Sound-Alike Words

Many words are misused because they look alike or sound alike. Here are some of the troublesome words.

accept/except

Accept means "to take or receive."
Except shows exclusion or omission.

A good hostess will *accept* all gifts graciously.

They invited everyone *except* Bill.

adapt/adopt

Adapt means "to become accustomed to or to adjust to."
Adopt means "to take on or to accept something."

When you live in the jungle, you learn to *adapt* to the environment.

After they *adopted* a child, they agreed to *adopt* a calmer lifestyle.

advice/advise

Advice is a noun, a recommendation regarding a decision or course of conduct.

Advise is a verb, an action word that means "to recommend or inform."

It is easier to give *advice* than to accept it.

Her lawyer may *advise* her not to sign the contract.

affect/effect

Affect is a verb meaning "to influence."

Effect, meaning "result," is a noun.

Effect is also used as a verb, meaning "to bring about or cause to happen."

John's job promotion did not *affect* his competence, sad to say.

Failing the exam had a disastrous *effect* on Lee's final grade.

The staff worked long hours to *effect* a quick solution.

capital/capitol

Capital refers to a city. It also has the meanings (1) "wealth; the group that controls wealth"; and (2) "uppercase letter."

Capitol refers to a building.

Harrisburg, the *capital* of Pennsylvania, has a lovely old *capitol* building.

Dan and Vera don't have the *capital* to buy that pharmacy.

choose/chose

Choose is the present-tense form.

Chose is the past-tense form of *choose.*

Today we have to *choose* wallpaper to go with the slipcover fabric we *chose* last week.

coarse/course

Coarse means "rough or uneven."

Course is a procedure or plan of action or a path.

The cement contains *coarse* gravel.

Physics is a hard *course.*

The road followed the *course* of the river.

We will follow a *course* of 090 degrees.

complement/compliment

Complement means "to add or to make better," as a verb, and "the full quantity or amount," as a noun.

Compliment means "to praise," as a verb, and "a statement of praise or admiration," as a noun.

> A béarnaise sauce will *complement* the flavor of the beef.
>
> The regiment has a full *complement* of foot soldiers.
>
> I love to hear *compliments* about how gracefully I ice-skate.
>
> A *complimentary* glass of wine was included with our meal.

council/counsel

Council refers to a group, usually one that has a governing or administrative purpose.

Counsel means "advice or warning," and a *counselor* is one who gives advice.

> The town *council* meets on Tuesday.
>
> If I had followed my banker's *counsel,* I'd be rich today.

desert/dessert

Desert as a verb means "to abandon"; it is also a noun used as a name for a dry wasteland.

Dessert, the noun with a double *s,* is a sweet last course of a meal.

> They could not *desert* their post because the army was in the middle of the *desert.*
>
> The gelatin *dessert* was topped with whipped cream.

its/it's

Its, unlike noun possessives, uses no apostrophe.

The contraction *it's,* which means *it is,* uses an apostrophe (to show that a letter is left out of the contraction).

> The investigation committee released *its* report.
>
> *It's* a shame we have to cancel the game, but I checked the field, and *it's* squishy with mud.

lead/led

As a verb, *lead* means "to guide, conduct, or direct," and is spelled like the noun *lead.*

The past-tense form of *lead* is *led,* which is pronounced the way the noun *lead* is. As a noun, *lead* also names a heavy metal.

> Jeff agreed to *lead* them to the abandoned lead mine.
>
> Napoleon *led* his troops across Europe.
>
> We followed his *lead.*

loose/lose/loss

Loose, an adjective, means lax or open or that which does not fit tightly.

Lose, a verb meaning "to misplace," has only one o.

Loss, a noun, refers to that which is lost, a deprivation, defeat, or bereavement.

> Wear *loose* clothing when you travel in hot climates.
>
> You will *lose* your way in the swamp.
>
> He was thought to have *loose* morals.
>
> The Cowboys' *loss* on Sunday eliminated them from the play-offs.
>
> She never fully recovered from the *loss* of her husband.

passed/past

Passed refers to the act of overtaking.

Past refers to time—the opposite of *future.* It is also an adverb meaning "by or close in passing."

> The Jaguar *passed* the Alfa Romeo on the final turn.
>
> He has done some strange things in the *past,* but what is *past* is *past.*
>
> He walked right *past* me on the street.

principal/principle

Principal means "primary, the most important person or thing." In this sense it names the administrative head of a school.

Principle means "rule, characteristic; moral attitude or belief."

> A high school *principal* has the principal responsibility for discipline.
>
> The experiment illustrated a *principle* of cell growth.
>
> The architect is a woman of *principle;* she wouldn't have taken a bribe.

right/rite/write

Right is used as a noun referring to a value or concept. It also names a direction (turn *right*) and describes correctness (*right,* not wrong).

A *rite* is a ceremony or ritual.

Write means "to inscribe letters, words, or symbols on a surface for the purpose of communication."

This *right* is guaranteed by the Constitution.

Human sacrifice was part of a religious *rite* among the Aztecs.

Being able to *write* well should be a goal of all college students.

sight/site/cite

Sight refers to any visual impression.

Site refers to location.

Cite means "to recognize or bring forward."

The first *sight* of you sent my blood racing.

The *site* for the new gym is on the south slope of the hill.

My drama teacher couldn't *cite* an example from a Greek tragedy.

The soldier was *cited* for bravery.

there/their/they're

There can refer to location.

Their is always used to show possession or ownership.

They're is always a contraction for *they are*.

He is over *there*, behind the parade marshal.

They're not planning to visit *their* relatives in Canada this summer.

to/too/two

To indicates motion toward, or it combines with a verb to make a verb form called an *infinitive*.

Too indicates extremes, more or less of some characteristic or quality than one wants.

Too can mean "also," as well.

Two is the number.

We went *to* town to buy coffee and sugar.

The soup was *too* cold, and the fish was *too* salty.

I forgot the vegetables, *too*.

The number is always *two*.

One and one are *two*.

who's/whose

Who's is a contraction for *who is*.

Whose is the possessive form of *who*.

Jan is the only employee *who's* never late for work.

You are a person *whose* promises I trust.

you're/your

You're is a contraction for *you are.*

Your is used to show possession.

You're going to lose *your* mind.

Use a good dictionary to check the meaning of any words you are still not sure of.

EXERCISE 7I: USING THE DICTIONARY

Check your dictionary for the difference in meaning between the following pairs of words.

curtly/courtly	gently/genteelly
staid/stayed	strait/straight
access/excess	allusion/illusion/elude
beside/besides	detract/distract
censor/censure	stationary/stationery
know/no	uninterested/disinterested
peace/piece	aloud/a loud/allowed
prosecute/persecute	altar/alter
bare/bear	cereal/serial
born/borne	patients/patience
device/devise	new/knew
farther/further	lend/loan

✓ Apostrophe to Show Possession

Although some words are troublesome because they look alike or sound alike, other words are troublesome because they require the use of the *apostrophe.* One important use of the apostrophe (') is to indicate letters that are left out of words such as *isn't, couldn't, don't, let's.* But there is another important use of the apostrophe: to show possession. It stands for "belonging to," as in *John's book* (the book belonging to John) or *children's hour* (the hour belonging to children). The following are rules for use of the apostrophe to show possession.

1. Add an apostrophe and an *s* to show possession in singular nouns.

my mother's dress	the room's atmosphere
Mary's job	the club's rules
the teacher's assignment	

2. Add an apostrophe and an *s* to singular nouns that already end in an *s*.

                    Charles's friend   Dickens's novels

3. Add an apostrophe without the *s* to form the possessive of plural nouns.

             my brothers' wives   the students' lounge
             the players' dressing room

4. Use an apostrophe and an *s* for plural nouns that do not end in *s*.

             the children's book   the group's decision
             the men's room

5. With compounds that are possessives, use an apostrophe for both if each word is a separate "belonging to"; use an apostrophe on the last one only if the possession is a joint one.

          Henry's and Robert's jackets   Henry and Robert's clothing
              are both ripped.   business failed.

6. Don't overlook the need for the possessive form in the following constructions using indefinite pronouns.

             somebody else's problem   anybody's opinion
             everyone else's house   in each other's way
             nobody's business   taking one another's part

7. Don't overlook the need for the possessive form in such expressions as these.

             a quarter's worth   forty years' labor
             ten dollars' worth   Queen of England's duties
             a day's work   Attorney General's job
             three weeks' wages   a remark of the author's

8. The apostrophe is also used
   a. to indicate plurals of numbers

             several size 16's   his name is spelled with two s's

   b. to abbreviate dates

             the blizzard of '96   the early 1900's
             the class of '98

Note: Do not use an apostrophe with the possessive forms of the personal pronouns, such as *his, hers, its, ours, yours, theirs.* It is also not used in some expressions in which the plural noun is considered to be a modifier, such as United States Marines and Veterans Administration.

EXERCISE 7J: USING WORDS CORRECTLY

In the following sentences, cross out the misused form(s) and write the cor-rected sentence on the line below.

1.   I do not except the philosophy of today's big business.

     _____

2.   I cannot adopt my liberal principals to they're conservative practices.

     _____

3.   Big business must choose between access profits and what is rite.

     _____

4.   My advise to them is "Change you're ways."

     _____

5.   Downsizing is the coarse theyve taken, and its not moral.

     _____

6.   Big businesses no longer value there employees; they let them go so
     they can up there profits.

     _____

7.   Good employees cannot be valued to much.

     _____

8.   They should be valued as much as it's customers or profits.

     _____

9. When a loyal employee loses his job to downsizing, he looses more than his pay; he looses his self-esteem.

_____

10. Business should not follow the council of money grubbers and dessert the workers who have always served them well.

_____

EXERCISE 7K: USING POSSESSIVE FORMS CORRECTLY

Rewrite the following sentences to eliminate the incorrect possessives. If the sentence is correct, write a *C* on the line.

1. Carla didn't like Elizabeth Rechards new book, *Every Day,* because the plots unrealistic.

_____

2. It's heroine, a woman named Leigh Adelman, reacts abnormally to her ex-lovers return.

_____

3. After a fourteen year absence, he wants to come back into Leighs life.

_____

4. He, Jim Fowler, had abandoned Leigh and their newborn son, but now he is in the last stages of Lou Gehrigs disease.

_____

5. Despite his neglect when she really needed him, he now wants Leighs help and support as well as her forgiveness.

_____

6. A normal womans reaction would be to make him squirm in remorse over what he has lost.

_____

7. But not Leigh: realizing that shes still in love with him, she decides to help.

   _____

8. During the year's of Jims absence, Leigh has married Simon and is raising three children.

   _____

9. When she tells Simon what her plan's are, Simons reactions are predictable: he's not pleased.

   _____

10. The couples marriage unravel's, and you can imagine the effect on the couples children.

    _____

11. "Leighs decisions are stupid; Jims expectation's are stupid; the entire books stupid," says Carla.

    _____

chapter 8

Defining

What Is a Definition?

A definition is the precise meaning of a word or term. The word *definition* indicates an outline that sets limits for something; *fin* is the Latin root of the word, meaning "end" or "limit."

THE ESSENTIAL DEFINITION

Definition is a precise form of exposition; like other forms of exposition, definition explains something. In order to explain something, one must be able to say *what something is* or *how it looks or works*. This makes up what is commonly called a limited or essential definition. An essential definition specifies what makes a thing what it is and distinguishes that thing from all other things.

One of the most famous definitions ever given, probably, is Aristotle's "Man is a rational animal." Aristotle's definition has the characteristics of being both *necessary* and *sufficient*. With only one of these characteristics, there would be no definition.

Man is an animal. (So are many other creatures.)

Man is rational. (He is many other things as well.)

Animal and rational are *necessary* qualities to define man, and they are *sufficient* to do so. Nothing else is needed.

THE IMPORTANCE OF DEFINING

"What do you mean?" is one of the most frequent and the most important questions that we ever ask. We all have an imperative need for precise
definitions if we are to understand ourselves, each other, and the world
around us. For example,

> "What do I really mean when I say that I am a 'conservative'"?
>
> "What does John mean by saying he's, 'on the fence'"?
>
> "What do you mean when you say it's my 'civic obligation' to tip
> public employees at Christmas who make more than I do"?

In both writing and speaking, it is necessary that the originator of a
term and the audience agree on its meaning. Otherwise, precise communication cannot occur, and there will be misunderstandings.

✓ Concrete and Abstract Terms

It is much easier to define a concrete term than an abstract term: A **concrete
term** is one that we can observe through the five senses, such as *automobile,
desk, television set, peach,* or *alley cat.* Because all of us perceive these items
in approximately the same way, their general characteristics are usually
agreed upon. If you were to say to several friends, "I just got a new laptop
PC," they would make similar associations and form similar mental pictures.

> *Basic definition:* A laptop PC is a portable computer that enables the user
> to perform full information processing functions from any
> location.

Note: Variables, such as brand, capacity, features, size, or cost are supple-
mentary information that would not be part of a laptop PC's *basic* definition.

An **abstract term,** however, is not so easy to define. Since the worlds of
education, business, and community operate through the communication of
ideas—ideas that are often expressed in *abstract* terms—you constantly need
to define, for yourself and for others, what those terms mean in order to
avoid misunderstandings.

Abstract terms are perceived intellectually rather than through the senses.
They name *qualities,* such as honor and pride; *concepts,* such as free will and
constitutional guarantees; and *conditions,* such as poverty and affluence.

Your instructors in history, economics, sociology, psychology, physics,
philosophy, and criminal justice might require you to define abstract terms
as they apply to varying circumstances:

What is *capitalism?*	What is *motion?*
What is *fascism?*	What is *work?*
What is *ecology?*	What is a *neurosis?*

What is *evolution?*   What do you mean by *freedom under law?*
What is *prejudice?*   What do you mean by a *liberal education?*
What is *integrity?*

The italicized words are symbols for abstract or intangible things—things you cannot see, hear, touch, or smell. You cannot buy an ounce of integrity or shed a pound of prejudice; you cannot extract liberal education from the blood of a Stanford graduate or put capitalism on the counter to pay for a pound of baked ham. You cannot eat fascism like cereal or see a neurosis the way you see a striped cat. Since abstract words stand for ideas or concepts rather than observable concrete phenomena, you must define them if you want to communicate your meaning precisely.

These words are abstract—what they represent cannot be seen, felt, heard, touched, smelled—or weighed.

In the following paragraph, Martin Luther King, Jr., applies his own definition to the abstract term *power* in order to make a particular point:

Power, properly understood, is the ability to achieve purpose. It is the strength required to bring about social, political, or economic changes. In this sense power is not only desirable but necessary in order to implement the demands of love and justice. One of the greatest problems of history is that the concepts of love and power are usually contrasted as polar opposites. Love is identified with a resignation of power and power with a denial of love. It was this misinterpretation that caused Nietzsche, the philosopher of the "will to power," to reject the Christian concept of love. It was this same misinterpretation which induced Christian theologians to reject Nietzsche's philosophy of the "will to power" in the name of the Christian idea of love. What is needed is a realization that power without love is reckless and abusive and that love without power is sentimental and anemic. Power at its best is love implementing the demands of justice.

✓ Two Kinds of Definitions: Limited and Extended

THE LIMITED DEFINITION

In writing or speaking, you often need to provide your reader or listener with a short definition without getting bogged down in long, detailed explanations:

> Mouse—"a small rodent resembling a rat, but one fourth the size of a rat."
>
> Fame—"great public recognition and esteem."

The most common forms of the limited definition are (1) *synonyms,* (2) *comparisons,* and (3) *formal definitions.*

1. Using Synonyms to Define   You should always include a brief definition when the word or term that you use might not be understood by the reader. The easiest way to define a word is to *explain it in terms of a more familiar word* that means the same thing or nearly the same thing—a **synonym.**

Be sure, when using a synonym, that it closely follows the original term. Try to find the *best* synonym that you can; a more difficult synonym doesn't help. A *thesaurus* can help you because it is a dictionary of synonyms.

Poor Synonym Choices

Dr. Andrews was indeed *loquacious,* an extremely *garrulous* man.

The speaker was *erudite,* a true *polymath.*

Good Synonym Choices

Dr. Andrews was indeed *loquacious,* an extremely *talkative* man.

The speaker was *erudite,* an extremely *learned* woman.

Note: Always consider your readers' ability to comprehend what you are writing, but don't insult their intelligence by overdefining or oversimplifying terms or ideas they already know.

EXERCISE 8A: NOTING DIFFERENCES AMONG SYNONYMS

Explain the differences in the meaning of these synonyms for *think.* The differences are not great, but an awareness of synonyms gives precision and variety to your language.

Among other synonyms are these:

to reason	to judge
to reflect	to expect

to ponder	to anticipate
to suppose	to remember
to regard	to recall

When combined with prepositions there are still more synonymous meanings.

to think over	to think so
to think through	to think better of

Choose some other general word and find ten synonyms that are more precise.

General word:

_____

Synonyms:

_____	_____
_____	_____
_____	_____
_____	_____
_____	_____

2. Using Comparisons to Define   Another way to define a word or term is to express it as part of a **comparison.**

> When he tried to convince *the woman* to leave her abusive spouse, she was adamant in her refusal, *like a tree with roots extending deep into the earth.*

> Occasionally, I encounter a student with a *photographic mind, whose memory, like a computer chip,* can process and store information indefinitely.

> The *Confederate soldier* defended his position against overwhelming odds, *like a lion at bay.*

Comparisons are effective because they use sensory imagery to show similarities. Comparisons stimulate the reader's imagination, making the connection between terms more graphic and meaningful.

3. Using Formal Definitions   A brief **formal definition** should, like the synonym, closely follow the original term.

*When he tried to convince the woman
to leave her abusive spouse,
she was adamant in her refusal,
like a tree with roots
extending deep into the earth.*

The **thesaurus,** a dictionary that alphabetically lists words and their synonyms, is a valuable reference for the college writer.

Consult your dictionary to write a formal definition, and then follow this three-part pattern:

1. Write down the term to be defined.
2. Place the term in a general *class* or *category.*

Term	General Class or Category
fascism	a form of government

3. List the *principal characteristics or details* that distinguish or differentiate the term from all others in the class. For example:

1 Term	2 General Class or Category	3 Differentiating Details
fascism	a form of government	totalitarian right wing nationalistic militaristic anticommunist limited individual rights 1930s–1940s Italy, Spain, and Germany

4. Write the formal definition based on the information in each of the three parts: term, class/category, differentiating details. Express the information in a sequence that your reader can clearly understand.

Complete formal definition: Fascism is a totalitarian form of government that is ultra-conservative and limits individual rights. During the 1930s and 1940s in Italy, Spain, and Germany, it fanatically embraced militarism and nationalism to sustain its anticommunist doctrine.

You can use the three-part formal definition for both concrete and abstract terms:

Term	Class or Category	Differentiating Details
Plimsoll mark	one of a set of lines on the hull on a merchant ship	indicating the depth to which a ship may be legally loaded under specified conditions
orangutan	one of the anthropoid apes	having a shaggy reddish-brown coat, very long arms, and no tail
paternalism	a policy or practice of treating or governing people	by providing for their needs without giving them responsibility, in a manner suggesting a father's relationship with his children
neurosis	a mental or functional nervous disorder	characterized by one or more of the following reactions: anxiety, compulsions and obsessions, phobias, depressions, disassociation, conversion

GUIDELINES FOR WRITING AN ACCURATE FORMAL DEFINITION

1. Be sure that your category is exact for the *specific* meaning that you intend.

Inexact categories: A hammer is an *object*
A phobia is a *feeling*
A Corvette is a *vehicle*

Exact categories: A hammer is a *tool*
                        A phobia is an *anxiety*
                        A Corvette is an *expensive two-seater sports car*

2. Be sure that your definition applies *only* to the term that you are defining. If it also applies to other terms:

> Your differentiating details are insufficient and vague—not specific enough

Vague and/or insufficient differentiating details:

Love is a strong feeling *that one person has for another.*

Other terms, however, can also fit under this definition:

> *Hate* is a strong feeling that one person has for another.
>
> *Passion* is a strong feeling that one person has for another.
>
> *Jealousy* is a strong feeling that one person has for another.
>
> *Sympathy* is a strong feeling that one person has for another.

To limit this definition only to *love*, add *more* details that pertain *specifically* to *love*—not to *hate, passion, jealousy,* or *sympathy.*

> Love is a strong feeling *characterized by fondness, deep affection, and strong liking of one person by another.*

Vague and/or insufficient details:

A hammer is a tool *used for hitting things.* (But so is a chisel.)

A phobia is an anxiety *provoked by some object, situation, or idea.* (But so is post-traumatic stress syndrome.)

A Corvette is *an expensive two-seater sports car.* (But so is the Ferrari 355 Spider, the BMW Z-3, the Mercedes SLK, and the Porsche Boxster.)

Specific and sufficient details:

A hammer is a tool *consisting of a solid metal head, set crosswise on a handle, used for driving nails, breaking rock, or beating metal.*

A phobia is an anxiety *that is irrationally fearful and provoked by some object, situation, or idea that is not actually harmful.* (Barbara Fried, *Who's Afraid: The Phobic's Handbook*)

The Corvette is an expensive two-seater sports car *that is made in America by Chevrolet, has a fiberglass body, is high performance, and is priced from $38,000 to $50,000.*

Many terms have multiple meanings. As a result, each definition for that term would have a new category and a new set of differentiating details. For example:

A hammer is a *padded mallet* that strikes the wires of a piano action to produce a tone.

A hammer is a *bone* of the middle ear in mammals that transmits vibrations from the ear drum to the spiral cavity of the ear.

A hammer is the *portion of a gunlock* that strikes the firing pin to ignite the powder charge.

A hammer is a *metal ball* attached to a long, flexible wire handle for throwing in competition.

3. Avoid *circular definitions*—using a term to define itself.

Circular: A circular definition is one that is circular.
Improved: A circular definition is one that uses the term to define itself.

Circular: A hay conditioner is a farm implement that conditions hay.
Improved: A hay conditioner is a farm implement that crushes the water out of freshly cut hay, thus enabling it to dry more quickly.

Circular: A certified letter is a piece of correspondence sent by certified mail.
Improved: A certified letter is a piece of business or personal correspondence guaranteed restricted delivery by the postal service.

4. Avoid the improper use of *where* and *when* in a formal definition. *Where* refers to location, and *when* refers to a particular time. Neither should replace a class or category.

Incorrect: Pruning is when you trim limbs and stems to make a plant or tree healthier.
Correct: Pruning is the practice of trimming branches and stems to make a plant or tree grow better.

Incorrect: The Olympics is when athletes from every nation compete for gold, silver, and bronze medals.
Correct: The Olympics are games in which athletes from all nations compete for gold, silver, and bronze medals.

Incorrect: Phipps Conservatory is where one can see some of the finest live floral exhibits in the country.
Correct: Phipps Conservatory is a one-hundred-year-old exhibition building that shows some of the finest live floral exhibits in the country.

EXERCISE 8B: CORRECTING LIMITED DEFINITIONS

A = Circular   D = Improper use of *when* or *where*
B = Inexact class or no class   E = Synonym more difficult than term being
C = Insufficient differentiating detail   defined

Identify the faults in the following sentences, using the blanks in the spaces before to place the appropriate letter. Rewrite the sentences to eliminate the errors and then make them formal definitions.

_____   1. The mouse is either a household pest or a part of a computer.

_____

_____   2. A synonym is another word for the same thing.

_____

_____   3. An organ-grinder is a person who grinds an organ and sometimes has a monkey.

_____

_____   4. Piano tuning is when you get someone to fix the piano.

_____

_____   5. A morel looks like a sponge but you can eat it.

_____

_____   6. Cowardly means pusillanimous.

_____

_____   7. Bifurcation means where something is bifurcated.

_____

_____   8. A malapropism is named for Mrs. Malaprop who is a character in a play called *The Rivals* written by R. B. Sheridan.

_____

_____ 9. Odium means hatred in a special way.

_____

_____ 10. An oxymoron is something writers use, especially poets.

_____

THE EXTENDED DEFINITION

Many terms represent ideas or concepts that are too complex to be defined in a limited definition. They require much more elaboration and supporting material to be clearly understood. Knowing that your defining paragraph is due in a week, you ask your sociology teacher how she would define a *radical* person. If she answers, "Oh, someone like Jesus Christ, Mahatma Gandhi, or General George Patton," you still would not know much about a radical. Your instructor obviously has some opinions about radical behavior, but all she is sharing with you are some examples that support her personal definition.

What your instructor is actually doing, however, is encouraging you to formulate your definition of a radical. Also, in naming alleged radicals, she is providing some sources—case studies—of radical behavior for you to examine.

> *First,* you must consult a good dictionary for a formal definition of *radical* in terms of behavioral characteristics.
>
> *Second,* with this basic knowledge, you can read biographical sketches of these individuals to determine whether or not they were indeed radicals according to how *you* interpret the definition.
>
> *Third,* choose a strategy for your defining paragraph.

Since you have now concluded from your research that each of these men was a radical, several methods of paragraph development are available for you:

a. *Compare* the radical characteristics of your subjects to see how they are similar and/or different. Compare ethical standards of the radical to those of the establishment of his time.
b. *Analyze* a subject in depth. Select key situations that *illustrate* his radical behavior. Or use one long *extended example*—an *anecdote.*
c. *Divide* radical behavior into types and discuss these categories in terms of your subjects. Perhaps each subject is a specific type of radical.
d. *Describe* how your radical subjects achieved their goals and how the establishment responded to their radical behaviors.

These are only a few of the many approaches you could take, but in each situation, you are *expanding upon and extending* the formal definition through personal and creative discussion.

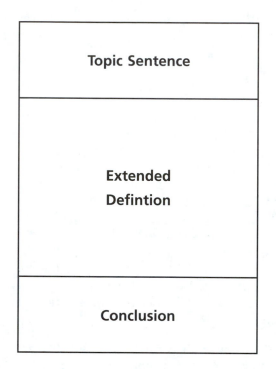

Topic Sentence

Extended Defintion

Conclusion

✓ Assignment

Write an extended definition of an abstract term.

1. Choose an abstract term that interests you, one that has a particular connotation that you can relate to.
2. Use a dictionary to write a formal three-part definition of the term based on its primary meaning *or* a secondary meaning that you want to discuss.
3. Discuss this term using any one or a combination of the types of paragraph development we have discussed.

Think of the possibilities for the word *freedom*. Freedom may be the name of a town, a patriotic feeling, a new liberation when you leave home and begin your own life, or even a sense of relief when you end a relationship. Perhaps you experience freedom when you earn a diploma, when you walk alone in the woods, when you drive down a lonely road, or when you spend a few minutes sitting alone in church. Janis Joplin once sang "Freedom's just another word for nothing left to lose" before her untimely death. What does freedom mean to you?

Consider the term *marriage* and its many possibilities:

good marriage	marriage vs. cohabitation
bad marriage	no marriage
the ideal marriage	marriage of convenience
marriage without kids	marriage to someone with kids
May–September marriage	marriage for the wrong reasons
abusive marriage	when to end a marriage
second marriage	when to get married
danger signals in marriage	interracial marriage

These are just some of the many aspects of marriage that one could write a defining paragraph about.

Remember: Your extended definition should have a point or purpose, either stated or implied. It does not necessarily have to be expressed in your topic sentence. It can be revealed as your paragraph progresses.

Here are some more abstract terms to consider:

responsibility	security
guilt	loneliness
patriotism	charity
happiness	duty
frustration	friendship
prejudice	fear
courage	self control
commitment	honor

STRUCTURE

Essentially, an extended definition follows the three-part structure common to all expository paragraphs: topic sentence, body, conclusion.

✓ Topic Sentence

1. After consulting a dictionary, write a precise three-part formal definition of the term that is your subject.
2. Your attitude evolves from the general meaning that you assign to the term. It may be expressed within the topic sentence or developed more fully in the body of your paragraph.

   Cultural relativity means respect for the ways of people who are different from ourselves.

Justice is rewarding or punishing people according to their deeds.

The *hypothalamus* is the part of the brain that is responsible for many of the brain's routine housekeeping chores.

These sentences can only introduce your topic. It will take a paragraph to discuss them. A good topic sentence for an extended definition should either:

a. Stimulate new thoughts about a familiar subject *or*
b. Bring an unfamiliar subject home to us in terms of our common experience.

✓ Body

EXTENDING YOUR DEFINITION

There is no set form for developing the body of a defining paragraph. Depending on the method of development you choose, you should follow the applicable rules you have already learned. Think of this as a solo flight; you can perform whatever maneuvers you wish as long as you do them skillfully and land the plane in one piece.

Here are some ways to develop your extended definition:

Use synonyms.   Alone, a synonym is usually not sufficient, but used in combination with other methods, it can be very effective. If you are defining *phobia,* synonyms like *dread, panic, horror,* or *hysteria* might help readers understand the meaning, especially if they are more familiar with these words than with *phobia.*

There are many ways to write an extended definition. Here is one student's definition of the word *normal.*

> **Normal is a word that people use to judge all manner of things—both concrete and abstract.** Everything from sizes of fruit and shapes of tree trunks to degrees of love and types of personalities have been described as either "normal" or "abnormal." People need a center, an average to make a comparison, and we call that center "normal." A great part of being normal hinges on acceptance. If, for example, it is accepted that a tip should be 10 or 15% of the cost of a meal, then it would be normal to tip around those amounts. Very seldom if ever would you see a person giving a $100.00 tip to the waitress who just served him a Denny's $3.95 Grand Slam Breakfast. The meaning of normal can vary from country to country or from group to group within the same country. The average American, for instance, thinks that Europeans drive on the "wrong" side of the road, but if an American moved to Great Britain and had to drive to work every day in London, he would soon get accustomed to driving on the "wrong" side of the road and it would no longer seem abnormal to him. To illustrate further, try this: open any book. Chances are there are words on the pages. No surprise there. Books are supposed to have words, but

say you open another book and you find no words . . . just rows of little bumps! You have just opened a braille book. Is that "normal"? Maybe not to you, but to a blind person, it is not strange at all: It is perfectly "normal." So maybe the question should not be "What is normal?" but rather "What is normal for *you*"?

Bryan Drake

Use examples.   As you have already seen, examples often help to clarify the meaning of a word. As a result, they are often useful in an extended definition. Your reader will gain a clearer understanding of the meaning of *phobia* if you provide specific examples of different kinds of phobias.

Acrophobia: a morbid fear of heights: standing on a bridge, a roof, a mountain ledge, or even on a chair

Misophobia: an irrational fear of contamination: dirt, dust, germs, radiation, infection

Claustrophobia: an excessive fear of enclosed spaces: closets, elevators, automobiles, or small windowless rooms

FEAR OF HEIGHTS   FEAR OF GERMS   FEAR OF CLOSED PLACES

Use word origin.   Much can be learned about using words correctly when you research a word's origin, or etymology. If you were defining *claustrophobia,* you could tell your reader that it is derived from the Latin word *claustrium,* meaning "lock, bar, bolt," and later, "a shut-up place, a cell or cloister," and from the French word *phobe,* meaning "fearing" or "dreading." You could also show how the meaning of the word has changed over the years.

Obviously, this student writer approaches her subject from the standpoints of origin, evolution, and variations of the term:

A pen is a familiar object in our everyday lives; however, thought of in its broader meaning, the word has several connotations. Naturally, most people think of a pen as an instrument filled with ink used to either write or draw with. This is true, although the original pen looked quite different from what we know of today. Our fore-fathers used a quill, a feather dipped into an ink-well, to sign the Declaration of Independence. In fact, the very definition of a pen means "something resembling or suggesting a feather or quill." After going through much modification, the writing instrument of the 1990s is generally thought to be either a ball-point or a fountain pen. A pen can be the instrument of writing or authorship, such as "The pen is mightier than the sword." It can also signify a person's style or quality of writing: "He writes with a witty, incisive pen." Sometimes the word, pen, can be used to express a writer or writers of information: "I leave this story to abler pens." A "pen-pusher" may be a clerk or journalist who does routine, boring, drudge-like writing. The profession of writing itself can even be termed with the word pen. "A master of the pen" means a highly skilled author, whereas a "master of penmanship" is one skilled in the art of handwriting. Also, some writers use an assumed name, a "pen name": Mark Twain was actually Samuel Clemens. One can be said to have "penned" an essay or a sketch, meaning to have "put down in writing" information or creative expression. At times, one can actually be a "penner" or "penman," the author of expressed thoughts in ink. The simple word, pen, has many connotations according to its use and the status of the user.

                                                                Patricia Butchki

Use comparison and/or contrast.   Although a phobia is not so serious a disorder as paranoia, being phobic about something can be compared to being paranoid because a person who suffers from paranoia often behaves much like a phobic. For example,

> A person with a paranoia complex has an unnatural obsession about being persecuted. He sees danger in harmless situations and enemies everywhere, whether they exist or not.

> A claustrophobic has such an irrational fear of enclosed spaces that an otherwise harmless room without windows suddenly becomes a suffocating trap.

Note how, in the following paragraph, the student writer uses contrasting situations and attitudes encountered by cynics and optimists to define cynicism. What method of contrast development is this writer using? Can you identify her transitional devices?

> **Cynicism can be defined as the attitude or belief that our world is basically a malevolent environment; however, the clearest way to define cynicism is to observe that the cynic's interpretation of life differs completely from that of an optimist.** Both the cynic and the optimist view circumstances from extremes, but that is where their similarities end. A cynic concentrates only on the bad side of life; whereas an optimist focuses only on the good side of life. A cynic has a cranky contempt for life, but an optimist has a grateful appreciation for the wonders of life. A cynic grumbles, "Life is a bitch," yet an op-

timist sees life as a series of satisfying challenges. A cynic denies the sincerity of people's motives and actions. An optimist, on the other hand, sees only sincerity in people's motives and actions. A cynic perceives a philanthropist as a self-serving person seeking a major tax deduction. An optimist, in contrast, sees that same philanthropist as an altruistic benefactor of society. A cynic observes something and interprets it negatively; conversely, an optimist observes the same thing and perceives it positively. H. L. Menken said, "A cynic is a person who, when he smells flowers, looks around for a coffin." However, when the optimist smells flowers, he is mesmerized by thoughts of spring and beauty. A cynic's glass of milk is half empty and probably sour; the optimist's glass is half full, sweet, and delicious. A cynic believes that behind every cloud is a potential life threatening storm. An optimist, however, believes that behind every cloud is the familiar "silver lining." For every pessimistic view of the cynic's world, an optimist sees the exact opposite. The fact that a cynic and an optimist view life with such polarity suggests that absolutes may be fallible and that truth and reality usually lie somewhere between these extremes.

Wendy Bullock

Use negation.   Sometimes you can help the reader understand what something *is* by explaining what it is *not*. For example, you can help the reader understand the meaning of *phobia* by pointing out that a phobia is *not* a superstition. A person who is more comfortable walking around a ladder rather than under it for fear of bad luck does not necessarily have a phobia about ladders. The sight of a ladder won't cause him to faint; however, if an individual had a severe case of acrophobia (fear of heights), the sight of a ladder might cause him to feel dizzy and perhaps faint.

In explaining to us what religion *is* for him, this student writer, through contrast, is also telling us what it is *not*.

> Each religion has a different view of its god or Supreme Being, but the God of my understanding does not quite mesh with any one of the known religious depictions. Each religion has a name for its God. The Jewish have Yahweh, the Muslims call God Allah, and the Christians call their God the Heavenly Father or the Holy Spirit. My God is nameless and is known only to me. Religious beliefs and lessons are learned by reading holy books and by attending ceremonies at worship sites, albeit I learn about God by looking for lessons in every leaf and rock and by listening for His voice in the winds. Some religions have paintings or statues showing God in human form, sitting on a throne in the sky. My understanding of God is that He, She, or It is purely spiritual and without form; consequently, I have no idea what God looks like. Many religions portray God as a God of wrath and vengeance—to be feared. My belief tells me otherwise. It tells me that I should revere God and never fear Him, for He is loving, understanding, and forgiving. Many practitioners of particular religions pray for material things, whereas I try to pray only for knowledge of His will for me and the power to carry that out. I feel that my God will always provide

my needs rather than my wants. I have also learned that some of God's greatest gifts are unanswered prayers. I do not always know the difference between
my needs and my wants, and if I were to receive all of my wants, I would be ill
equipped to handle them. My belief in God draws bits and pieces from some of
the known religions, but my view is different enough that joining a particular
sect would not meet all of my needs.

David Sabina

Use process.   If you were trying to define the term *fax machine* to readers who had never heard of one, you could do so by explaining how it oper-
ates and what it produces. You might help your readers to understand *phobia*
if you describe how a phobia can progressively affect a victim's behavior.

Use anecdotes.   An entertaining way to explain what a term means is
by *anecdote,* a short narrative that shows the term in action. The anecdote
might be a personal experience or an imaginary situation in narrative form.
In either case, it should hold the reader's interest and relate directly to the
term being defined. Perhaps, in defining phobias, you could relate an anecdote (humorous or serious) about your own or someone else's phobic ad-
ventures.

In the following paragraph, the student writer uses anecdotal development to define the abstract term *imagination.*

**Imagination is the mind's ability to form pictures or ideas of things
that are not yet known.** It is inspiration, it is invention, it is the stuff that
dreams are made of. It can also be a major source of joy in a child's life, as I
know so well. One summer when I was young, my father conceived a wonderful idea; he wanted to build a treehouse for my brothers and me. He even constructed a miniature model of it out of balsa wood so that we would have an
idea of what it would look like. It was elevated on four legs and had three windows, a deck, and a detachable roof that enabled us to peer inside at the two
rooms, one equipped with a set of built-in bunkbeds. Oh, the many wonderful
hours my brothers and I spent imagining what we would do with that treehouse! My brothers were going to form a club (No girls allowed!) complete with
secret meetings and passwords. They dreamt of fierce battles against neighborhood enemies determined to take over their clubhouse. With toy guns, swords,
and shields, they would defend their property "to the death," and when cornered by their enemies, they would slide down the pole that my father designed as an escape route for embattled young warriors. I, on the other hand,
envisioned the beautiful lace curtains that I was going to sew for the windows
and the matching tablecloth that I would make for my child-sized table and
chairs set. I would have elegant tea parties with my friends and exciting
overnight camp-outs. My friends and I would stay up all night long giggling and
whispering little girl secrets, far from the prying ears of my parents. I cannot
even begin to count the hours and years that my brothers and I spent thinking,
planning, and dreaming about that treehouse, or all the joy that those hours

brought us. The treehouse model still sits on my father's desk in his office. Whenever I visit, I often walk over to it, look inside, and lovingly smile. Needless to say, the treehouse was never actually built, but in our minds, that treehouse was as real as any that was built of wood and nails. My father unintentionally gave us a gift that would last forever: the gift of imagination.

Mary K. Hobbs

Using combined methods of defining.   When writing an extended definition, you are not limited to any single form of paragraph development. You could develop an extended definition of *charity,* for example, by combining methods of development you have used in previous assignments.

Narration:	Tell about the work of one man or woman whose efforts exemplify true charity.
Description:	Show the joy that a poor child gets from receiving one small gift.
Factual details:	Use factual details and statistics to show how much Americans donate to charity.
Explaining with examples:	Use examples to show how various charitable organizations help those in need.
Comparison/contrast:	Use comparison/contrast to show the difference between genuine charity and that which humiliates and degrades people.
Classification:	Divide contributors to charity into various groups according to their motives for giving—guilt, pity, self-aggrandizement, love of people.

DEFINING ABSTRACT TERMS

Concrete and technical terms often have precise, restricted meanings. With many words, however, the interpretations will vary according to the background and experience of the person using the words. What might seem like *prosperity* to a very poor person might seem like *poverty* to a very wealthy person. Thus, meaning can lie not in the words themselves but in the people who use the words, This is especially true in dealing with *abstract* terms, such as *love, beauty, honor*—words that refer to ideas rather than tangible objects. Because of the many ways to define abstract terms, it is best to select one particular aspect of meaning and develop that aspect as fully as possible. For example, look at the possible ways to define a common term, *courage,* and some of the approaches you might take in defining it:

Physical Courage	Moral Courage	Intellectual Courage
in battle	with friends	in conversation
on the streets	in a difficult situation	in the classroom
at home	when all are against you	within yourself

✓ Conclusion

The conclusion for your extended definition should sum up your impressions of the term in the topic sentence. You have defined this term in a special way, and you should end by stressing the relevance or significance of your personal interpretation.

HOW TO WRITE AN EXTENDED DEFINITION PARAGRAPH

1. Choose an interesting term to define (e.g., a word that is rich in meaning, a term or concept that is often misunderstood, a slang expression that your readers use but know little about).
2. Write a topic sentence that places your term in a logical category and includes some specific distinguishing detail.
3. Select those methods of definition that will be most effective in explaining the meaning of your term (examples, synonyms, process, anecdotes, negation, word origin, comparison or contrast).
4. Review your definition to see if it really makes the reader think about the meaning of the term and to make sure that it doesn't sound like a rewrite of a dictionary definition.
5. Add a concluding sentence that sums up your understanding of the term and its significance.

✓ Some Do's . . .

1. *Do* make your basic definition as clear as possible. Place the term in a logical class and add details that really distinguish the term from other members of the same class. If you think it necessary, use another sentence or two to present the differentiating details.
2. *Do* recognize the difference between defining a concrete object (a chalkboard) and defining an abstract term (education). Remember that the meaning of an abstract term is subject to different interpretations. Therefore, in order to communicate *your* meaning precisely, choose words that say exactly what you mean and provide your reader with enough information to understand your definition fully.
3. *Do* remember that a circular definition tells your reader nothing: "A circular definition is a definition that is circular."
4. *Do* choose an interesting or entertaining subject. It has been said by experts that there are no boring subjects, just boring treatments of sub-

jects. True as that may be, you have a better chance at a successful paragraph if you choose a subject with some appeal.

✓ . . . and Don'ts About Defining

1. *Don't* rely on only one method of definition. Decide which methods are most useful for your topic, and then use those methods to expand your basic definition.
2. *Don't* define a term simply by rewriting a dictionary definition of the term. Your readers expect and deserve more.
3. *Don't* choose a word that can be defined in one sentence.
4. *Don't* stop your basic definition after placing the term in a class. Remember that clear, distinguishing details are often the key to a good basic definition.

SUGGESTED ACTIVITIES AND ASSIGNMENTS

1. Throughout history, female beauty has always been a highly sought and carefully cultivated attribute—but, has beauty always been defined in the same way? An old saying states: "Beauty is in the eye of the beholder," yet differences in time and location have revealed many contrasting perceptions of what a beautiful woman should look like. For example, a beautiful woman, judged by the standards of sixteenth-century Europe, might be considered unattractive by today's standards, and the glamorous model on the cover of *Cosmopolitan* might be absolutely repulsive to a tribe in the jungles of New Guinea. To see how much the standards for physical beauty have changed during this century, compare photos of bathing beauties from the 1920s to photos in the latest *Sports Illustrated* swimsuit issue. Surprisingly, however, many women today would give anything to have the classical features of Queen Nefertiti, wife of the Pharaoh Akhenatem, who reigned in fourteenth-century B.C. Egypt.

   Write a brief paragraph that defines the characteristics of female beauty for one of the following:

   > a woman of ancient Egypt
   >
   > a woman of ancient Greece or Rome
   >
   > a woman of the Renaissance
   >
   > a woman of the Victorian age
   >
   > a woman of the Nuba, Sudan

2. Abstract terms are fun to define because no two people will define one in exactly the same way. The following are some brief, thought-provok-

ing definitions of a number of abstract terms. Find a definition that interests you and then build on that definition with examples, negation, synonyms, and so forth. If you disagree with the writer's conception of the term, write your own basic definition and build on that.

> "A committee is a cul-de-sac to which ideas are lured and then quietly strangled." (John A. Lincoln)
>
> "Advertising may be described as the science of arresting the human intelligence long enough to get money from it." (Stephen Leacock)
>
> "An appeaser is one who feeds a crocodile—hoping it will eat him last." (Winston Churchill)
>
> "Defeat is not the worst of failures. Not to have tried is the true failure." (George Edward Woodberry)
>
> "An enemy is anyone who tells the truth about you." (Elbert Hubbard)
>
> "A fanatic is a man who does what he thinks the Lord would do if only he knew the facts of the case." (Finley Peter Dunne)
>
> "A classic is something that everybody wants to have read and nobody wants to read." (Mark Twain)
>
> "Litigation . . . a machine which you go into as a pig and come out of as a sausage." (Ambrose Bierce)

SENTENCES

Although this entire book is devoted to clarity, this chapter especially concentrates on **precision**. To achieve precision, sentences of definition make frequent use of modifiers to pinpoint their precise meaning. You must choose precise nouns and verbs, then, to clarify further, limit, or specify these words. That is, you use modifiers.

Modifiers make your subjects and verbs even more specific and add color and interest to your paragraphs. The following section explains the correct use and placement of modifiers.

✓ Modifiers

Modifiers are words, phrases, or clauses that, when placed with other terms, change or limit those terms.

> The *gray* goose escaped. (Adjective modifying goose)
> The goose *barely* escaped. (Adverb modifying escaped)

The goose *from the newly hatched egg escaped.* (Phrase modifying goose)

The goose, *which had just emerged from its shell,* wobbled *across the chicken yard* and escaped. (Clause modifying goose and adverbial phrase modifying wobbled.)

As these few examples indicate, all modifiers limit or specify in some way the terms they are modifying.

Modifiers are important words in a sentence because they help to make the nouns and verbs clearer to readers. "The car" is not so clear a subject as "the antique green Caddy." To make sure that the modifier does clarify your meaning, place it as close as possible to the word being modified.

Remember that modifiers can be

single words	the *back* door
phrases	the door at your *back*
clauses	the door *which is at your back*

DANGLING MODIFIERS.   A serious—and frequently ridiculous—error in the use of modifiers is labeled *dangling,* which occurs if the modifiers do not have a word to modify *or* are placed incorrectly in the sentence. For example:

Whispering through the pines, the lovers were charmed by the soft evening breezes.

Although swimming valiantly upstream, the canoe was unable to reach him in time.

Modifiers are correctly placed closest to the words they are intended to modify.

The lovers were charmed by the soft breezes whispering through the pines.

Although swimming valiantly upstream, the man was. . . .

You can also correct dangling modifiers by making them dependent clauses, that is, by adding a subject and a verb.

> Although the man was swimming valiantly upstream, the canoe was unable to reach him.
>
> Although the man was swimming valiantly upstream, the current swept him over the falls before the canoe could reach him.

To check if you have a dangling modifier at the beginning of your sentence, place the modifier directly after the subject and see if the sentence is clear.

> The canoe, swimming valiantly upstream, was. . . .

You must provide a sensible "doer" of the action. Obviously, the canoe is not the doer.

If the modifier is used correctly, it can be placed on either side of the subject, and the sentence will be clear:

> Having signed up for the match, I waited to be called.
>
> I, having signed up for the match, waited to be called.

EXERCISE 8C: FINDING A SUBJECT FOR DANGLING MODIFIERS

For each of the following sentence beginnings, provide a subject and use it in an interesting and correct way.

1. After losing my keys down the elevator shaft,

   _____

2. Since winning the Pulitzer Prize,

   _____

3. Remembering to phone Marylin,

   _____

4. By stopping for gas,

   _____

5. Having spent all her money and breaking her heart,

_____

6. While waiting for your phone call,

_____

7. To make her understand,

_____

8. Forgetting his wife's birthday,

_____

9. Since losing my nerve,

_____

10. Despairing of help,

_____

MISPLACED MODIFIERS. Modifiers should be placed as close as possible to the words they modify. They should also be placed so there is no doubt as to the words they modify. Sometimes words can be placed in several different positions and still be clear.

> *On November 22, 1963,* John F. Kennedy was assassinated.
> John F. Kennedy, *on November 22, 1963,* was assassinated.
> John F. Kennedy was assassinated *on November 22, 1963.*

Be careful to place your modifier in a position that will indicate the meaning you intend. Look at the following sentences:

Only he said that he loved my sister.	He said that he *only* loved my sister.
He *only* said that he loved my sister.	He said that he loved *only* my sister.
He said *only* that he loved my sister.	He said that he loved my *only* sister.
He said that *only* he loved my sister.	He said that he loved my sister *only.*

Note: The meaning of the sentence changes each time the position of the modifier *only* changes. When a modifier can modify different words in a sentence, make sure you place it where it will give the meaning you intend.

In the following sentence, the modifier is misplaced.

> They played while I was reading with the new pups in the basket.

It should be:

> They played with the new pups in the basket while I was reading.
>
> or
>
> While I was reading, they played with the new pups in the basket.

They played while I was reading with the new pups in the basket.

EXERCISE 8D: CORRECTING DANGLING AND MISPLACED MODIFIERS

Revise all sentences to make them clearer.

1. Dejected and worried, his marriage proposal wasn't very optimistic.

   _____

2. Since he had been turned down three times, it wasn't a bit hopeful.

   _____

3. By selling all the stock options, the finances were completed.

   _____

4. Getting there an hour late, the party was in full swing.

   _____

5. Having been stored in the garage for three years, my father was afraid his tools were badly rusted.

   _____

6. Never having had any lessons, my game was barely adequate.

   _____

7. Being old and worn out, I had no reason to keep the car.

   _____

8. Dave decided to phone Diana while out of town.

   _____

9. The ducks hid among the bracken huddled against the cold.

   _____

10. Having studied hard all semester the exam was aced by Jo.

    _____

MAINTAINING A CONSISTENT POINT OF VIEW

Avoid needless shifts in point of view by being consistent in:

Person:	Using the right pronouns (first, second, or third person)
Number:	Using a singular pronoun to refer to singular terms and plural pronouns to refer to plural terms.
Tense:	Using verb forms that keep the reader in the same tense (present, past, or future)
Voice:	Staying in active voice and using passive voice only when necessary.

✓ Shifts in Point of View

> **Point of view** is made up of *person, number, tense,* and *voice.* Sometimes your meaning requires you to make changes in one or more parts of your point of view, as it does in this example of changes in person.

> *I* screamed when *he* fell off the deck; indeed, *everyone* cried out.

> However, when changes are not demanded by context, they are awkward and confusing.

NEEDLESS SHIFTS IN PERSON

Shift:	As *you* came across the bridge, *we* could see the spire of the cathedral in the distance.
Consistent:	As *we* came across the bridge, *we* could see the spire of the cathedral in the distance.

NEEDLESS SHIFTS IN NUMBER

Shift:	Each one has *their* directions and *know* how to get to the lodge.
Consistent:	Each one has *his* directions and *knows* how to get to the lodge.

NEEDLESS SHIFTS IN TENSE

Shift:	The drill instructor *called* us to attention and then *announces* a fifteen-mile hike.
Consistent:	The drill instructor *called* us to attention and then *announced* a fifteen-mile hike.

NEEDLESS SHIFTS IN VOICE

Shift:	Today we *discussed* medical terminology; pharmacology *will be discussed* tomorrow.
Consistent:	Today we *discussed* medical terminology; tomorrow we *will discuss* pharmacology.

Shifts in sentence structure often lead to statements so clumsy and confusing that the only way to correct them is to rewrite the sentences completely.

Awkward and confusing:	Why doesn't the State Department at least send out people who understand the language is what he wondered.
Rewritten:	He wondered why the State Department didn't send out people who at least knew the language.

Awkward and confusing:	The cause of the widespread unrest in the country, which was largely the result of our misguided policy, offered little hope for a stable government.
Rewritten:	The widespread unrest caused by our misguided policy threatened the stability of the government.
Awkward and confusing:	It would do little good to have a college degree for a person if he or she has accomplished nothing and little to show for it.
Rewritten:	Having a college degree does little for the person who fails to make use of his or her education.
Awkward and confusing:	These transportation costs when ordering in large quantities the supplier may be able to absorb.
Rewritten:	The supplier may be able to absorb the transportation cost on orders for large quantities.

EXERCISE 8E: CORRECTING SHIFTS IN POINT OF VIEW

Underline the word or words that shift. Then rewrite the sentences to eliminate the inconsistencies.

1. Each child has their lunch box and their costume, and they must be responsible for them.

   _____

2. She turned away after a kiss and breaks into sobbing.

   _____

3. Sara feeds the dogs and put out fresh water every morning.

   _____

4. The two men hike all day; they hike all day yesterday too.

   _____

5. Balancing between the subway cars, the drunk had been in danger.

   _____

6. As you come over the hill, they could see the village spread out beneath them.

   _____

7. Lou screamed when the bum snatched her bag like a banshee.

_____

8. The hairdresser washed her hair then cuts it in bangs.

_____

9. Mary had once owned a little lamb, and it has a fleece of snow.

_____

10. The bankers are conservative because you can't trust everybody, you know.

_____

✏ WORDS

✓ The Dictionary

In the search for precise definition, the writer seeks the best possible sentence to convey his idea, a sentence that in turn, searches for the right word. The right word is easily found—in the dictionary.

Speakers, readers, and writers all depend on the *dictionary,* a reference book that contains an alphabetical, explanatory list of words. When you speak, you need to know how words are pronounced; when you write, you need to know how words are spelled. More important, however, whether you are speaking or reading or writing, you need to know the *meaning* of words because word meaning is the foundation of clear communication. All these things the dictionary supplies.

Although pronunciation, spelling, and meaning are the things you most frequently look up in your dictionary, it also informs you of many other things about a word. Look at this typical entry:

> **love** (luv) n. **1.** An intense affectionate concern for another person. **2.** An intense sexual desire for another person. **3.** A beloved person. Often used as a term of endearment. **4.** A strong fondness or enthusiasm for something: *a love of the woods.* **5.** *Capital L* Eros or Cupid, the god of love in classical mythology. **6.** *Theology* **a.** God's benevolence and mercy toward man. **b.** Man's devotion to or adoration of God. **c.** The benevolence, kindness, or brotherhood that man should rightfully feel toward others. **7.** *Capital L Christian Sci-*

ence God. **8.** A zero score in tennis. —**fall in love.** To become enamored of or sexually attracted to someone. —**for love.** As a
favor; out of fondness; without payment. —**for love or money.**
Under any circumstances. Usually used in the negative: *He would
not do that for love or money.* — **for the love of.** With loving regard for; for the sake of. —**in love.** Feeling love for someone or
something; enamored. —**make love. 1.** To copulate. **2.** To embrace
or caress. —**v. loved, loving, loves.** —**tr. 1.** To feel love for. **2.** To
desire (another person) sexually. **3.** To embrace or caress. **4.** To like
or desire enthusiastically; delight in. **5.** To thrive on; need: *The
cactus loves hot, dry air.*— **intr.** To experience loving tenderness or
sexual desire for another; be in love. —See Synonyms at like [Mid-
dle English *love,* Old English *lufu.* See leubh- in Appendix.]

    Synonyms: love, affection, devotion, fondness, infatuation.
These nouns refer to feelings of attraction and attachment experienced by persons. *Love* suggests a feeling more intense and less
susceptible to control than that associated with the other words
of this group. *Affection* is a more unvarying feeling of warm regard for another person. *Devotion* is dedication and attachment
to a person or thing; contrasted with love, it implies a more self-
less and often a more settled feeling. *Fondness,* in its most common modern sense, is rather strong liking for a person or thing.
Infatuation is extravagant attraction or attachment to a person or
thing, usually short in duration and indicative of folly or faulty
judgment.

love affair. 1. An intimate sexual relationship or episode between
    lovers. **2.** An enthusiastic liking or desire.

love apple. *Archaic.* A tomato.

love-bird (luv'burd') n. Any of various Old World parrots, chiefly of
    the genus *Agapornis,* often kept as a cage bird.

love feast. 1. Among early Christians, a meal eaten with others as a
    symbol of love. **2.** a similar symbolic meal among certain modern
    Christian sects. **3.** A gathering intended to promote good will
    among the participants.

love game A tennis game in which the winner loses no points.

1. The first word of the dictionary entry is the word to be defined—*love.*
2. Next to it, in parentheses, is the indication of its pronunciation—(lŭv). It
   is one syllable and is phonetically spelled with a u under the diacritical
   mark ˘. (In almost all dictionaries, diacritical marks are printed at the
   bottom of each page.)
3. The lowercase n. identifies the word as a noun. Eight differing definitions follow.
4. There follow six phrases indicating special uses.

5. Next comes the letter v., which shows that the word *love* is also a verb and gives its principal parts.
6. It then gives the abbreviation tr, indicating a transitive verb, and several examples of its uses as a transitive.
7. Following these, *love* is defined as intr, meaning intransitive and giving its usage.
8. It then suggests looking at synonyms under the word *like.*
9. Next, in square brackets, the entry gives the derivation of the word.
10. There follows a list of synonyms OE and distinctions among them. (In some dictionaries pertinent quotations are given.)
11. Finally, several phrases include *love,* as in *love bird* and *love apple.*
12. *Love apple* is marked *Archaic,* meaning no longer in current use.

Dictionary entries for other words will contain comparable pertinent information. Some words will require more, some less. Within a few inches of space, the dictionary codifies a wealth of information to become an indispensable—and daily—reference tool.

THE DICTIONARY AS A GUIDE TO MEANING. Dictionaries, in the strictest sense, do not define words but, rather, record the meanings used by the majority of educated speakers and writers. That is, dictionaries are recorders rather than policymakers in the usage of words. They give their readers information concerning meaning and usage through the various methods described below.

Simple definition. Suppose your English instructor uses the word *syntax* in class, and you are not sure what he means. You look it up and find the dictionary gives as a first definition: "1. orig., orderly or systematic arrangement." This does not fit into the context of your instructor's lecture, so obviously you must read on. The next item in the dictionary is: "2. Gram. (a) the arrangement of words as elements in a sentence to show their relationship to one another; (b) sentence structure; (c) the branch of grammar dealing with this." Item 2 is clearly what your instructor was talking about.

For several reasons, it is important to read the *entire* dictionary entry and not stop at the first definition. First, as in the example with *syntax,* you might get an incorrect meaning for your purpose. Second, in all Merriam-Webster dictionaries, the first meaning is the oldest meaning, and therefore, might be out of date for your purpose. Finally, if you read the entire entry, you learn more about the word, which helps you to remember it.

Etymology. Etymology is the history of a word. It may be simply the derivation of a word, that is, the languages through which it passed before it came into modern English. The following examples show the derivation of words as given in *Webster's New World Dictionary.*

Woman [ME wumman < OE wifmann, later wimman < wif, a female + mann, a human being, man . . .]

This coded information means that *woman* comes from Middle English (language of England from c. 1200 to 1500), which comes from Old English (language of England from c. 400 to 1200), and that it is a compound word made up of the words *wif* (female) and *mann* (human being). The changes indicated in ME *wumman* from OE *wifmann* and from *wifmann* to *wimman* occurred because the later forms are easier to pronounce.

In the case of the word *woman,* the derivation is just through the chronological periods of English. Such words are said to belong to the "native stock" of English. Probably about 60 percent of your vocabulary comes from the native stock of words, but many others came into modern English through other languages.

>   *discipline* [ME < from OFr descipline < L. disciplina < L. discipulus]

This means that the modern word *discipline* came into our language from Middle English, which derived it from an Old French word, which in turn came from two Latin words.

SYNONYMS.   One of the best ways to use your dictionary to enlarge your vocabulary and so improve your writing is to pay close attention to the entries that list synonyms and discuss the distinctions among them. If you read the synonyms, you may be able to vary your word choice to avoid being monotonous. Even more important, an awareness of synonyms will make your writing more precise.

The great Roman orator, Quintilian, said that a good writer did not try to see that the reader *might* understand but that the reader *must* understand. To guarantee that your reader understands you, you must be precise; you must choose the exact word. Since no two synonyms are identical, you must select with care the one that best suits your purpose.

In the *New World Dictionary,* the entry under *give* presents twenty definitions for the word as an intransitive verb and an additional five definitions for it as a transitive verb. Then it gives the synonyms, which also vary enough so that the careful writer would not interchange them.

>   SYN.—**give** is the general word meaning to transfer from one's own possession to that of another; **grant** implies that there has been a request or an expressed desire for the thing given [to *grant* a favor]; **present** implies a certain formality in the giving and often connotes considerable value in the gift [he *presented* the school with a library]; **donate** is used especially of a giving to some philanthropic or religious cause; **bestow** stresses that the thing is given gratuitously and often implies condescension in the giver [to *bestow* charity upon the poor]; **confer** implies that the giver is a superior and that the thing given is an honor, privilege, etc. [to *confer* a title, a college degree, etc.].

EXERCISE 8F: USING SYNONYMS

Look up the following words to find their synonyms. List five synonyms and use each of them in a sentence to reveal the different shades of meaning among them.

1. fun _____

_____

_____

2. attraction _____

_____

_____

3. mixture _____

_____

_____

4. fix _____

_____

_____

5. dialect _____

_____

_____

6. chew _____

_____

_____

7. intention _____

_____

_____

8. struggle _____

_____

_____

9. fight _____

_____

_____

10. disposition _____

_____

_____

LABELING

Still another way in which your dictionary helps you write precisely and correctly is known as *labeling*. If, for any reason, the use of a word is limited, the dictionary will label it to indicate what its limitations are. If no label appears, the word is correct in all usages.

Subject labels. In most dictionaries, if you looked up the phrase *home run,* you would find the label *Baseball.* The word *homeostasis* is labeled *Physiology.* Such labels appear for many words in business, law, finance, sciences, and other fields.

Usage labels. The labels *obsolete* and *archaic* indicate that the words are limited by *time.* For example, the word *ere,* meaning "before," would probably be marked archaic, and so you would not use it. The labels *dialect* and *provincial* indicate that the words are limited by *geography.* For example, the word *cornpone* you would find marked *Dialect southern U.S.A.*

Other labels indicate the level of *formality* at which the word is appropriate.

1. *Colloq.* means correct for speech but probably too informal for writing. For example, "*picky* [colloq.] fussy."
2. *Slang* means limited to informal speech and often limited to a specific group. For example, "*hooch* [slang] alcoholic liquor."
3. *Substandard* means limited to *uneducated* speech. For example, "*you'uns* [substandard] you, you all."

Your dictionary will never let you down if you use it with care.

chapter *9*

From Paragraph

to Essay

INTRODUCTION

To go from writing a single paragraph to writing a short essay involves little more than applying the principles you have already learned in this book. All you need to do is expand the basic pattern of *introduction— body—conclusion.*

An essay, just like a paragraph, requires *one* clear controlling idea. In the paragraph, we call the statement of the controlling idea the *topic sentence.* In the essay, we call it a *thesis statement.* The thesis statement, then, is a statement of the controlling idea for the whole essay, whether it be three, four, or dozens of paragraphs in length.

No matter what the length or purpose of your essay, you must make a clear statement of your central idea almost immediately. In your single paragraph, the topic sentence is the introduction. In the essay, your thesis statement, the statement of your controlling idea, is a part of the introduction.

Paragraph	**Essay**
Topic sentence first as introduction	Thesis statement at end of introduction

Usually, it works best if you put your topic sentence first in a paragraph and put the thesis statement at the end of your introduction.

✏️▷ BODY

The body of the essay may be just one well-developed paragraph.

Introduction·   with thesis statement at end
Body paragraph: with supporting details
Conclusion

More frequently, however, the body of the essay has more than one paragraph.

Introduction: with thesis statement at end
Body paragraphs: each with its own topic sentence
                  each with supporting details

Conclusion

A celebrated French writer of short stories, Guy de Maupassant, wrote an unusual book of hunting anecdotes called *Love: Pages from a Sportsman's Notebook*. This poignant memory from it follows the basic structure of the essay.

Introduction

"The sun had risen, and it was a bright day with a blue sky, and we were thinking of taking our departure, when two birds with extended necks and outstretched wings, glided rapidly over our heads. I fired, and one of them fell almost at my feet. It was a teal, with a silver breast, and then, in the blue space above me, I heard a voice, the voice of a bird. It was a short, repeated, heart-rending lament; and the bird, the little animal that had been spared, began to turn round in the blue sky, over our heads, looking at its dead companion which I was holding in my hand.

Body paragraphs

"Karl was on his knees, his gun to his shoulder watching it eagerly, until it should be within shot. 'You have killed the duck,' he said, 'and the drake will not fly away.'

"He certainly did not fly away; he circled over our heads continually, and continued his cries. Never have any groans of suffering pained me so much as that desolate appeal, as that lamentable reproach of this poor bird which was lost in space.

"Occasionally he took flight under the menace of the gun which followed his movements, and seemed ready to continue his flight alone, but as he could not make up his mind to this, he returned to find his mate.

"'Leave her on the ground,' Karl said to me, 'he will come within shot by and by.' And he did indeed come near us, careless of danger, infatuated by his animal love, by his affection for his mate, which I had just killed.

"Karl fired, and it was as if somebody had cut the string which held the bird suspended. I saw something black descend, and I heard the noise of a fall among the rushes. And Pierrot brought it to me.

Conclusion
"I put them—they were already cold—into the same game-bag, and I returned to Paris the same evening."

✓ Topic Sentence to Thesis Statement

The first part of the paragraph to be expanded is the topic sentence. As you are now well aware, the topic sentence must be grammatically complete, clear, and specific. It must also have a subject narrow enough to be adequately developed in the length planned for, and that subject must be treated with a consistent attitude.

So must the essay. The thesis statement must have all the qualities of the topic sentence, but in addition, it must be expandable.

Suppose, as your probable first step, you decided on a topic—comedy. Examples of the paragraph's topic sentence and the essay's thesis statement follow.

Topic sentence: Mark Twain once commented that we laugh in order not to cry.

Introduction and   Comedy, as somebody once remarked, is no laughing matter. A
thesis statement: reviewer of a book of Woody Allen's commented, "Woody Allen is too funny not to be taken seriously." In the eighteenth century, Prime Minister Horace Walpole observed that "comedy is the style for the man who thinks as opposed to tragedy which is the style for the man who feels." *But Mark Twain made the most poignant analysis about the seriousness of comedy when he said, "We laugh in order not to cry."*

✓ Form of the Paragraph

Mark Twain once commented that we laugh in order not to cry. In traditional comedy, although things always turn out well for the hero in the end, he suffers and suffers greatly until the end. We laugh only because we know it will finally come out all right. In a very specialized sense, a number of the world's great religions follow this pattern. Mohammed and Jesus, among other great leaders, suffer greatly and succeed magnificently. With their glory, they bring a great good, a boon, to all mankind. In a far more secular sense, Charlie Chaplin in *The Gold Rush,* one of the greatest movie comedies, suffers cold, starvation, and rejection, but, in the end, he sails away home with the gold in his pocket, the girl on his arm, and wearing *two* fur coats. Charlie's success is gratifying to us because we can recognize ourselves as poor, little, incapable, rejected Charlie . . . who wins in the end. The aim of comedy is to improve what can be improved and to make bearable that which can't by laughing at it.

✓ Form of the Essay

Comedy: No Laughing Matter

Comedy, as somebody once remarked, is no laughing matter. A reviewer of a book of Woody Allen's commented, "Woody Allen is too funny not to be taken seriously." In the eighteenth century, Prime Minister Horace Walpole observed that "comedy is the style for the man who thinks as opposed to tragedy which is the style for the man who feels." *But Mark Twain made the most poignant analysis about the seriousness of comedy when he said, "We laugh in order not to cry."*

Critics at least as far back as the Greeks have tried to define comedy. Its definition remains elusive, but a few of its basic characteristics can be identified.

First, classical comedy is a form of literature in which things turn out well for the hero, the leading character. No matter what the hero suffers during the action, his ending is successful as opposed to the tragic ending, in which the hero goes down to defeat and death.

In a very specialized sense, a number of the great religions of the world follow this pattern. Mohammed and Jesus, among other great leaders, suffer greatly and succeed magnificently. With their glory, they bring a tremendous good, a *boon,* to all mankind.

The bringing of a *boon* to mankind was a very important characteristic of comedy for several hundred years of English stage comedy. The boon was symbolized by ending the plot with a feast, usually a wedding feast, at which the actors pelted each other and the audience with food.

This seems to be just genial horseplay, but the feast, especially if it is a wedding feast, promises that the hero's world is now in happy moral order after his struggles with moral disorder. Frequently, the poor young man has just won the young woman from the rich old man. This goes back to the earliest *situation comedy,* the myth where spring, represented by a comely young man, drums out the crabby old man, winter.

The *comedy of situation* and the *comedy of character* are two vast divisions of comedy. In great comedy, the two usually come together. Charlie Chaplin's *Gold Rush,* one of the greatest movie comedies, is a superlative example of the comedy of situation in which disorder is resolved into order. Charlie suffers cold, starvation (he's starved into boiling and eating one of his boots), violence (he's pummeled by every other male character), and disaster (his house slides over a cliff and he barely leaps free).

Above all, he suffers rejection both social and sexual. Nevertheless, with the help of nothing much but a tender heart, Charlie wins equilibrium. He sails away (to a happier land) with the girl on his arm, the gold in his pocket, and *two* fur coats.

But Charlie is so individualized a character that his movies are not only comedies of situation but of character as well. Charlie's success is gratifying to us as individuals; we recognize ourselves all along in poor, little, incapable, rejected Charlie. It is also gratifying to us as a society because moral order has been established as the good guy wins.

Comic characterization is the second great classification of comedy. Comic characters range from tremendous creations like Shakespeare's Falstaff to types like the "little souls" of Chaplin and Woody Allen, to Dorothy Parker's women made cynical by men, to men victimized by women.

One of the great comic individuals is Geoffrey Chaucer's *Wife of Bath,* probably the first comic heroine in English literature and certainly the first fictional feminist. The Wife has it made in a man's world—she's a business and social force. Her interest in men is earthy and long-lived; she says she has had "five husbands by the Church door," which implies a few more by the back door. Yet when she tells her tale, its theme is that women should have "sovereignty" in marriage. As she speaks, her "sovereignty" is somewhat challenged because her fifth husband is twenty-five years younger than she is. However, she loves him dearly and is just amused as he capers around kicking up his heels in his "green and yellow stockings." He is, she smiles, "so fresh abeddye." She is ultimately endearing because she says "yes" to life. "I have had," she assures us, "my life in my time."

The Wife represents another characteristic of comedy—the frequent theme that love is a game and sexuality is the funniest joke ever played on the human race. This lighthearted characteristic goes back to the origin of comedy, the celebratory drama of fertility rites.

Comedy is an affirmation of life because of its attitude towards error and incongruity, towards evil and death. Comedy is a way of making life possible in this world, despite what we know about it. Comedy recognizes human limitation, neither in broken pride nor in saintly humility, but in the spirit of ironic acceptance. This is what Walpole meant when he said that comedy was for the thinking man. Comedy is the intellectual perception that the world does not bend to fit our desires, and we can do nothing but make the best of it. Many jokes and much literature are directed at making the best of the human condition.

The purpose of comedy is both criticism and acceptance. The aim of criticism is to improve what can be improved; the aim of acceptance is to make bearable, through laughter, that which can't.

Comedy is undefined because limits cannot be put to it. Still, it can be characterized as intellectual, earthy, heart-broken, tough. When Camelot fell, when all the knights lay dead, only two men survived to walk away—Merlin, the wise man, and Dagonet, the comedian.

✓ Organization Within the Essay

You will recall in the Sentences section of Chapter 6 a discussion of paragraph development using subtopic sentences. The following essay by Malcolm Forbes is similarly analyzed with topic sentences replacing the subtopics.

Title	Wild Bill Hickok
	May 27, 1837–August 2, 1876
Introduction	Amid widespread reports that he had been shot to death at Fort Dodge, Kansas, in 1873, quick-draw lawman Wild Bill Hickok wrote this letter to the St. Louis *Missouri-Democrat:* "Wishing to correct an error in your paper of the 12th, I will state that no Texan has, nor ever *will* 'corral William.' I wish you to correct your statement, on account of my people.— P.S. I have bought your paper in preference to all others since 1857."
Thesis statement in first sentence of second paragraph	Stories about Hickok were legendary in his own time. As a deputy U.S. marshal over much of the Plains territory, Hickok developed such a reputation as a fast shooter that other men would follow him around looking for a show-down. Hickok, a tall, broad-shouldered man who carried two pistols in his vest and a pair of .36-caliber Colt revolvers around his waist, took to walking down the middle of the street and avoiding open windows. The former Union spy even sat in the barber's chair with his shotgun in his lap.

Still, Hickok relished his dangerous job. In fact, some say he used his deputy's badge simply as a license to get involved in gunfights. He once advised, "Young man, never run away from a gun. Bullets can travel faster than you can. Besides, if you're going to be hit, you had better get it in the front than in the back. It looks better."

Topic sentences begin paragraphs 3–5	As the frontier towns grew more settled and hired their own lawmen, Hickok was called on less and less. He performed in some of Buffalo Bill's Wild West stage shows, but mainly he wandered the West in search of some action. In 1876, Hickok was in Deadwood Gulch, where gold had been discovered in the Black Hills of the Dakota Territory. He had gotten married that March and hoped to strike enough gold to settle down. But meanwhile Hickok pursued his passion for gambling.

On August 2, Hickok walked into the Number 10 Saloon just after noon to join a poker game. He always sat at the table with his back to the wall. But this time when he asked one player to get up and give him that stool, the other players just laughed it off, and Hickok finally took a seat that faced the front door but didn't give him a full view of the barroom.

At about 3 P.M., Jack McCall entered the saloon and walked to the end of the bar behind Hickok. Hickok had played against McCall the day before, and had even given him money for dinner after McCall went broke, so the former deputy continued to concentrate on his cards. Suddenly, McCall pulled a pistol and fired at Hickok, shouting, "Damn you, take that!" The bullet struck Hickok in the back of his head, exited through his right cheek, and then lodged in the wrist of the card player across from him, Hickok, killed instantly, fell off his stool and slumped on his side on the floor.

Conclusion
is in the last
paragraph
    McCall, who said later he shot Hickok for killing his brother, ran out of the saloon and jumped on a horse. But he was caught when the saddle fell over, and he later was hanged. Hickok, meanwhile, left part of his legend on the poker table. The cards he was holding—a pair of aces and a pair of eights—are known as the "dead man's hand."

✓ A Few Suggestions for Conclusions

Remember that a conclusion is a summing up. You don't just stop as if you had run out of gas; you want to get where you are going, which is back home again. However, you return home having accomplished something: you have informed or entertained your readers.

Because it is the last thing you say to your readers, you want to write a conclusion that is strong and interesting. Most of all, you want to convince them that you have satisfied the promise you made in the thesis statement.

✓ Outlining

An **outline** is the blueprint for your paragraph or essay. At first it may seem to be additional work, but it saves you time and prevents you from including irrelevant ideas or omitting ideas necessary for clear and adequate development. Since your outline is the blueprint from which you will construct your essay, the outline should contain all the points you will make in the essay and contain nothing that will not appear in your essay.

Thus, each of the basic parts of the single paragraph is expanded in developing a complete essay. The topic sentence becomes the thesis statement (statement of the controlling idea for the whole essay), which is the focal point of the introductory paragraph. The subtopics of the single paragraph become topic sentences for paragraphs of development (each, of course, requiring detailed support). The concluding sentence becomes a concluding paragraph to tie together the various parts of the essay and reinforce its controlling idea.

For the longer, more formal essay, you need a more detailed outline; the pattern needs to be further expanded. Regardless of the length or purpose of your essay, however, you must first decide on your subject and your attitude—your thesis statement. That is the first thing you write down for your outline.

After writing your thesis statement, write down the most important points you intend to cover in your essay. Make sure each of these main points supports the controlling idea expressed in your thesis statement. Working from main headings to subordinate ones, proceed to develop your outline with supporting details until you have a complete skeleton for your essay.

The relationship among the supporting details is made clear with a standardized form of numbering:

Thesis statement: _____

_____

I. First major support for thesis statement
   A. First major support for I
      1. First detail supporting A
      2. Second detail supporting A
      3. Third detail supporting A
   B. Second major support for I
      1. First detail supporting B
      2. Second detail supporting B
II. Second major support for thesis statement
   A. First major support for II
      1. First detail supporting A
      2. Second detail supporting A
   B. Second major support of II
      1. First detail supporting B
      2. Second detail supporting B
      3. Third detail supporting B
      4. Fourth detail supporting B

If a *conclusion* is included in the outline at all, it is not numbered or subdivided. A brief statement of the purpose of your conclusion, however, may be helpful to you.

Note: Since outlining consists of dividing the whole writing into its parts, each element in your outline must have at least two parts. (After all, you can't divide anything into fewer than two.)

EXERCISE 9A: FINDING THE OUTLINE

After reading the following excerpt from Josephine Miles's introduction to *Classic Essays in English,* first circle the thesis statement and then underline the topic sentences, the main body supports. (Paragraph 2 is an extension of the thesis statement.)

If you have ever tried to work out an idea that seemed to you worth-while, you realize the pleasure of seeing it take shape. This is the pleasure of the essayist—first the tentative thought, then the steps of development through positive and negative evidence, finally the restatement and clarification of the thought in its developed form.

You may ask, how generally true is your idea? What connections and associations does it have? Who cares about it? How may it grow, take on breadth and depth, lead others to think about ideas like it? What is your feeling toward it, your manner in writing of it?

You may ask, what are the main concerns of your ideas? They may be what you like to do—"Fishing is pleasanter than hunting," or "It's a good plan to read the end of a book first." Or they may be concerns about people, with puzzling complexities of character, with a question such as "Why do I like the people I like?" or "What is the difference between an acquaintance and a friend?" Or they may be about concepts of groups and organizations—"Why do people enjoy excluding others?" "How does a church differ from a religion?" "How important are settings in theatrical productions?" "What are the consequences of one vote in an election?"

If you think as you read these suggestions that no one of them is an idea that would ever cross your mind, then ask yourself what you think about instead, when you are philosophizing on matters larger than one person or one event, when you are thinking, that is, about matters that may be at least proposed to be generally true.

An essay tries to develop an idea. The concept of trying, of tentative effort, is in the term *essay* itself—*essaier* in French is *to attempt*. So it differs from a formal report or a technical work of any kind which supplies evidence as complete and thorough as possible. The evidence offered by the essay is usually just that available to the author at the moment of writing. He searches his mind, maybe asks his friends what they think, but does not necessarily do further research. An essayist's main interest is his idea, his argument; he is more interested in developing an attitude, a clarification of a thought, than in adding to knowledge.

✓ Organization Through Transition

Just as you need unity and adequate development, you must have *coherence* for your writing to be clear. And coherence is achieved through transition. A transitional word or phrase moves the readers easily from sentence to sentence in a paragraph. Those words or phrases may be expanded to one or two transitional sentences, which, in like fashion, move readers from paragraph to paragraph. Transition achieves coherence.

DEVICES OF TRANSITION

Transition in the body of your essay links part to part in two different ways. First, there are *devices of transition,* with which you are familiar: enumeration, pronoun reference, parallel structure, and repetition of key words or phrases or their close synonyms (These are discussed on pages 232-240; refer to them if you wish a refresher.)

LOGICAL SEQUENCE

The second method of transition is a part of the structure of the paragraph or essay. It is *organizing the whole in logical sequence.* The organization is your own; it can use narration or examples, description or definition, or any method you choose. But whatever it is, you need a reasonable and consistent order to your thoughts.

Each paragraph in the body of the essay has, as you know, a topic sentence with a subject and an attitude and transition. Each topic sentence in the body of an essay has ideas that link it to what has gone before.

Often these topic sentences begin with a subordinate clause that looks backward to the preceding paragraph. The independent clause of the topic sentence announces the subject for the current paragraph.

Here are some typical subordinate clauses with the conjunctions that introduce them:

> Although I was fond of movies, I liked stage plays better.
>
> If you will be late, phone me.
>
> Once they were graduated, they never looked back.
>
> As soon as he got a job, he bought a house.
>
> Until the snow melts, the skiers will hit the slopes.
>
> As we understand it, there will be an increase in taxes.
>
> Where there's smoke, there's fire.
>
> When it's cool, I'll serve the cake.
>
> While the cat's away, the mice will play.

If the old adage about the absent cat were a topic sentence in an essay, the subordinate clause *(while the cat's away)* would be referring to its preceding paragraph about the cat's travels. The independent clause *(the mice will play)* points forward to the development of this paragraph describing the carousing of the mice.

TRANSITIONAL PARAGRAPHS

Sometimes within the body of an essay, coherence requires that you write an entire paragraph—usually short—to act as a transition. In the essay on comedy on page 295, the purpose of the second paragraph is purely transitional. It bridges the gap from the generalizing first paragraph to the following paragraphs that support the thesis of the first.

TRANSITIONS OTHER THAN SUBORDINATE CLAUSES

In addition to subordinate clauses, there are other transitional links you might use. The simplest transitions are words like *and, but, for, nor, so,* and *yet.* Demonstrative adjectives *(this, these, that, those)* also can link previous

Transition bridges the gap.

sentences to those that follow. As effective as these words may be as transitions, remember that you don't want to use them frequently as subjects of sentences.

TITLES

Another difference between paragraphs and essays is that paragraphs have no titles, but essays have titles with a threefold purpose. First, a title should gain the readers' interest. Second, it should indicate the subject of the essay. Third, it should at least hint at its attitude.

Sometimes a title is only a label. If the author intends a factual or technical essay, he wants his title to inform only. Here are two such titles: "The Perils of Free Trade" and "Chemical Signaling in the Brain."

Far more often, however, a good title is allusive or imaginative to show the author's style and attitude. An excellent title is E. M. Forster's "Two Cheers for Democracy." Forster identifies his subject, democracy, and his attitude of unenthusiastic approval with "cheers," but only two instead of the customary three cheers.

A long-winded title is seldom as appealing as a short, snappy one. But once in a while a long title provokes curiosity, like "Lying in a Hammock at William Duffy's Farm in Pine Island, Minnesota." A title is effective when it reveals something of its attitude as well as its subject.

EXERCISE 9B: TITLES

Just guessing, try to match the titles with the brief descriptions of the writings.

    Example: 1. The Oldest Stories in the World _____

                  f. Babylonian, Hittite, and Canaanite myths and legends of 3,500 years ago.

1. Patriotic Gore _____

2. "The Art of Political Lying" _____

3. "The Story of the Red-Headed League" _____

4. Medieval Households _____

5. The Private Papers of Henry Ryecroft _____

6. "Anglers" _____

7. Progress into the Past _____

8. Leave It to Psmith _____

9. The Moon Is Shining Bright as Day _____

10. Horse Feathers _____

a. An anthology of amusing verse for children selected by the comic poet, Ogden Nash.
b. The records of three anthropologists about their discoveries of the Mycenaean civilization.
c. A novel in the form of a diary about an ordinary but reticent man.
d. A fine essayist presents his philosophy of life while fishing.
e. An intriguing Sherlock Holmes story where the solution depends on the hair color of the villains.
f. A social history of the Middle Ages based on domestic life.
g. A farcical movie starring the Marx Brothers.
h. A wildly comic and somewhat bawdy novel about a man who disguises his name to impress luscious babes.
i. A great satirist expounds his bitter belief that the vast majority of men will lie for their own self-interest.
j. An analysis of the literature of the American Civil War.

✓ Some Do's . . .

1. *Do* begin your essay with an introduction that has a good chance of interesting your readers. The introduction is important because it and your title will probably determine whether or not you will have readers.
2. *Do* stick to your controlling idea for the sake of unity.
3. *Do* be consistent in your attitude.

✓ . . . and Don'ts for the Expanded Essay

1. *Don't* forget that your title should be meaningful and appealing.
2. *Don't* forget to support each topic sentence in the body of your essay.
3. *Don't* end without a real conclusion.

EXERCISE 9C: COMBINING SENTENCES

As your papers become longer, you do not want to use a series of short simple sentences. Practice your transitional skills by combining the short sentences given here, as shown in this example.

Choppy:	We have a new cordless phone. It was a prize we won last Saturday. We didn't pay anything for it. Our grocery store gave it as a prize. It was a prize we won for being the hundredth customer to come into the store to buy something. It doesn't work very well. My husband says we got exactly what we paid for.
Revised for coherence	Last Saturday we won a cordless phone from our grocery store, which awarded it to their hundredth customer. It doesn't work very well; my husband says we got exactly what we paid for.

1. My uncle likes to go to the movies. There are five movie theaters in a mall near us. He thinks that is just nifty. He is very indecisive. He can't decide which one he wants to see.

   _____

   _____

   _____

2. That mall wasn't meant for indecisive movie patrons. When you first enter the movie area, you buy your ticket. The ticket is good for any one of the five. Then you go into a long corridor. The five movie theaters lead off that corridor.

   _____

   _____

   _____

3. My uncle frequently goes to that mall. He eagerly buys his ticket. He scurries into the corridor. He scans the marquees to see what movies are playing. They all look wonderful. He can't make up his mind. My uncle is not a decisive man.

   _____

   _____

   _____

4. His ticket is good for any one of the movies. They all appeal to him. The first one he spots is a spy movie. He had read the novel that spy movie was made from. It was a great novel. It would make a great movie.

   _____

   _____

   _____

5. Next to that is a horror show. He had always loved those. He used to go to the movies with his grandmother. She had been very keen on horror movies. A horror movie is a good choice.

   _____

   _____

   _____

6. From one of the theaters comes a roar of big guns. Then there is the crackle of rifle shots. There is a drone of men's voices. He hears the bark of a command. A war movie is a fine way to spend an evening.

   _____

   _____

   _____

7. From the theater across the corridor comes the sound of a familiar song. My uncle listens to the song. He remembers it. That movie house specializes in "oldies." They are re-running an old show of Gene Kelly's. What a great show!

_____

_____

_____

8. My uncle is an indecisive man. He is bewildered by choices. He really can't make up his mind. Then he gets a superb idea. His ticket is good for three hours. He will go into each movie for thirty or thirty-five minutes. The indecisive man has made a decision.

_____

_____

_____

EXERCISE 9D: UNITY AND COHERENCE

Although the sentences in the following paragraphs relate to the controlling idea, the paragraphs as a whole appear choppy and disjointed. Using whatever transitional words and phrases necessary, rewrite the paragraphs to improve unity and coherence without changing the basic ideas.

I have a friend to whom ridiculous things happen. She is not silly or careless. Things just happen to her. She was driving home from bowling once, humming to herself. She'd had good scores. She stopped, still humming, at a red light. A car crashed into the rear of her car. She roared out of her car to complain. She observed that the other car was driven by her teen-aged son. He was driving his father's car. He had been told not to drive it. He had been told that car was off limits for him for a week.

She was upset. She breathed in deeply. The button popped off her skirt band. Her skirt fell to the street. The spectators cheered.

One time she and her daughter took a short trip. They stopped in New York City for a couple of days. She bought her daughter some clothes to wear back to school. While she was gone, her husband made out the salary checks for the employees of his little business. He accidentally made them out on their personal account.

The bank phoned to say that their account was overdrawn by several thousand dollars. She was appalled. "Oh, heavens," she moaned. "I knew I was spending too much money. I never dreamed it was that much." She fainted dead away.

These are trivial things. They are never her fault, really. They make her feel that she can't control anything in her life. She feels that she is a victim of circumstances.

✓ How to Write an Essay Examination

Once you understand how to expand the paragraph into an essay, you can apply this skill to any type of essay writing, including the essay examination. Everyone wants to do well on an examination and to see an A or a B on the returned exam booklet. It can be managed, if you realize that *taking exams is a skill that you can learn.* To take an essay exam, the initial step is to give a form to your answer—a form that is exactly like the form of your essays: first, a brief introduction presenting your thesis statement; second, the body, which is the support for your thesis statement; third, a conclusion that reaffirms your thesis statement. Not only is the writing of good examinations a skill that can be learned, *it is a skill which you have already learned.*

First, of course, you must know enough about the subject to have the raw materials for an answer. But facts, and opinions based on facts are just that—the raw material only, which by itself is only good enough for a C or a C+. With raw material only, you can't get that A. If you are aiming for a good grade, then you must know how to present your material.

Read the whole examination carefully. Make sure you understand the directions before you start answering any questions. You might see five essay questions on a test, but that doesn't mean you should automatically answer all five questions. If you read the directions first, you might find that you are supposed to choose only two of those questions.

Budget your time. Decide how much time you can spend on each question, and don't panic—it only wastes time. If you have a half-hour to spend on each question, you can't spend ten minutes worrying about how you are going to answer the question. One way to help ease test anxiety is to answer the first question successfully, so begin with the question you know the most about.

Read the question. What does it ask you to do? Look closely at the verb. Notice some of the activities required by the verbs:

Explain:	Give the reasons for something.
Evaluate:	Decide on the value or significance of something.
Analyze:	Break something down into its parts.
Illustrate:	Give examples of some generalization.
Define:	State the precise meaning of a term.
Compare:	Point out similarities.

Contrast: Point out differences.
Discuss: Tell all you know about a subject.

Think before you write. Jot down any details you can think of that might help you answer the question. Listing major points in a rough outline will help you get a general answer in mind before you begin to develop it. Think about your topic sentence (subject plus attitude). Think about what the topic sentence commits you to. If you can't come up with a good topic sentence of your own, you can frequently make an acceptable topic sentence by turning the question around, as in the following example.

Identify and discuss the monarchs of England who did the most to strengthen the throne during the eleventh and twelfth centuries.

Your topic sentence begins:

During the eleventh and twelfth centuries, the monarchs of England who did the most to strengthen the throne were. . . .

Then you might devote a paragraph to each of the monarchs you identified.

Develop your topic sentence. Once you have decided on a topic sentence, develop it as completely as time allows. If you have approximately twenty-five minutes to answer an essay question, you can be sure your professor expects more than a one-paragraph answer. The key to writing a good answer on an essay test is learning how to select the most important information and how to present it in a limited amount of time. Therefore, try to avoid long, rambling introductions. Get to the point.

Don't pad your answer. Remember that complete development does not mean padding an answer. *Padding* consists of wordiness, repetition, and irrelevant detail.

✓ You Can Write

By applying the principles of composition illustrated throughout this book, you can do the writing necessary for success in college. Furthermore, the same principles of organization used in writing the paragraph and short essay can serve you in writing on any subject at any length. The simple three-part organization of introduction, body, and conclusion can be adapted and expanded to suit various types of expository writing, including on-the-job writing of business and technical reports.

Your ability to write clearly will determine, to a greater extent than you may imagine, your chance of success in whatever career you choose. With the principles of organization and development firmly in mind, you can proceed confidently toward further developing your skill as a writer—a skill that can go a long way in determining your future.

chapter *10*

Persuading

PURPOSE OF PERSUASION

Persuasion is always with us, for better or worse, and it occurs in many variations. It can target an individual or a vast population. **To influence thought and action is the purpose of most persuasion.**

Examples of persuasion are everywhere. A car dealer emphasizes the needs that his product satisfies. A candidate for state senator travels around the state informing voters what her policies can do for them. The town council explains its conservative politics; the school board justifies its liberal policies.

Basically, **persuasion** is an attempt to convince, to motivate, and to gain agreement or assent. Persuasion is not just used by other people to influence you. You use persuasion every day: coaxing the baby to stop crying, explaining why your term paper isn't finished on time, convincing your boss that you deserve a raise, urging your friends to go to one movie instead of another.

TYPES OF PERSUASION

We are constantly bombarded by propaganda and advertising, the two most obvious forms of persuasion. Some is blatant, some subtle, some true, some false, some important, some trivial. We are the targets of individuals and groups all trying to influence our thoughts and our behavior, all trying to persuade us to think what they want us to think, to do what they want us to do.

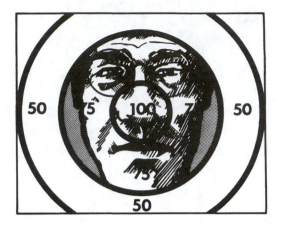

We are the targets.

Persuasion is not necessarily bad. *"Exercise!" "Protect the environment!" "Save the whales!"* Persuasion is not always used by powerful groups for their own benefit. When a mother says, *"Eat your vegetables," "Don't stay out too late,"* or *"Take an umbrella,"* it is not because she doesn't want to take out more garbage, or spend less on electricity, or get rid of an umbrella, it is because she cares deeply for the well-being of her children.

Advertising is not necessarily bad either, even though its purpose is to sell you something. Because of advertising, we can select from many choices. As a result, we can often get the highest quality products at the best prices. Advertising is also informative. For example, the front of a cereal box is intended to appeal, but the back of the box informs of its nutritional qualities.

Persuasion does not always bring immediate results. Sometimes you can persuade in a moment: "Let's go to McDonald's; it's cheaper and better." Sometimes attempts to persuade can take years: "Vote for me," "Become active in our group," "Change your life."

But persuasion is always with us. It is a process that affects most of our everyday decisions and actions, and it is a process that we use constantly and sometimes unconsciously. Because persuasion is so influential, and because it has both positive and negative aspects, it is important to learn not only how to use basic persuasive techniques but also to recognize some of the methods that others use to influence our thinking and behavior.

ORGANIZATION

In all of the writing you have done up to this point, you have had some restraints:

First, you were required to use one method of development for each assignment—narration, description, process, examples, classification, and definitions.

Second, you had to confine your writing to a single paragraph.

Well, graduation day has arrived! For your final assignment

1. You may select any single method of development
2. You may combine methods of development
3. You may write as many paragraphs as you need to make your point, using the *essay* format.

✓ Tips for Successful Persuasion

To be successful when convincing others, you must examine several variables as you plan your strategy. Here are a few points that experienced persuaders always consider before they write.

I. Know Your Purpose.

A. Know exactly why you want to persuade someone and the results that you want to achieve.

B. Use the strategy that will best achieve your purpose.

Casper wants his neighbor to stop spilling garbage in his driveway and to clean up the mess. How successful do you think this note to his careless neighbor will be?

Dear Neighbor:

Excuse me, I'm sorry to bother you, but I think that your garbage can has been spilled in my driveway for over a week. It sure looks like the can that has been sitting on your porch; it has your name painted on it, but I could still be mistaken. Maybe we could decide whose it is and what to do about it. I know it isn't mine though. I could even help you clean it up if you wanted me to. Again, I'm sorry to bother you about this because I don't want to be a nuisance. Please call if you want to talk to me about this. Thanks!

Your friend and neighbor,
Casper Milquetoast (next door)

After reading Casper's note, his irresponsible neighbor will probably have a good laugh and then forget about Casper's request. A simple, unapologetic phone call asking the neighbor to clean up the garbage and not to let it happen again would be a more effective first step. If the phone call was unsuccessful, what other persuasive options do you think Milquetoast should pursue?

II. **Know Your Reading Audience.**

Your reading audience is important in all writing, but it is especially important in persuasive writing. If you know certain characteristics of your reading audience, you can choose the most effective persuasive techniques for that audience.

A. Determine how much your readers know about your subject.

1. If they are knowledgeable, provide *less background* and *more new information.*

2. If they know little or nothing about your subject, provide the necessary background and clear examples to clarify complex concepts and issues.

You won't need to define "full court press" to a sports-minded audience, but you should define it for a general reading audience, which might include members who are not sports-oriented.

B. Knowing demographic information about your reading audience enables you to adapt your persuasive methods to that particular audience.

Demographic information includes *age, gender, educational level, ethnic,* and *racial background,* and *economic status.* For example, *obfuscation* might be the appropriate word to use if your readers are English majors, but the wrong word for a general reading audience.

C. Determine your readers' attitude toward your subject and your point of view.

1. If your readers are opposed, you must first gain their respect if you expect to persuade them.

a. Identify with your readers by establishing a common ground, something that you both can agree on.

For example, suppose you are attempting to persuade them that capital punishment is a necessary deterrent to crime, but you already know that they favor imprisonment and rehabilitation for all capital offenders. In this situation, make a point on which both you and your readers can agree: "The innocent citizen must somehow be protected from convicted murderers who might kill again." Once this *common ground* is recognized, your readers may be less hostile toward your argument.

b. Never insult or demean those who oppose your point of view. A rational approach and respect for your readers' intelligence give you a better chance for success. How effective is this method of persuasion?

Smoking is a rotten, dirty habit, and those of you who smoke are a menace to society. You have no business smoking either at home or in public places, endangering the health of innocent people and little children. Do you want to die of lung cancer or emphysema, and do you want it on your conscience that you have probably killed someone else as well? Smoking reflects poor breeding, questionable morals, and lack of intelligence. Anyone with half a brain knows that smoking kills. Because of your selfishness, our healthcare rates are skyrocketing. Your habit is not only harming you, but all of us, physically and economically, and we don't deserve it. If you who smoke won't clean up your acts, then someone will have to do it for you.

> How could you modify this approach to convince your smoking readers that you were sincerely interested in *their* welfare as well as that of the nonsmoker in our society?

2. If your readers are neutral
   a. try to interest them in your subject
   b. try to convince them that your viewpoint is the best
3. If they are already in agreement
   a. reinforce this agreement
   b. increase their enthusiasm
   c. motivate them to take action to support your argument

D. Never underestimate your readers' intelligence, yet be aware of their limitations.
   Everyone appreciates clear, simple language, but oversimplification can be insulting.

   1. A memo from the boss regarding changes in office procedure should not sound like the instructions you give your three-year-old son for keeping his room clean.

   but

   2. Persuading your new secretary, just out of school, to adopt different office procedures will not require the same degree of persuasion as convincing the secretary who has run the office for twenty years.

E. Adapt persuasive techniques to your readers.
   Try to determine which kind of convincing will work best on your reader.

   1. For example, a soft subtle touch is obviously the best approach for asking Aunt Matilda to sit with the kids, dog, cat, canary, and

fish while you and your spouse escape for a second honeymoon in the mountains.

but

2. Stronger language may be needed to motivate the local dealer to complete warranty repairs on your new car, which is falling apart after four months of normal use. Threats to call the manufacturer and the Better Business Bureau may be the only way to get results.

III. **Know Your Subject.**

To persuade effectively, you should know the issues and the situation that form the subject of your argument.

A. Learn as much as you can about the subject that you will discuss. Lack of knowledge can weaken or destroy your efforts to convince. How quickly do you think the mayor will react to this citizen's plea, which contains no specific information—just vague assumptions with no factual basis?

Mr. Mayor, we are here to complain about the great increase of crime on our street. We are all concerned for the safety of our families and homes, and we hope you can do something about it. Obviously, the whole problem is caused by the kids in the gangs who are pushing drugs. It just isn't safe to walk the streets anymore, and our kids are afraid to go out to play. We have heard a rumor that you were decreasing patrols in our area, but surely there must be enough money in the budget to find us some kind of protection. We also think that too many offenders are getting off on suspended sentences. Something must be done because we have had lots of muggings and shootings in the last year or so. All kinds of terrible things have been going on for a long time.

Instead, wouldn't the following letter containing specifics be much more informative and thus more persuasive?

Mr. Mayor, as spokesperson for the citizens' committee of Quaker Street, I am here to ask your help in making our neighborhood safe. In the past month, we have had fifteen burglaries, seven muggings, six knifings, and two fatal shootings. Incidents of harassment are too numerous to mention; I am speaking here only of the crimes that were reported. Our senior citizens are afraid to leave their homes. Our women and children feel intimidated whenever they step outside, day or night. Much of the problem is the lack of police patrols. Groups of teenage boys and young men who are not from the neighborhood gather on corners or on lawns. They make remarks to or about passersby, especially adolescent girls and younger women. They drink beer and play their radios at top volume far into the night, and they are, by their very presence, threatening. They gather here because there are no police patrols. When a seldom-seen patrolman walks the streets and the occasional police car drives through the area, they move on. We want your help, Mr. Mayor.

I would like to take you down to the street this week to see for yourself the problems of your neighbors on Quaker Street. Please respond to this letter at your earliest convenience, or call me at home after six.

B. Reinforce knowledge with confidence.
   Confidence, combined with knowledge, is a key ingredient in the art of persuasion. Compare the following two appeals, and decide which is more effective. Explain why.

   1. I think we need to ask the police for more protection on our street. It seems that there has been a lot of crime around here lately, and this is a very bad situation, isn't it? Maybe some of you have some ideas that might work and wouldn't upset anyone.

   2. During the last three months, we have had five muggings, one auto theft, and two burglaries on our street. Police protection has been inadequate, and the promise of increased patrols has not been kept. I propose that tonight we form a citizens' committee to attend the next council meeting to demand the protection that our tax money has already paid for.

C. Arrogance alienates.
   Avoid giving the impression that you know everything or are overly impressed with your own importance. This can either insult the reader or bore him to death. For example, how would you react to this person's statement?

   Let *me* speak personally to Ralph Jones, our mayor and a close personal friend, about the crime on our street. *I* can do more good alone because *I* know how to communicate with public officials. Having fourteen months in the military police and six credits in psychology, *I* know that *my* feel for the dynamics of the situation will be much more useful since the rest of you may not fully understand a complex social problem such as this. *I* will let *you* know what is going to happen as soon as Ralph and *I* work out the details with Chief Hawkins whom *I* played football with in high school.

ASSIGNMENT

Your assignment in this chapter is to write a persuasive essay using factual library sources to support your controlling idea. Try one of the following:

1. Convince your readers that your stand on an issue is the correct and logical one.
2. Convince your readers to agree with you and take action on an issue.

THESIS STATEMENT AND INTRODUCTION

1. Choose an issue that you feel strongly about and state your position in a clearly worded thesis statement.
2. You may introduce your thesis and expand on it in an introductory paragraph that does any of the following:
   a. Captures your reader's attention.
   b. Provides background information.
   c. Establishes a common ground or point of mutual assent.

BODY

1. Select your persuasive details based on *your* knowledge of
   a. *The Subject*
      (1) Its relevance and importance
      (2) The views or arguments of your opponents
   b. *Your Readers*
      (1) Their level of sophistication
      (2) Their knowledge of the subject
      (3) Their views on the subject (pro, neutral, con)
2. Use facts that you have researched—not judgments and generalities to support your thesis. **Note:** Your thesis can be an opinion, but *facts* will give it credibility.
3. Avoid extremes of tone and language that are

   a. overly sentimental   c. insulting
   b. overly emotional   d. hateful or spiteful

4. Avoid using fallacies (false notions based on mistakes in logic or perception).

CONCLUSION

1. Write a brief concluding paragraph that
   a. Sums up your argument.
   b. Makes a plea for action/involvement.

Persuade someone to share your point of view on either side of one of the following controversial issues. Choose an issue about which you have strong feelings. You can assume that your reader is a rational, intelligent person who is either uncommitted or slightly opposed to your point of view. This means that you have a good chance of success *if* your essay is effective.

United Nations peacekeeping   High salaries in sports, TV, business
Censorship for pornography   Income tax reform
Gun control   Prenuptial agreements
Curfews for teenagers   Terrorism as diplomacy
Police and the use of deadly force   Teenage gangs
Legalization of marijuana   Nuclear power
   and/or cocaine   The need for space exploration

A lowered (or raised) drinking age

School vouchers

Abortion

Smokers'/Nonsmokers' rights

Mandatory crash helmets for cyclists,
seat belts and/or air bags for motorists

Legalized gambling

U.S. as world peacekeeper

Sex education/prayer in public schools

Capital punishment/mandatory
sentencing

Euthanasia

Gay rights

Rights of illegal aliens

Foreign- versus American-made automobiles

Exploiting college athletes

Government perks

Sexual harassment

Child abuse

Cloning

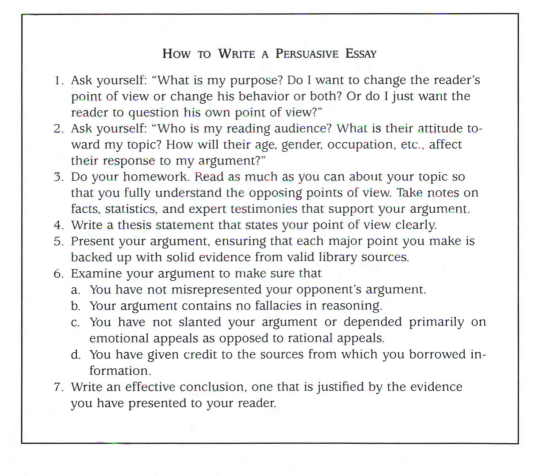

How to Write a Persuasive Essay

1. Ask yourself: "What is my purpose? Do I want to change the reader's point of view or change his behavior or both? Or do I just want the reader to question his own point of view?"
2. Ask yourself: "Who is my reading audience? What is their attitude toward my topic? How will their age, gender, occupation, etc., affect their response to my argument?"
3. Do your homework. Read as much as you can about your topic so that you fully understand the opposing points of view. Take notes on facts, statistics, and expert testimonies that support your argument.
4. Write a thesis statement that states your point of view clearly.
5. Present your argument, ensuring that each major point you make is backed up with solid evidence from valid library sources.
6. Examine your argument to make sure that
   a. You have not misrepresented your opponent's argument.
   b. Your argument contains no fallacies in reasoning.
   c. You have not slanted your argument or depended primarily on emotional appeals as opposed to rational appeals.
   d. You have given credit to the sources from which you borrowed information.
7. Write an effective conclusion, one that is justified by the evidence you have presented to your reader.

When writing your essay, you may use any combination of methods of paragraph development that you have studied in this book. Remember to limit or narrow your controlling idea to a point of view that can be adequately supported. Do not make your topic too general, too broad, or too difficult to prove. Finally, be sure to proofread your essay carefully. Examine your reasoning and strengthen any weak links that you might find.

Consider the following examples:

Babe Ruth was the best baseball player who ever lived.

This would involve comparing Babe with other baseball players of every position. Was he better than Ty Cobb? Grover Cleveland Alexander? Roberto Clemente? Hank Aaron? Can you prove it? Impossible!

Babe Ruth was the best athlete ever.

Again, impossible. How can you prove that a baseball player is better than a boxer or a runner or a swimmer? You can't! The judgment is too broad.

Babe Ruth was a great man.

Again, this is too broad. There are too many aspects of a "man" to be proved. Narrow your controlling idea until you have provable judgment, such as "Babe Ruth was a great baseball player." Only then will you be able to convince your readers with facts such as these:

Babe Ruth: Hit sixty home runs in one year—never surpassed until the season was lengthened.
Hit 714 home runs in his career.
Got 2,056 bases on balls.
Called his shot, a home run, in the 1932 World Series.
Earned $2,000 a week in 1932—considerably more than the President of the United States.
Pitched eight times against Walter Johnson and won six of the games, three by scores of 1–0.
Pitched twenty-nine scoreless innings in World Series competition—a record that still stands.
Led the American League in homers nine out of ten years.

✓ Research

"BORROWING" FACTS FROM LIBRARY SOURCES. Among the best sources of factual information are the writings of men and women who have studied extensively and have become recognized authorities in their respective areas of knowledge. Other factual information can be found in the bulletins, surveys, and reports compiled by government and private agencies. Still more facts are contained in encyclopedias, newspapers, magazines, and journals and in the staggering number of reference works found on the shelves of libraries.

Because of the wealth of information available, you should have no trouble finding enough supporting material for your essay. Seeking and gathering this information is a process called *research,* and the best place to begin is your school library.

1. Once you have chosen your topic, use the library computer to help you locate material on that topic.
2. If your library does not use a computer-locater system, look up your topic in the subject index of the library card catalog, and copy down the titles and authors of books related to that subject. (Don't forget to copy the call number for each source so that you can find the book on the shelf.)
3. You can also look up your subject in an index called the *Reader's Guide to Periodical Literature,* which lists magazines, past and present, that contain articles pertaining to your topic. These sources of facts should provide a starting point for your search. There are, however, additional places to look, and the *reference librarian* can guide you to them.

PLAGIARISM.   Let us now assume that you have located several sources of factual information and would like to copy some facts onto note cards so that you can later incorporate them into your essay. Are you allowed to

Plagiarism doesn't pay.

"borrow" these facts for your own use? Absolutely—but with proper *documentation*—giving credit to the person or persons from whom you borrowed them.

The guidelines for borrowing library information are as follows:

1. You may borrow the opinions and research of others if you wish.
2. You should never alter or distort the borrowed material in order to make it say something other than that which its author originally intended.
3. You must give credit in your essay to anyone from whom you have borrowed information.

Facts that you have borrowed from library sources must be acknowledged in a notation—either in the text of your essay (in text) or at the end of your essay (in endnotes). Ask your instructor which method he or she prefers, or refer to the latest edition of the *MLA Handbook for Writers of Research Papers.*

Schools think of themselves as communities of learners. This common interest in learning means that there is an intense wish to *share* learning, and such sharing is ruled by a few laws that must be obeyed. *To violate these rules is to plagiarize—to present someone else's learning as your own.* This is the ultimate sin in academic life.

There are two ways to incorporate the thoughts of others into your own work:

1. Quoting Verbatim.   You can *quote them* directly, word for word, and place quotation marks around the quotation to show that you have made no changes in the original wording.

   The Edwardian Age was "the period in English literature between the death of Victoria in 1901 and the beginning of the first World War in 1914, so-called after King Edward VII, who ruled from 1901 to 1910."

2. Paraphrasing.   Instead of quoting directly, you may *paraphrase,* putting the author's thoughts into your own language and style. This involves completely rewriting the original material, not just changing a word or two. Also, when paraphrasing, you must *not* change the intent or the opinions of the original source. Finally, when paraphrasing, you do *not* use quotation marks. Note the difference between the direct quotation above and the paraphrase of the same material.

   The Edwardian Age, named after King Edward VII, is the period in English literature extending from the death of Queen Victoria in 1901 to the outbreak of World War I in 1914.

Remember: Whether you choose to quote verbatim or paraphrase, you are *still* using borrowed material and *must* give credit to the source of that information.

DOCUMENTATION—GIVING CREDIT TO YOUR SOURCES

Informal Documentation.   In a single paragraph or short essay, your instructor may allow you to give credit to your source *informally* within the text. Here are several ways of acknowledging your sources within the paragraph or essay.

1. According to *Handbook to Literature* (Holman 1972, 190) the "Edwardian Age" is the name given to . . .
2. According to C. Hugh Holman's *Handbook to Literature,* 3rd ed. (180), the "Edwardian Age" is the name given to . . .
3. For example, the December 1989, *Popular Mechanics* explains how the owner and restorer of an old house may be able to list it on the "National Register of Historic Places." (36)
4. During his October 1997, White House press conference, President Clinton made the following remarks about international terrorism: ". . ."
5. In her article, "An Executive's Guide to Volunteering" (*Working Woman,* December 1989, 86) Pamela Kruger advises, ". . ."
6. In "Distance Casting" (*Field & Stream,* December 1989, 82), Ken Schultz stresses that a long cast does not necessarily make one a better fisherman.

Note: When documenting your sources, remember to underline or italicize book and magazine titles. Put quotation marks around the titles of articles or chapters.

Here are some excerpts from an essay that attempts to show that athletes are treated differently from other people. The author used *informal* documentation.

> Athletes receive preferential treatment in all phases of their lives. The following paragraph from *Necessary Roughness* shows exactly what I mean by "treated differently." (Mike Trope and Steve Delsohn. *Necessary Roughness.* Chicago: Contemporary Books, Inc., 1987)

> "People do things for athletes that they don't do for others. When an athlete needs some credit, even if his finances are in a shambles, he walks into a bank and gets it. Best table in a crowded restaurant? No problem. You can't make that appearance you promised you would? It's okay, we understand you're busy. To you and me, people say no, make us suffer the consequences of our behavior. Not athletes. Until they retire, 'no' isn't a word they hear much." (24)

> In a feature article, "Why Sports Heroes Abuse their Wives," in the September, 1995, issue of *Redbook,* author Joan Ryan says of a sports hero, "Adored and accommodated most of his life, he believes he can have whatever he wants, whenever he wants it—and he may lose his temper if his wife confronts him. . . ." David Meggyesy, former linebacker for the St. Louis Cardinals, says, in the same article, "If a person at a fair young age is identified as

special, as many athletes are, and there are no consequences of living outside the rule structure—in other words, 'The rules don't apply to me'—then it's fairly predictable there will be problems. . . ." (85)

Another section of the student's paper gave examples of the preferential treatment given athletes by the justice system.

"Darryl Strawberry broke his wife's nose in a fight and was arrested for waving a .25-caliber semi-automatic revolver in her face. Later, he was arrested for hitting his live-in girlfriend. Strawberry wasn't charged." (*Redbook*, 84)

The article "Fiesta Brawl," *Time* 8 Jan. 1996, reported that although Nebraska's star running back Lawrence Phillips was arrested for assaulting his exgirlfriend, he was allowed to play in the championship game. Some people even treated *him* as the victim. "I don't think people will ever look at me the same," whined Phillips at a news conference. His teammate, center Aaron Graham, felt Phillips had to pay too great a price, it seems. He said, "It cost the guy a million bucks [in future endorsements] . . . it cost him kids coming up and asking for autographs." (51)

And another quotation from the same article, ". . . in the past three years alone, . . . Nebraska has housed six players who have faced charges for crimes ranging from sexual assault to attempted second-degree murder. None of them has served time in jail." (*Time*, 51)

The essay goes on with example after example of athletes committing, but not being punished for, crimes. Here are a few more, all documented by the informal method.

William Nack and Lester Munson give some examples of sports heroes and the law. ("Sports Dirty Secrets," *Sports Illustrated*, 31 Jul. 1995) Their conclusion, "Whether stopped for speeding or arrested for battering a woman, the athlete encounters a legal system in which the scales are tipped in his favor." (70)

To support this claim, the student used the following excerpts from magazines.

"Barry Bonds petitioned a San Mateo Superior Court judge to have his family support payments cut in half—from $15,000 to $7500 a month because of the baseball strike. The judge granted the reduction, then asked Barry for his autograph. Barry, at that time was baseball's highest paid outfielder, making 4.75 million a year. He had already been paid about three million." (Joan Ryan "Why Sports Heroes Abuse Their Wives," *Redbook*. Sep. 95: 130)

From the article "Sports Dirty Secrets" (*Sports Illustrated*, 31 Jul. 1995), authors Nack and Munson report on how the vocabulary of abuse changes if the perpetrator is an athlete. "A *neck-wringing* was minimized as a *domestic dis-*

pute. An *assault* was masqueraded as an *argument*. A crime is perceived and treated like no other in America, especially, it seems, when it is committed by an athlete." (66)

Here are examples of factual essays using in-text documentation that refers to a *works cited list* at the end of the essay. *Works cited lists* are usually required for term papers. Your instructor will tell you if he or she wants a works cited list with your persuasive essay. The first essay is informative; the second is persuasive.

There are three qualities about the cemeteries in New Orleans that I found fascinating: their unusual appearance, their vital origin, and their unique burial methods. New Orleans has practiced the present above-ground burial system since 1827. The appearance of these cemeteries suggests narrow residences with peaked roofs ranged along side streets. They are often referred to as cities within a city or "cities of the dead." (Kane, 296) The tombs are often built of brick, then plastered or stuccoed to preserve the masonry. Some of the more expensive tombs are made of granite or marble, and most of the tombs are surrounded by iron gates or metal chains. Often, iron benches or chairs are arranged in front of the tombs as if the residents within are awaiting the arrival of guests. Some of the more expensive tombs have statues of trumpeting angels, marble girls in Grecian robes, Egyptian figures of men and animals, or Corinthian motifs. (Kane, 296) The walls surrounding the cemeteries are six-foot brick walls with the "oven tombs," or vaults, built in. They look somewhat like filing cabinets arranged in two or three tiers. The poor can rent these vaults for a few dollars a month; however, if they fail to pay the rent, the casket is removed, and the remains and the casket are burned. (Kane, 299)

There are two reasons why the above-ground tombs came into existence. In the late 1700s, New Orleans buried the rich in chapels or cathedrals. The poor were buried along the riverbank in low swampy sites surrounded by ditches; the bodies were simply wrapped in shrouds or placed in cheap wooden caskets and dropped into the earth. (Huber, 118) Since the water level was only two feet below ground surface, the water would pour into the gravesites as fast as the holes were being dug. Sometimes, holes had to be bored into the wooden caskets, and men would have to stand on them to force them to settle into the swampy earth. The bodies were then literally devoured by crayfish and catfish. (Cable, 126) Since the bodies disintegrated so quickly, it was possible for the gravesites to be used repeatedly. Because of the cholera and yellow fever epidemics in the early 1800s, the cathedrals and churches became overcrowded. In 1827, city officials made it mandatory that all burials be above ground, and this rule initiated the burial practices that prevail in New Orleans today.

The uniqueness of these cemeteries really lies in the tombs themselves. One tomb may contain as many as forty to fifty relatives spanning ten generations. It is possible for a tomb to hold this many bodies because, after a year and a day, the tombs can be reopened. The remains are then removed from the casket and deposited into a lower vault beneath or are pushed to the back; the caskets are then burned. The dust and bones of all the prior burials are mingled together, and this fact accounts for the many inscriptions on the front of the tombs. It may sound a little grim, but it works. If another relative dies before the year and a day has expired, the family can rent an "oven tomb" temporarily. (Kolb, 71–2)

Above-ground burial has solved both the problems of the water-filled graves and those of the overcrowded churches and cathedrals. This method of burial may seem a little odd to us, but to the people of New Orleans, it is practical and essential.

Linda Welsh

Works Cited

Cable, Mary. *Lost New Orleans.* Boston: Houghton Mifflin, 1980.

Huber, Leonard V. *New Orleans, A Pictorial History.* New York: Crown Publishers, 1971.

Kane, Harnett T. *Queen New Orleans, City by the River.* New York: Bonanza Books, 1978.

The right to die without pain or use of life-prolonging equipment is a fundamental right of every living person. It is a right acknowledged by the medical profession, terminally ill patients and their families, and the many right-to-die organizations. While most people assume that when it is their time to die they will pass away peacefully, the reality is that the last days of life for most terminally ill patients are often filled with pain and suffering as doctors needlessly prolong their deaths, seemingly oblivious to their wishes. According to a recent twenty-eight million dollar study of almost five thousand seriously ill patients, half of the patients who died were in moderate to severe pain, and thirty-eight percent spent more than ten days in intensive care, where the average cost of treatment of a patient who dies is nearly one hundred thousand dollars. Of the thirty-one percent of patients who did not wish to be resuscitated, fewer than half of their doctors knew of their wishes. (Study) It seems senseless and cruel to continue life-saving treatments that cause unnecessary suffering, both physically and financially, for the patient and his family, when the treatments do not benefit the patient anyway.

The failure of the medical profession to fulfill the patient's last wishes can be attributed to various reasons. Many patients and their families are not willing to discuss end-of-life issues with their physician, and many physicians are not acknowledging that their patients are dying. (Study) Fear of lawsuits is another reason many physicians will opt to use all available means to prolong the patient's life. The perception is that doctors risk more if they do not put a patient on life support, but the reality is that more physicians are sued by the families of patients who died when doctors did too much. (Terminally) Finally, the responsibility of whether to allow life-producing procedures may ultimately rest on the shoulders of the patient's closest relative, who may not know the patient's wishes or who can not make a rational decision because of the heavy burden of guilt associated with it.

There are several things that can be done to facilitate fulfillment of a dying patient's wishes. First, a living will can be drawn up stating exactly what procedures are to be followed when the patient is dying. Several options of care include: total life support, which includes intensive care unit admission, cardiopulmonary resuscitation (CPR), artificial respiration, and dialysis; limited life support, which includes all of the treatments described in the total support category with the exception of CPR; and no extraordinary measures, in which only comfort measures are given, such as morphine for pain. (Terminally) Living wills do not always ensure that the patient will get the care that he requests, though, because some are too vague to be useful. A better method would be to make it a standard procedure to ask patients at the admitting desk if they have any advance directives, or if they do not then who should be the one to make any decisions if the patient is unable to participate. (Terminally) Finally, frank discussions between the patient and his physician ahead of time to decide which interventions the patient does or does not want implemented can be very beneficial if the patient is willing and able to discuss such things. Physicians must start taking the initiative and realizing that decisions about death are an important part of a patient's care plan and the last thing that the terminally ill patient has control of.

In conclusion, terminally ill patients should be able to end their lives the way that they wish. Decisions about life support and resuscitation should be up to them and life should not be prolonged if the patient is going to die nonetheless. Changes must be made within the healthcare system to make certain that every terminally ill patient can die as quickly and painfree as possible. Ultimately, society as a whole must take a more creative and willing approach to end-of-life decision making, for we all have to face these hard decisions one day, either with our own deaths or those of our loved ones.

Mary Hobbs

Works Cited

"Study: Patients' Deaths Prolonged." *Beaver County Times* 23 Nov. 1995: C2.

"Terminally Ill Put Wishes for Treatment in Writing." *Pittsburgh Press* 11 Jun. 1990: A5.

THE PERSUASIVE ESSAY

✓ Thesis Statement and Introduction

A thesis statement, like the topic sentence, should capture the readers' attention and interest so they will want to read everything that you have to say.

1. Limit your topic to a single area or issue of discussion. Consider the following sentences, all of which introduce a specific subject that requires persuasive supporting details:

> The BMW is superior to the Harley because it vibrates less, handles more precisely, and has a stronger drive train.
>
> By giving just $25.00 a month, you will ensure that a needy third world child has the food, clothes, and medical care that his or her family cannot provide.
>
> This office can no longer function effectively because we have only one secretary to support twenty-five people.
>
> Strap on the 380 Vulcan twelve, with six on the floor, command module cockpit, antiquagmire all-wheel traction in three ranges, dual celestial roof ports, and hypersonic load compensators.
>
> Marry me—you know that I'm the only one who understands you.

2. Include your thesis statement in a brief paragraph that introduces your controlling idea to the readers. It should contain

A. A clear statement of subject and/or issue
B. Any necessary background information
C. Your attitudes toward the subject/issue
D. An attempt to identify with your readers

✓ Body

The support for the attitude of your thesis statement is the most important part of your persuasive essay:

1. Have a clear purpose.
2. Know your subject.
3. Use facts and logic for support—not opinions. For example, note how George tries to persuade Sam to agree with him about the "three strikes and you're out" law.

> Sam: Wow, the new three criminal convictions and you're in jail for life is great.
>
> George: I don't think so; it would be too expensive.

> Sam: No. What's too expensive if you can walk the streets in safety?
>
> George: I don't think it's necessary to keep someone in prison for life to keep the streets safe.
>
> Sam: You want to let career criminals out to commit more crimes? You haven't convinced me. I'm all for life sentences for three-time losers.

Sam is right! George really has not said anything substantial. All George has done is pile one unsupported opinion on top of another.

But what if George had used one or two facts to support his argument?

> George: Sam, do you realize it costs $35,000 to $45,000 per year to keep one inmate behind bars? Building the 25,000 new cells to house the "lifers" would cost 2.5 billion!

George has just supplied facts about the expense that Sam cannot dispute and probably didn't even realize.

> George: Also, I think the money could be better spent on things we need rather than housing sixty- and seventy-years-olds who are no longer a threat to society. According to Philip B. Heymann, a former deputy attorney general, "The vast majority of 'street violence' is committed by robbers who grow out of the occupation at a relatively early age."

Here George has presented a logical argument supported by quoting an authority on crime. Thus George continues to build his case, and you can do the same—by using facts to reinforce or provide validity for your opinions, beliefs, and recommendations.

Once your readers get the facts, they are more likely to be convinced that you know what you are talking about. In the 1950s, when the popular police series *Dragnet* was first on TV, viewers loved to imitate Detective Sergeant Joe Friday, who, at some point during each program, would intone, "All I want is the facts, ma'am—just the facts." Once Sergeant Friday got the facts, he *always* solved the case.

Facts can be used effectively to strengthen any written presentation by *informing* (presenting actual details that prove, explain, clarify, or simply provide additional knowledge about a subject), or *persuading* (convincing someone to accept your point of view on a particular issue). Whatever your purpose, however, the skillful use of facts to support and strengthen your controlling idea will greatly improve the possibility that your reader will accept what you have to say.

> *What is a fact?* A fact is a piece of information that has been or can be verified (proved to be true).

How is a fact used in an informative or persuasive essay? A writer whose purpose is to inform or to persuade can select key details (facts) to support his controlling idea.

Why is it important to use facts whenever possible? A fact provides correct information to readers. Once careful readers see that you are using solid facts to support your controlling idea, they will be more willing to accept what you have to say.

Where decisions are being made, in business, in government, or in the military, reliable, convincing facts must support any proposal. Any statistics in support of facts that you present must be correct; they should clarify, not confuse. As you select facts for the body of your essay, apply these common-sense tests:

1. Have sufficient facts to support your controlling idea fully.
2. Have relevant facts that relate directly to your purpose. A fact that distracts won't convince, but a specific, relevant fact helps your reader focus on your subject.
3. Have interesting facts that will hold your readers' attention. Persuasion and boredom are incompatible.

✓ The Difference Between Fact and Judgment

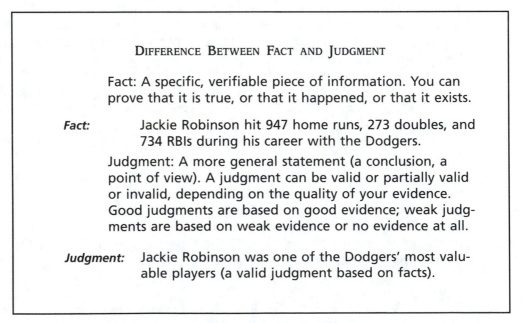

DIFFERENCE BETWEEN FACT AND JUDGMENT

Fact: A specific, verifiable piece of information. You can prove that it is true, or that it happened, or that it exists.

Fact: Jackie Robinson hit 947 home runs, 273 doubles, and 734 RBIs during his career with the Dodgers.

Judgment: A more general statement (a conclusion, a point of view). A judgment can be valid or partially valid or invalid, depending on the quality of your evidence. Good judgments are based on good evidence; weak judgments are based on weak evidence or no evidence at all.

Judgment: Jackie Robinson was one of the Dodgers' most valuable players (a valid judgment based on facts).

A **fact** is something done, a reality that can be verified.

> "When John became a father, he stayed home every weekend for three months to babysit."

> "During John's first six weeks as a father, he arose at five o'clock every morning."

Why are these facts? Because they can be verified.

A **judgment** is an assertion, opinion, judgment, belief, or a conclusion.

> "John's life changed drastically when he became a father."

Why is this only an opinion or a conclusion? Because this statement cannot be verified without factual support. ***Remember:*** Your opinions and conclusions about an issue are more respected if you support them with facts.

Here are some examples of the differences between facts and judgments.

Fact: Sherry wine is produced in both California and New York.
(An encyclopedia or a reliable handbook on wines can prove that this is true.)

Judgment: The *best* sherry wine is produced in New York State.
(There may be differences of opinion on this preference.)

Fact: Frank demolished three cars last year.
(Read the insurance reports.)

Judgment: Frank is a *reckless* driver.
(Was it his fault?)

Fact: In addition to providing the B complex vitamins, spinach is also a source of vitamin A and vitamin C.
(Research proves this.)

Judgment: Spinach is *good* for you.
(Is it good for everyone?)

Fact: I got an A on my last psychology test.
(Check the teacher's grade book.)

Judgment: My last psychology test was *easy.*
(Does everyone else who took it agree with this?)

Notice how the words *best, reckless, good,* and *easy* imply judgment on the part of the writer, whereas a sentence such as "Sherry wine is produced in both California and New York" reveals no particular feeling—just information.

It is perfectly all right for your controlling idea to be a general statement, a judgment, or an opinion. The facts that you use to support it are what convinces the reader to accept or believe it.

EXERCISE 10A: DISTINGUISHING BETWEEN FACT, JUDGMENT, AND GENERALIZATIONS

Examine the following statements carefully to decide which are facts and which are judgments or generalizations. On the blank before each statement, indicate your opinion by an F, a G, or a J.

_____ 1. Mystery stories are the most popular type of fiction in the United States.

_____ 2. There is no one who doesn't love a good mystery.

_____ 3. The Gotham City Library Association reports that mystery books are checked out even more frequently than romances.

_____ 4. Probably that's because men don't like romances.

_____ 5. Only women are interested in romance.

_____ 6. Men only like police procedurals, the stories in which the cops have all the brains.

_____ 7. The reference work *Books in Print* lists more books about Sherlock Holmes than any other mystery writer.

_____ 8. Some of the other great detectives of fiction are Hercule Poirot, Miss Marple, and Morse, who never uses his first name.

_____ 9. Most of the great fictional detectives have only a vague shadow of romance in their lives.

_____ 10. On the other hand, heroes of spy stories really should be called undercovers, not undercover, agents.

✓ Using Facts to Prove, Explain, or Clarify When Informing or Persuading

Most generalizations are far more convincing if facts are used. For example, one student decided to write her essay on the connection between domestic violence and the violence taught in sports. Having herself been abused by her amateur athlete husband and having noted the number of professional athletes accused and convicted of beating their wives and girlfriends, she felt that her thesis could be supported. She also realized that facts would convince her readers better than generalities.

Television, newspapers, and magazines provided her with many examples of such abuse. Few people can forget seeing, during the murder trial of O. J. Simpson, the battered face of his wife, Nicole, and hearing her crying for help from the 911 operator. The student put this in her paper. She also used the following examples in her persuasive essay:

> Many people remember the arrest and trial of Lawrence Phillips, star running back of Nebraska's 1996 championship team. Phillips "burst into a former girlfriend's room at 4:30 A.M., knocked her to the floor, dragged her down three flights of stairs, and slammed her head into a mailbox." ("Fiesta Brawl" *Time* 8 Jan. 1996: 51)

> On August 25, 1993, in Atherton, California, 911 received a call from the wife of Barry Bonds, a San Francisco Giant baseball star. After an argument, Mrs. Bonds had fled into the driveway of the Bonds' home. Barry caught up with her and "pushed her against [the car] and then grabbed her by the neck . . . threw her to the ground and kicked her. . . ." (Joan Ryan, "Why Sports Heroes Abuse Their Wives," *Redbook,* Sept. 1995: 95)

> Even Warren Moon, "anointed the NFL's Man of the Year in 1989 . . . admitted he had 'lost control' and made a 'tremendous mistake' after an assault on Felicia Moon, his wife of fourteen years." One of his children had called the police. ("Sport's Dirty Secrets" *Sports Illustrated,* 31 Jul. 1995: 62)

✓ Using Statistics—Numerical Facts—to Inform and Persuade

When the student writer decided that she needed information on men like her abusive husband, she set out to get evidence on former amateur athletes, not the celebrity athletes featured on TV and in magazines. To get this evidence, and thus add interest to the paper, the student sent out her own questionnaires to women who had spent time in women's shelters. After multiple mailings (many women were reluctant to admit there was a problem in their marriage, let alone that their husbands were abusers), she finally received 100 questionnaires to work with. She charted in simple bar graphs the yes or no answers to her questions.

The 100 Questionnaires

Does your abuser push to win at everything, even a card game?
Yes 85%

Does he ever get violent during a game in which he is playing?
Yes 91%

Does he ever abuse you during a sports broadcast on television?
Yes 62%

Did he ever abuse your children during or after a game?
Yes 71%

Did he ever abuse you during or after playing a game?   Yes 66%

Do you think sports is the reason for your abuser's aggressive behavior?   Yes 70%

Do you think his violence stems from his training in sports?
Yes 87%

The survey was a local one and could not be used to show national tendencies, but it was certainly more convincing than saying, "Many women are abused by men who have participated in sports."

The following short paragraphs also illustrate how statistics can inform and persuade:

> The increasing number of women's shelters appearing in cities and small towns across the country is a reflection of the increasing level of domestic violence in America. Statistics show that domestic violence is the single largest cause of injury to women, affecting the lives of three to four million women a year. According to emergency room figures, almost half of all the injuries sustained by women in the U.S. occur in the context of abuse. In fact, the nation's police spend one-third of their time responding to domestic calls; an incident of domestic violence is reported somewhere in this country every fifteen seconds. One of the most common forms of domestic violence in America is wife battering: two thousand to four thousand women are beaten to death annually, and four out of five of these murders are committed in the home. Statistics such as these help explain why there are currently over twelve hundred shelters nationwide available for victims of domestic violence.

> Women's Shelter of Greater Pittsburgh

You should learn to read and learn to read well, not only for the pleasure it will give you but also for the monetary rewards it will give you. According to an article by Carl Sagan and Ann Druyan, the best readers get the highest salaries.

> Only 4% of those at the highest reading level are in poverty, but 43% of those at the lowest reading level are. Although it's not the only factor, of course, the better you can read, in general the more you make—an average of about $240 a week at the lowest reading level, about $650 a week at the highest reading level. And you are much more likely to be in prison if you're illiterate or barely literate.

> "Literacy—The Path to a More Prosperous,
> Less Dangerous America," *Parade*

✓ Using Interviews—The Experience and/or Expertise of Others—to Inform and Persuade

In addition to using TV, magazines, newspapers, and questionnaires as sources, the student who wrote on the correlation between sports and domestic violence decided to interview some of the women who had answered her questionnaires. From these interviews, she got *specific* and *startling* answers.

Although fewer than 40% of the women reported that their husbands still talked about their coaches, others quoted verbatim what their coaches had said years before:

> In one such interview, an ex-athlete's coach told him if he didn't break his opponent's leg, he would sit out for three games. He broke the man's leg and was so proud of doing it that he told the story over and over again—and was still telling it. (Carol H. Personal interview. Beaver County Women's Center, 4 Apr. 1997)

> Another wife reported her husband's coach telling him, "If you ____ up, your ass is mine for the rest of your life." (Peg S. Personal interview. Beaver County Women's Center, 5 Apr. 1997)

> Sometimes the coaches use threats. "I'll remember your name, and don't forget someday you'll have kids on this team, too." (Fran R. Personal interview. Beaver County Women's Center, 30 Mar. 1997)

For the question "What is the most violent thing your husband ever did while watching a game?", some of the more interesting answers follow:

> My husband jumped up and stepped on the cat and broke its neck. He just pushed the cat aside until the game was over. When the kids found out, he told them the cat was hit by a car.

> He threw a bowl of potato chips across the room and said he would break my arm if they weren't cleaned up by the next quarter. I wasn't allowed to use the vacuum cleaner because it made too much noise. He threw me against a plate glass window, and I went through it and had to go to the hospital.

> He threw a beer can at my son because he walked in front of the TV and made him miss a play. My son needed six stitches, but he would not take us to the hospital until the game was over. My son had to apologize for walking in front of the TV.

In preparing for your research essay, you need not rely on library sources alone. For some subjects you can look for sources elsewhere. *Be creative.*

✓ Specific Facts Are Always More Convincing than a Series of Judgments

It's easy for the reader to disagree with your opinions if they are not supported with facts, but if you back up your judgments with factual details, your reader will find it more difficult to argue with you.

On a sociology examination, a student was asked to prove that primitive cultures suffer when they come into contact with advanced civilizations.

> It's really tough on a primitive culture when an advanced culture moves in. The primitives can't do things their own way anymore, and they get troubled and sick and they die off. This has happened many times and in many places around the world.

The student's answer is true; however, you can't be sure that it is true because the writer has not given you any facts as verification. He uses general and nonspecific terms. You would be surprised to find a paragraph like that in your sociology textbook—and your sociology professor would be disappointed to find that paragraph on your test.

Consider the following paragraph as an answer to the essay question.

> Contact with an advanced civilization has virtually destroyed some primitive cultures and peoples. When the British came to Melanesia, they abolished headhunting, a major aspect of the Melanesian culture. Because of this, the Melanesians lost interest in living. On one island, the number of childless marriages increased from 19% to 46%, on another from 12% to 72%. Also, in the early 1900's, the Australians began migrating from their coastal cities into the interior of the continent. As a result, the aborigines, who had lived there for centuries, disappeared because of the encroachment on their tribal homelands. Also, the native population of Tahiti was decimated by diseases which their immune systems could not withstand after the arrival of de Tocqueville and the French explorers. Our own American Indian population dropped from an estimated 200,000 to less than 30,000 during the 1800's when the white man's westward movement destroyed the buffalo, the Indians' main source of food, fuel, and shelter. When an advanced civilization meets a primitive one, it is the latter that suffers.

This paragraph may or may not convince you, but because it contains facts (verifiable information) and not just judgments, you can check to determine if the statements are true.

4. Always provide enough support to convince your reader fully. Two or three carefully chosen examples are often better than a long list. The quality is much more important than the quantity. For example, the student writer of the following paragraph has selected three good reasons, instead of a long, rambling list, to support the controlling idea:

**I strongly believe that an essay test is a far more effective method of de-
termining a student's ability to put to practical use the information and material he or she has learned in freshman composition than a multiple-choice
or a true-or-false test.** First, an essay test is composed of questions that force a
student to put forth his or her ideas in paragraph form, which is the objective of
the entire course of study in freshman composition. Second, the essay test requires the student to use many basic skills, such as proper punctuation, proper
sentence structure, proper sequencing of sentences, and a smooth flow of ideas
with easy transition throughout the paragraph. Finally, an essay test forces a student to think creatively—a rare occurrence for the average student. The multiple-choice and the true-or-false tests, on the other hand, rarely force a student
to think. The student is merely confronted with a choice of answers, and the
most common method used to arrive at the correct answer is to eliminate the
obviously wrong answer and choose among the others. Or simply to guess.
The guessing accomplishes nothing, but there is a good possibility of choosing
the correct answer. In a multiple-choice test, possible answers may be so closely
related to other choices that the question is ambiguous. The student benefits
more from an essay test than a true-or-false or multiple-choice test.

Peter Beach

5. Explain each reason fully enough so that the reader will know exactly why you think it is important. A bare list of unexplained reasons won't
impress your reader. Also, think of any objections the reader might have to
your point of view, and include reasons with explanations that will satisfy
these objections.

How convincing is the following paragraph?

The death penalty is not the solution to the problem of serious crime.
Capital punishment is simply barbaric revenge. Sometimes the wrong person is
executed. Besides, the penalty is not fairly imposed. Anyway, the death penalty
is not a deterrent to crime.

Now read the revised version. What are the differences between the two
paragraphs?

As the crime rate increases, so do demands for the death penalty, but capital
punishment does not provide a rational solution to the problem of increased
crime. Putting a man to death by hanging, electric shock, shooting, or lethal in-
jection remains a barbaric form of revenge in which the entire society partici-
pates. Besides, there is always the chance that an innocent man may be put to
death; after all, that has happened a number of times in the past. Furthermore,
any objective examination of the record on capital punishment shows clearly that
it is usually the poor and ignorant who suffer the death penalty, not the wealthy
and clever criminals. Most important of all, the idea that the death penalty is a deterrent to crime simply doesn't hold true. In states that have abolished the death

penalty, there has been no consistent increase in the murder rate, nor has the murder rate declined in states that have restored the death penalty. The record provides no proof that the death penalty serves as a deterrent to crime. Whatever social and legal reforms may be needed to cut down the appalling crime rate, imposing the death penalty is not the way to solve the problem.

Are you convinced yet? Or would you like to see specific facts and statistics to support these arguments?

6. Arrange your reasons in the most effective order for convincing. Use a sequence that will best allow your reasons to relate to the controlling idea and to each other. Many successful persuaders like to save their most important reasons until last, but the arrangement can change according to the writer's purpose.

Suppose, for example, that you are campaign manager for a local political candidate and that you must write an article based on the following positive attributes that he claims to possess. To be most effective, in what order would you list them? (Consider the attitudes of the people and the area in which you live.)

> civil rights champion
> conservationist
> law and order advocate
> crusader for truth
> labor activist
> civic and church leader

7. Avoid using fallacies to persuade. A *fallacy* is an error in reasoning, a false notion based on a mistake in logic or perception. Here are some commonly used fallacies that lead to false conclusions because they distort the logical reasoning process. Do not accept these fallacies when they are used to try to influence you, and do not attempt to manipulate others into agreeing with you by the use of false reasoning (fallacies) or other deceptive tactics.

Hasty generalization.   The *hasty generalization* is a false assumption that results from jumping to conclusions about a group or issue. It is a blind, all-inclusive assumption based on too little evidence.

> "All women are poor drivers." (Are *all* women poor drivers?)
>
> "The British people are nothing but a pack of snobs." (Are *all* British people snobs?)
>
> "Police departments all over the country are corrupt; cops really don't care about the average citizen." (What about the many cops who do an excellent job?)

Ad hominem (substitutes the individual for the issue). The *ad hominem* is a false assumption that focuses on individuals instead of issues. It is a distracting tactic used to trick people into making faulty judgments. Watch for this one in political campaigns.

> "I always vote for Tom Smith to be township supervisor; he's very good to his children." (Would his being a good father necessarily make Tom a good supervisor?)

> "Byron's poetry is not fit to be read, for he led a disgusting, immoral life." (What does Byron's lifestyle have to do with his writing ability?)

Begging the question (circular reasoning). In *circular reasoning,* the conclusion simply repeats or rephrases the beginning assumption; thus nothing is really proved.

> "This pickup is the most rugged one on the market because our people in Detroit designed it to be rugged!" (But what are the reasons why it is the most rugged pickup?)

> "Furthermore, my candidate is honest because he is a man of integrity!" (The speaker still hasn't proved that the candidate is honest.)

Polarization. *Polarization* is a type of one-sided reasoning that is often highly emotional and offers no alternative action—nor does it allow consideration of the middle ground in any argument. Everything is either one way or the other, with no consideration for the broad areas between right and wrong, good and bad.

> "West Aliquippa—love it or leave it!" (This type of all-or-nothing approach offers no choice between extremes.)

> "Juvenile delinquency is the direct result of a breakdown in the public school system." (What about other possible reasons for delinquency?)

> "All manufacturing of strategic arms must stop immediately; if not, civilization is doomed." (The speaker ignores the fact that *some* arms manufacture is necessary to ensure national security.)

Non Sequitur (false conclusion). A *non sequitur,* or *false conclusion,* is one that does not logically follow from the reasoning provided. This type of argument overgeneralizes, and it often indicates hasty and overemotional conclusions.

> "John does not smoke; therefore, he will make an excellent tennis player." (John could be a lousy tennis player as well as a non-smoker.)

"No wonder the country is in a mess; look at all those college-trained punks who are running it." (Those who attended college are not the only ones capable of poor administration.)

"Sex education in schools is a subversive liberal plot to undermine the morality of our youth." (No evidence of a subversive plot is given.)

Is sex education really a subversive plot?

Post hoc, ergo propter hoc (after this, therefore because of this). The *post hoc* fallacy contains a misplaced cause or effect. The mere fact that one thing takes place first and another follows does not necessarily mean that the first event caused the second. The post hoc fallacy is faulty reasoning because it does not permit the possibility of other causes or effects.

"Kay, do you know that Jack asked me out to dinner Friday night! It just had to be that new perfume I wore yesterday." (Maybe it was—or perhaps Kay was the only one on Jack's list who wasn't busy on Friday night.)

"I attribute my 95 healthy years to the fact that I don't drink, smoke, or chase women." (What about heredity or just plain luck?)

Bandwagon (join the crowd). The *bandwagon* technique attempts to impress by the claim that everyone is doing something and that you will be left out if you don't participate. This is largely an emotional appeal and is used extensively in both advertising and politics.

"Everyone knows that Judge Zink is the man for the job; become a member of his team when you pull lever 9A on November 4." (Did you ever wonder who *everyone* was?)

"Join the 'now generation' of swinging singles at Swampy Point Yacht and Racquet Club; you too can share this carefree experience already enjoyed by so many others." (Will joining the club really make you a swinger? And how do you know that everyone else likes the club?)

Appeals based on incompetent or biased authority. An appeal using an authority is not necessarily a fallacy if that authority is competent and reliable. The fallacy occurs when the authority is not knowledgeable in that particular subject. Also, advertisers often associate celebrity names with products in the hope that the consumer will be dazzled, identify with the personality, and therefore buy the product.

"Nine out of ten veterinarians agree that Stringles provides the best nutritional balance your dog can possibly get." (Which ten veterinarians were asked for their opinions?)

"If Hunk Flechette says that Dodge pickups are the best, then that's good enough for me." (How much does this celebrity really know about Dodge pickups, and how much is he getting paid for the endorsement?)

False analogy (illogical comparisons). An analogy is a specific form of comparison: finding similarities between two things that are normally classified under different categories. Properly used, a good analogy can provide strong support for your argument. The *false analogy*, however, can be misleading and deceptive. The false analogy does indeed make a comparison, but it bases the comparison on trivial similarities that ignore fundamental differences.

"Consider the United States and Switzerland, for example. Here we are with high unemployment and high crime rates, wasting billions of dollars a year on welfare programs and defense budgets. In Switzerland there is very little crime or unemployment, and the government isn't wasting billions on welfare and defense. The country has very few natural resources, but the people live comfortably. Why can't we have a well-run economy like that of Switzerland?"

(Even if the claims about Switzerland are true, the analogy is a poor one. For one thing, Switzerland is only about as large as Massachusetts, Connecticut, and Rhode Island. This analogy also ignores other enormous dissimilarities between the United States and Switzerland, such as the United States' reluctant roles as world policeman and free trade advocate, which makes American goods and labor less competitive.)

> "The acts of terror perpetrated by extremist Middle Eastern reli-
> gious sects or nationalistic groups are as patriotic and as justifiable
> as American colonial efforts to overthrow the British Crown."
>
> (Can the kidnapping and/or murder of innocent civilians be logically
> compared to the resistance of desperate citizens who fought mili-
> tary engagements against an oppressive colonial government?)

Rationalization (self-delusion).   *Rationalization* is a device that is used
to avoid unpleasant realities. Rationalizations are usually easier to swallow
than the truth. For example, there is always a student who justifies a low
grade in the following manner: there was no time to study; the teacher was
prejudiced; no transportation to class was available because the car always
broke down; the teacher expected too much; the student misunderstood the
assignment; there was a conflict with basketball practice, and so on. All this
is a substitute for the truth—that the student didn't care enough to do the
work.

> "Why should I buy this suit, even though it fits perfectly now, when
> I know that I will be ten pounds lighter by this time next month?"
> (Next month? Next year? Or ever?)
>
> "A couple of drinks does not affect my driving—and one more be-
> fore we go won't make a bit of difference." (Tell it to the judge
> and the victim's family.)

The slippery slope.   The *slippery slope* fallacy is an argument that re-
lies primarily on scare tactics rather than evidence. It points to a specific
action and claims, without support, that this action will lead inevitably to
tragic results. Once you let action A occur, you will initiate a grim series of
events, each one worse than the other, until you eventually find yourself in
a real crisis. The listener becomes so caught up in the magnitude of the im-
pending disaster that he or she overlooks the fact that the argument contains no evidence whatsoever—no proof that the "inevitable" disaster will
actually occur. Here is a typical slippery slope argument:

> "If you start letting doctors remove life support systems from termi-
> nally ill patients, then who's next? Pretty soon they'll be killing de-
> formed babies and the severely retarded 'for their own good,' of
> course. And before you know it, no hospital or rest home in this
> country will be safe. It's genocide!"

Even though each of the preceding examples illustrates a particular fallacy, you have probably noticed that several of them fit into more than one
category. Watch for fallacies that are used on you, and avoid using them to
convince others. A discerning reader will not be fooled by fallacies, and your
credibility could be destroyed if you're caught using them.

✓ Conclusion

The persuasive conclusion can be very flexible, and it should be adapted to your purpose.

1. Perhaps your reader should be handled gently with a final appeal that is sensitive and moving.

    And so I beg all of you to join me in what may be the final opportunity to save this, our proudest natural resource.

2. On the other hand, you may emphatically demand compliance through threats and warnings.

    Finally, if you do not vacate the premises by noon on May 31, I shall have the constable evict you, forcibly if necessary, that same day.

3. In most cases, however, your conclusion will come somewhere between the two extremes:
    a. You can *summarize your main points and/or reasons,* in order to emphasize how effectively they support your controlling idea.
    b. You may *restate your controlling idea* after having convinced your reader, point by point, that he or she should agree with you.

A sincere, direct, strong final impression is especially necessary for the persuasive paragraph, as the following example illustrates.

In conclusion, let me again remind you, as parents, that teaching social responsibility is not completely a function of the schools. It is a process that must begin in the home and continue throughout the child's formal schooling. The teacher cannot be a parent, a policeman, a therapist, and still be expected to teach fundamental skills. Social responsibility must be brought from the home to the classroom, and, unless this happens, learning cannot take place in our public schools.

Note the effective conclusions in the following student paragraphs:

Racial segregation of the public schools in the United States must be ended because of the illogical implication that skin color indicates potential. This is tantamount to saying that the color of a cow determines the quality of her milk. This premise, however, can be easily proven false. If a dairy farmer puts all his brown cows into one barn, feeds them a generous diet of silage and hay, and keeps them warmly protected from extreme weather conditions, the brown cows will produce an abundant supply of fine, sweet milk. If, on the other hand, he fences all his red cows in an open field which offers only loco weed and sourgrass as sustenance, and which provides no protection from the elements, the milk produced by the red cows, if any is produced at all, will be unfit for consumption. If the farmer then concludes that all red cows are poor producers of milk and have no place in his dairy herd, he has judged solely on the basis of color, and his conclusion is invalid. Obviously, the difference in the quality of the milk produced by the two groups of cows resulted from the farmer's uneven investment of food and shelter. *Similarly, if society allows an uneven educational investment to be made in its children on the basis of color, the contributions of the deprived group will bear no relation to that group's underdeveloped potential.*

Rosemary Weber

Hitchhiking poses a tremendous danger in the United States. Every summer, innocent vagabonds toting only a small backpack take to the highways unaware of the dangers of getting into a car with a stranger. No one can separate the potentially dangerous from the well-meaning motorist until it is too late. Most often, hitchhikers accept a lift from any stranger who appears presentable, despite repeated warnings from law officials that one simply can't judge a person by appearance alone. Consider the case of a California girl who "thumbed" a ride to school with a clean-cut, well-dressed, friendly motorist. One hour later, she was found on a deserted road, severely beaten, with a 36-inch stake driven through her chest. Her assailant, who had a Jekyll-and-Hyde personality, is now in a mental institution. The ever-present risk of an accident is also frightening. In a five-month period in California, there were 441 accidents involving hitchhikers. Some of the fatalities included drivers who crashed into the rear of an automobile that had stopped unexpectedly on a busy freeway to pick up a hitchhiker. Other accidents occurred when hitchhikers accepted rides from intoxicated drivers or drivers who fell asleep at the wheel. Police and highway officials across the country have declared that violence against young hitchhikers—particularly girls—has become a major problem. For example, the most recent statistics in Los Angeles show the following crimes involving hitchhikers over a one-year period: 825 robberies (everything from picking pockets to auto theft), 292 kidnappings, 288 rapes, 101 attempted rapes, 123 sex offenses (other than rape), 146 assaults with deadly weapons, 49 beatings, 13 attempted kidnappings, and 1 murder. Also, a recent study in California reported the following conclusions: hitchhikers were involved in one out of every 160 major crimes in California, one half of all hitchhiking victims were female (even though only one out of ten hitchhikers was female), and hitchhikers were three times more likely to be the victim than the perpetrator. *Despite the growing number of crimes and accidents involving hitchhikers, young people can still be seen on curbs and roadways with their thumbs up, risking their safety for a ride. Unfortunately, the hitchhiking menace will probably continue to increase unless those thumbs up become thumbs down.*

Joseph Mano

EXERCISE 10B: FINDING ERRORS IN LOGIC

Carefully examine the following arguments and identify the fallacy or fallacies, if any, on the line below.

1. Jimmy Jingler, that nifty new singer at the Cola House, advertises a new car named Whoops. He earns a lot of money so he certainly can drive a great car. I'm going to get one too, even though I really can't afford it.

   _____

2. I advise you not to go to that opera. I've heard the tenor cheats on his wife. She's his second wife, too. He probably was also unfaithful to his first.

   _____

3. Mae is urging us to reelect Senator Wift; he has such an honest face.

   _____

4. We are not going to study for Thursday's exam. Two days more studying won't help much; relaxation is better.

   _____

5. My brother Jamie is extremely neat; he always hangs up his clothes and even puts shoetrees in his shoes. He will make a wonderful husband.

   _____

6. Episcopalians are only interested in social status, not religion.

   _____

7. Reformers are really just in it for themselves.

   _____

8. Tom Sanders is my choice for class president. He's really presidential material.

   _____

9. The Patriots' Party only wants a government handout.

_____

10. A new grocery store opened in our neighborhood. It also sells beer, which clearly shows the neighborhood is going down hill.

_____

11. All your neighbors are using Turfo. Make your lawn as lush as theirs. *Get Turfo!*

_____

12. A woman's life is an easy one if she doesn't have a job. I always tell my wife that taking care of a home and family really isn't work, it's pleasure.

_____

13. Bobby's brother-in-law is coming to visit him for the weekend. He aced all his courses in college and played sports too. He's probably a real snob.

_____

14. Tim Robertson bought a house in a really nice area; he will want fancier friends now.

_____

15. Lydia Languish recommends Pep-Up Pills. She's such a good actress I'd trust her judgment in anything.

_____

✓ Some Do's . . .

1. *Do* make sure that you know your audience before you decide how you're going to persuade them. You can't develop a convincing argument in a vacuum. You have to know whom you're talking to before you can make wise decisions on how to approach your topic.

2. *Do* understand the difference between fact and opinion. Remember, an opinion is only an opinion until it is backed up with facts—with evidence. Only then does your opinion become a valid judgment.

3. *Do* check over your argument to make sure that it contains no logical fallacies. Even one error of reasoning in an otherwise logical argument can destroy your credibility with your readers.

4. *Do* anticipate possible objections to your argument and deal with them in your essay. Place yourself in the position of your opponents and imagine how various types of people would react to your argument.

✓ . . . and Don'ts About Persuading

1. *Don't* try to write a persuasive essay on a topic you know little about unless you plan to investigate that topic thoroughly.

2. *Don't* let any unsupported generalizations creep into your argument. Piling opinion upon opinion is not persuasion. If you want to convince an uncommitted or hostile audience, you must substantiate your opinions with facts.

3. *Don't* rely on only one source to document an important point. An intelligent reader knows that only one source can be biased or inaccurate. If you're making a controversial point, back it up with several objective, credible sources.

4. *Don't* include irrelevant facts in your argument. Facts are only useful when they are directly related to your purpose.

5. *Don't* overly slant your argument. Trying to get the reader on your side by using words designed to provoke purely emotional responses is a cheap way of trying to win an argument. Besides, it doesn't work. As soon as your readers discover that you are manipulating their emotions instead of appealing to their reason, they become angry and insulted—and they lose respect for you and your argument.

SUGGESTED ACTIVITIES AND ASSIGNMENTS

1. Bring in an editorial from your local newspaper. Make a list of all the facts used in the editorial; then list all the judgments. Does this listing change your reaction to the editorial? Do you now agree? Disagree? Can you find any hidden assumptions in the article?

2. Spend three to five days (or evenings) monitoring TV commercials, and note the errors in reasoning that occur most often. Then see if your classmates reached similar conclusions about the commercials they saw. What sort of generalization can you make about advertising strategies based on what you and your classmates observed?

3. Have an argument with yourself. Choose a point of view that you feel strongly about and then try to talk yourself out of it. See what sort of persuasive strategies you end up using on yourself.

4. The real test of your ability to persuade occurs when you have to face an audience that doesn't share your opinion. It doesn't take much effort to convince an audience that already agrees with you, but it does take some skill to convince an unsympathetic audience. In each of the following topics, you must take an unpopular (in terms of your audience) stand on a specific issue. Write a persuasive paragraph on one of these topics. Be sure to back up your opinions with good solid evidence and to direct your arguments to the prescribed audience.

Try to convince a group of parents that a third-grader who has acquired immune deficiency syndrome (AIDS) should be allowed to attend school with their children.

Try to convince a group of unemployed workers in California who are U.S. citizens that the government should not deport illegal aliens who are doing their former jobs at half the cost.

Try to convince the annual convention of the National Rifle Association to support a strong bill on handgun control.

Try to convince a group of executives from the American Tobacco Company that smoking in public places should be prohibited.

Try to convince a conservative Roman Catholic cardinal that the priesthood should be open to women.

Try to convince a high school dropout who is making $50,000 a year selling cosmetics that education is important.

Try to convince a man who has been married and divorced three times that alimony laws are necessary.

Try to convince your local bartender that all bartenders should be subject to legal action for serving drinks to someone who is clearly intoxicated.

Try to convince the president of the Society for the Prevention of Cruelty to Animals that the progress of medical research would be seriously impaired without the widespread use of animals in laboratory testing.

Try to convince a group of angry taxpayers that teachers have as much right to pay raises as the members of any other occupation.

WORDS

✓ Choices in Writing

As the introduction to this chapter tells you, persuasion is always with us. Very often, we write or speak to inform, as in such sentences as "I've a new car" or "The hypotenuse is the side of a right triangle opposite the right angle." More often, probably, we write or speak to persuade, as in such sentences as "Let's go to the movies" or "You really ought to read the small print."

In persuading, you attempt to convey your ideas and attitudes to someone else. To persuade successfully, try to present your ideas pleasingly and forcefully.

All writing is a process of selection—of choosing one subject, one attitude, one kind of development over others. Some of this selection is almost subconscious, depending on the writer's personality and experiences. For example, three men look at an old house set far back on a huge, tree-shaded lawn. One man is an architect whose main interest is restoring old buildings. The second man had lived there as a child. The third man is a developer of housing projects. If these three men each described the house, their selection of details would vary widely.

SLANTING

Slanting is a conscious level of choosing. In slanting, the writer wants to emphasize an attitude toward the subject—usually hiding that this is the intent. (For you as a reader, it is important to be aware of slanting, so that the writer does not convince you unfairly that his attitude is correct.)

Slanting is achieved through

1. selection of subject and attitude
2. emphasis to support attitude
3. choice of words to support attitude

Almost all communication has some degree of slanting. The slanting is determined by the intention of the writer, who selects both the subject and the attitude. You may choose to slant *for* something (favorable slanting) or *against* something (unfavorable slanting).

EMPHASIS

Another persuasive device is **emphasis,** the stress you put on a word or a fact to highlight its importance. "Socrates was old but wise" emphasizes his wisdom, not his age. "Socrates was wise but old" emphasizes his age. *The position of words within the sentence changes the emphasis.*

Suppose you are trying to describe a teacher you think is strict and fair. Notice the difference as you rearrange these two facts:

> Mr. Green was a fair, strict teacher.
>
> Mr. Green was a strict, fair teacher.
>
> Mr. Green was fair but strict.
>
> Mr. Green was strict but fair.

Perhaps the most persuasive choosing you do in writing is selecting words to support your attitude. By choosing the right word, you can, as critic I.A. Richards says, "smuggle in emotion." (Notice that even as he describes such choosing of words, he is affecting your attitude. What is your reaction to "smuggling"?)

Suppose you are describing Franklin D. Roosevelt. If you say he was an "elected official," that is *neutral.* If you say he was a "statesman," you are smuggling in *approval.* If you say he was a "political hack," your choice of terms smuggles in your *disapproval.* Or, again, is the dog (neutral) that is running across your yard a "mutt," a "mongrel," or a "cur"? These are terms of increasing disapproval, which reflect your attitude toward dogs, or at least toward this particular dog. If you want to describe a romantic sunset, you might mention its "rosy glow." If you want a sunset as a background for a murder story, you might comment on its "lurid glare." Such slanted words reinforce your attitude and help your reader to follow your thinking.

DENOTATION AND CONNOTATION

To express attitude accurately, you must be aware of denotation and connotation. **Denotation** is the dictionary meaning—the explicit, objective meaning of a word without any suggestions of emotional reaction. **Connotation** is implicit, subjective—the meaning that stirs emotional overtones.

The words of the scientist, investigator, or objective observer are chosen for their *denotation.* Such words are used to present facts and observations without bias or slant, to represent things as they are without emotional tones. The words of the poet, politician, advertiser, or anyone wishing to persuade are chosen for their *connotation.* Such words are used to appeal to characteristics like pride, patriotism, charity, affection, and self-esteem.

Remember: A word is the right word only if it has the right denotation and the right connotation. It is accurate only if it conveys to the reader the meaning that the writer intended.

To illustrate the difference between denotative and connotative meaning, consider the words *house* and *home.* Both words refer to the same object, a building where people live, but *home* has a connotative meaning because it suggests warmth, protection, and family affection. The word *house* is primarily denotative because it suggests nothing beyond the literal definition: a building where people live.

Consider the following lists of words:

Law Enforcement Officer	Government Employee	Girl
police officer	public servant	doll
cop	bureaucrat	chick
pig	political appointee	broad

Which words carry a generally favorable connotation? Which words carry an unfavorable connotation? Which words are relatively neutral?

Now consider the following two sentences.

1. The reporter *exposed* the *cop's* past record.
2. The reporter *presented* the *policeman's* past record.

The words *exposed* and *cop* convey built-in disapproval. The reader expects the cop's record to be bad; thus, by choosing these connotative words, you have already interpreted the facts instead of letting the facts speak for themselves. Be aware of the possible connotations of every word you write.

The following are terms with a neutral meaning. That is, they have no emotional overtones; they are denotative only:

> my mother   automobile
> the law enforcement officer   lawyer

Now they are changed to have a connotation of approval:

> my mom   limousine
> the police officer counselor

And here they have a connotation of disapproval:

> my old lady   clunker
> the pig   shyster

Verbs can be connotative:

> John tiptoed   John revealed
> John sneaked   John squealed

So can adjectives:

> He was confident.   He was proud.
> He was pushy.   He was arrogant.

So can adverbs:

> He moved quietly.   He moved decisively.
> He moved stealthily. He moved ruthlessly.

And so can whole phrases or sentences:

I thought that I was persevering.   I thought that I was firm.
They thought that I was stubborn.   They thought that I was pigheaded.

EUPHEMISMS

A **euphemism** is a word or phrase that is used in place of a more blunt term that might be offensive. Euphemisms are sometimes justified, but often they are misleading, vague, or phony. For example, in an effort to hide what some consider to be an unpleasant occupation, the neighborhood refuse collector has been called a "sanitary engineer." Nothing is wrong with this, but the term *sanitary engineer* may confuse anyone who still thinks of an engineer as a highly skilled, technically oriented professional.

Similarly, euphemisms may be deliberately used to cloud the truth—to make something appear more acceptable than it actually is. No one likes to endure a depression in this country, so government officials carefully refer to a depressed period as a "mild recession" or a "downward trend in the economy." Thus the euphemism acts the same as the sugar coating on a bitter pill.

Finally, euphemisms are used, in some instances, to deceive—to hide the truth altogether. Recently, in modern warfare, the term *protective reaction strike* has been used to explain what actually might have been an unprovoked bombing raid to support illegal seizure of territory. In the same way, those who feel that our penal codes are too harsh prefer to think of the habitual criminal as "a socially maladjusted person" or "a victim of his environment" who should not be denied personal freedom even though he threatens the safety of every other member of society.

There are many euphemisms that we do not recognize as such because they have become an accepted part of our daily language. Many have resulted from the efforts of advertisers to create markets for their products. Now you no longer have to settle for any ordinary used car; you can buy a "previously owned" or "reconditioned" automobile. Some of us who like to eat no longer need to worry about being fat or overweight; now we simply have a "problem figure" or a "weight problem." The local "practitioner of funeral arts," or "aftercare provider" who buries people when they die, prefers to "lay the loved ones to rest after they have passed away."

How many of the following euphemisms can you supply a standard definition for?

strategic withdrawal	networking
misspeaking	your services are no longer required
halitosis	revenue enhancement
exceptional child	memorial park
culturally disadvantaged	recreational drugs
scammed	altercation
downsizing	antipersonnel device
distortion of the facts	passive restraint
meaningful relationship	emotionally disturbed
liquidate	surgical strike

EXERCISE 10C: EXPRESSING APPROVAL OR DISAPPROVAL

For each word listed, give a word of similar meaning (the same denotation) that expresses your approval and one that expresses your disapproval (connotative meanings).

	Neutral Term	**Approval**	**Disapproval**
Example:	*to teach*	*to enlighten*	*to indoctrinate*
1.	thin	_____	_____
2.	heavy	_____	_____
3.	fussy	_____	_____
4.	privateer	_____	_____
5.	didactic	_____	_____
6.	candid	_____	_____
7.	stern	_____	_____
8.	fallacious	_____	_____
9.	credulous	_____	_____
10.	to fail (a course)	_____	_____

EXERCISE 10D: CHOOSING THE RIGHT CONNOTATION

In each of the following sentences you will find a word or phrase with the wrong connotation, given the level of the sentence. Decide which word is inappropriate and substitute a better word for it.

Example:　In these days when police officers are being bad-mouthed constantly, it is reassuring to have one cited for bravery far beyond the requirements of his duty.

Inappropriate Word	**Appropriate in This Context**
bad-mouthed	criticized unjustly or castigated

1. With the United States falling behind other industrialized countries, many college people—from chancellors to freshmen—consider extracurricular activities a real bummer.

   _____

2. Others, of course, regard such entertainments as hot stuff, cultural and educational, and a vital element in college life.

   _____

3. Many such schools, in a sweat lest Jack be a dull boy, will enhance his work with play by offering a bridge club, an arts and crafts club, a photo club, a chess club, a dramatic club, and a multitude of sports clubs.

   _____

4. Higher education should have the guts and the idealism to widen and ennoble life.

   _____

5. Ours is an age of science, and one of the bases of science is mathematics, which, regrettably, some students think of as a real drag.

   _____

6. In *Vanity Fair,* which we are reading in English class, the author appears to be passionately intrigued by his heroine, the unethical whorish bimbo, Becky Sharp.

   _____

7. Charles Dickens created characters from the lowest levels of the English-speaking world, but he made these scumbags appear likable because he revealed their universal humanity.

   _____

8. Dickens from his youth saw life from just above the starvation level and, though later he earned megabucks and international hoopla, all his characters were based on his poverty-stricken childhood.

   _____

9. Recent movies have made the novels of Jane Austen popular. She presents a human society vivid and real. One of the greatest pleasures she gives us is to eavesdrop on gossip, to listen to and retell the trials and tribulations of our buddies.

_____

10. Jane Austen, Thackeray, and Dickens are only three of a vast mob who supply us with more lives than just our own.

_____

Credits

Bragdon, Henry. "George Washington: Monument or Man?" *American History Illustrated.* Feb. 1967.

Day, Clarence. "Life with Mother." *The Best of Clarence Day, Including God and My Father, Life with Father, Life with Mother, This Simian World, and Selections from Thoughts Without Words.* New York: Knopf, 1935.

de Maupassant, Guy. "Love: Three Pages from a Sportsman's Book." *Affinities: A Short Story Anthology.* Eds. John Tytell and Harold Jaffe. Crowell, 1970.

"Fiesta Bowl" *Time.* 8 Jan. 1996: 51.

Forbes, Malcolm. *That Went That-A-Way: How the Famous, the Infamous, and the Great Died.* New York: Simon & Schuster, 1988. 152–3.

Fried, Barbara. *Who's Afraid?: The Phobic's Handbook.* New York: McGraw-Hill, 1941.

King, Martin Luther. "Where Do We Go from Here?" *The Voice of Black America: Major Speeches by Negroes in the United States, 1797–1971.* New York: Simon & Schuster, 1972. 1070.

"Literacy—The Path to a More Prosperous, Less Dangerous America." *Parade* 6 Mar. 1994:5.

McElroy, John. *Andersonville: A Story of Rebel Military Prisons.* New York: Fawcett Publications, 1962.

Miles, Josephine, ed. *Classic Essays in English,* 2nd ed. 1965.

Norris, Frank. "The Epic of the Wheat." *The Octopus: A Story of California.* New York: Doubleday, 1901.

Roosevelt, Theodore. Speech before the Hamilton Club in Chicago on April 10, 1899. *Lend Me Your Ears: Great Speeches in History.* Ed. William Safire. New York: Norton, 1992. 478.

Ryan, Joan. "Why Sport's Heroes Abuse Their Wives." *Redbook* Sept. 1995: 84+.

Seuling, Barbara. *You Can't Eat Peanuts in Church and Other Little-Known Laws.* Garden City, NY: Doubleday, 1975.

"Sport's Dirty Secrets." *Sports Illustrated* 31 Jul. 1995: 62.

Stegner, Wallace. *The Sound of Mountain Water.* New York: Doubleday, 1969. 146–7.

Steinbeck, John. *Cannery Row.* New York: Viking-Penguin, 1973.

Thomas, Lewis. "The Lives of a Cell: Notes of a Biology Watcher." *The New England Journal of Medicine.* 1972.

Trope, Mike, and Delsohn, Steve. "Unnecessary Roughness." Chicago: Contemporary Books, Inc., 1987. 24.

Ulmer, Curtis. "Teaching the Disadvantaged Adult." Washington, D.C.: AAACE, 1969.

White, E.B. "Here Is New York." *Collected Essays of E.B. White.* New York: Harper Row, 1949. 123.

Index of Exercises

1A Identifying subject and attitude, 4
1B Narrowing a broad topic, 7–8
1C Making subjects and attitudes clear, 8–10
1D Subjects and attitudes, 10
1E Identifying and correcting fragments, 19–20
1F Choosing specific terms, 22–23
1G Choosing more specific words, 24
2A Identifying clear controlling ideas, 38–39
2B Using various methods to correct sentences, 47–49
2C Punctuating comma splices and fused sentences, 49–50
2D Punctuating run-on sentences, 50–51
2E Recognizing fragments, comma splices, and fused sentences, 51–53
2F Using the active voice, 55–56
2G Making wordy sentences shorter and clearer, 56–58
2H Replacing weak verbs, 59–60
3A Topic sentences for description, 70–71
3B Using specific and descriptive details, 73–74
3C Using logical order for description, 76–77
3D Using subordination effectively, 89–90
3E Combining equal and subordinate elements, 91–93
3F Using specific and concrete terms, 96–97
3G Selecting vivid words, 98–99
4A Choosing effective controlling ideas, 104–5
4B Combining sentences using relative pronouns, 117–19
4C Combining sentences using verbals, 120–22
4D Combining sentences through apposition, 123–24
4E Combining sentences to show relationship of ideas, 125
4F Eliminating useless words, 128
4G Using verbal phrases, 130–31
5A Choosing effective controlling ideas, 137–38
5B Choosing relevant examples, 143–44
5C Organizing ideas using subtopics, 149
5D Developing supporting details, 155–56
5E Developing supporting details, 156–57
5F Punctuating restrictive and nonrestrictive clauses, 159–60

5G Punctuation review, 164–65
5H Eliminating errors in word usage, 173–75
5I Eliminating nonstandard usage, 175–76
6A Choosing effective controlling ideas, 183–84
6B Acceptable controlling ideas, 184
6C Eliminating irrelevant details, 192–93
6D Choosing the correct verb, 201–2
6E Correcting agreement of subjects and verbs, 202–3
6F Correcting agreement of pronouns and antecedents, 206–7
6G Making comparisons clear and complete, 207–9
6H Identifying effective metaphors, 213
6I Writing your own metaphors, 213–14
6J Eliminating clichés, 214–15
6K Eliminating clichés and slang, 215–16
7A Choosing effective controlling ideas, 226–27
7B Classifying topic sentences, 227
7C Using parallel structure, 240–42
7D Correcting faulty parallelism, 242–43
7E Parallel construction, 243–44
7F Transitions, 244–45
7G Putting ideas in logical order, 245–46
7H Using transitions, 246
7I Using the dictionary, 252–54
7J Using words correctly, 254–55
7K Using possessive forms correctly, 255–56
8A Noting differences among synonyms, 260–61
8B Correcting limited definitions, 266–67
8C Finding a subject for dangling modifiers, 280–81
8D Correcting dangling and misplaced modifiers, 282–83
8E Correcting shifts in point of view, 285–86
8F Using synonyms, 290–91
9A Finding the outline, 299–300
9B Titles, 302–3
9C Combining sentences, 304–6
9D Unity and coherence, 306–7
10A Distinguishing between fact and judgment, 330
10B Finding errors in logic, 343–44
10C Expressing approval or disapproval, 351
10D Choosing the right connotation, 351–53

Index

Abstract terms, 94, 258–59, 275–77
Active voice, 53–54, 127
Actor-action sequence, 53–54, 127, 197
Ad hominem fallacy, 337
Adjectives, 18, 95–96, 163, 301, 349
Adverbs, 18, 43, 45–47, 81–83, 95–96, 162, 349
Advertising, 309, 310
After this, therefore because of this fallacy, 338
Agreement:
  pronouns-antecedent, 203–6
  subject-verb, 197–201
Ambiguous antecedent, 205–6
Analogy, 195
Anecdotes, 274–75
Antecedents, agreement with pronouns, 203–6
Apostrophe, 169, 252–54
Appositive words and phrases, 122–23
Attitude toward subject, 4–5

Bandwagon technique, 338–39
Begging the question, 337
Block method of comparison, 184–92, 194–95
Body of essay, 293–94
  in persuading, 326–29
Body of paragraph, 3
  adequate development of, 13–14
  in classifying, 227–29
  in comparing or contrasting, 184–92
  in defining, 270–75
  in describing, 71–73
  in explaining a process, 105–7
  in explaining with examples, 138–43
  in narrating, 28, 36–37
  in persuading, 316
  unity, 11–12
Brainstorming, 1, 138

Central impression. *See* Controlling idea
Choppy writing, eliminating, 125–25
Chronological order, 12, 36, 39, 75–76
Circular definition, 265, 276
Circular reasoning, 337
Classifying, 217–56
  adequate development in, 228–29
  approaches to, 220

body of paragraph, 227–29
conclusion of paragraph, 229–31
details, 227–28
"Do's and Don'ts," 231
logical order in, 228, 231
organization, 217–19, 231
purposes of, 221–22
topic sentence, 223–26
Clauses:
  dependent, 18, 80–81, 84
  independent, 41, 43–45, 79–81, 84, 301
  punctuation between, 44–47, 164
  reducing to phrases, 128–29
  subordinate, 301
Clichés, 211–13
Climatic order, 147, 148
Coherence of paragraph or essay, 12
Collective nouns, agreement with, 199–200
Combining sentences, 117, 120, 122–25
Comma, 44, 162–64
Comma splices, 40, 41, 45, 163
Comparing or contrasting, 177–216
  bases for, 182, 195
  block method, 184–92, 194–95
  body of paragraph, 184–92
  choice of topic, 178–81
  conclusion of paragraph, 193–95
  defined, 177
  defining and, 272–73
  details, 192
  "Do's and Don'ts," 195
  point-by-point method, 184–85, 187–91, 195
  topic sentence in, 181–83
  two subjects in, 181–82
  uses of, 178
Comparisons:
  defining and, 260, 261, 272–73
  incomplete and illogical, 206–7
  metaphor and simile, 209–11
Compound subjects, 199
Conclusion of essay, 298, 299
  in persuading, 341–42
Conclusion of paragraph, 3, 14–15
  in classifying, 229–31
  in comparing or contrasting, 193–95
  in defining, 276

in describing, 77
in explaining a process, 114–15
in explaining with examples, 151
in narrating, 28, 37–38
in persuading, 316–17
Concrete terms, 94, 258
Conjunctions:
  coordinate, 42–47, 80–82, 162
  correlative, 200, 240
  subordinate, 43, 46, 81, 82, 84–87
  use in dependent clauses, 18
Conjunctive adverbs, 43, 45–47, 81–83, 162
Connotation, 348–49
Context, defined, 54
Continuity, in sentences, 232–33
Contrasting. *See* Comparing or contrasting
Controlling idea, 2
  adequate development, 13–14
  coherence, 12
  in comparing or contrasting, 177
  in describing, 67–68
  in explaining with examples, 151
  in narrating, 27, 39
  narrowing, 6–7
  specific, 5–6, 22–23
  unity, 11–12
Coordinating conjunctions, 42–47, 80–82, 162
Correlative conjunctions, 200, 240
Crediting sources. *See* Documentation of sources

Dangling modifiers, 279–80
Dash, use of, 163
Defining, 257–91
  abstract terms, 258–59, 275–77
  anecdotes used in, 274–75
  body of paragraph, 270–75
  combining methods of, 275
  comparisons in, 260, 261, 272–73
  conclusion of paragraph, 276
  defined, 257
  dictionaries and, 286–91
  "Do's and Don'ts," 276–77
  examples in, 271
  extended definition, 260, 267–71, 275
  formal definition, 260–65
  importance of, 258

limited (essential), 258,
260–65
negation in, 273–74
shifts in point of view,
283–85
synonyms, 260, 270
topic sentence, 269–70
use of modifiers, 278–82
word origin in, 271–72
Demonstrative adjectives, 301
Demonstrative pronouns, 88
Denotation, 348–49
Dependent clauses, 18, 80–81,
84
Describing, 61–69
body of paragraph, 71–73
conclusion of paragraph, 77
details, 71–73
"Do's and Don'ts," 78
objective vs. subjective, 62–65
patterns of organization,
75–76
through senses, 66–67
topic sentence in, 63–64,
67–70
use of subordination, 84–87
uses of, 61–62
Details:
in classifying, 227–28
in comparing or contrasting,
192
in defining, 264
in describing, 71–73
in explaining a process,
107–9, 116
in explaining with examples,
133, 144–49
ordering of, 74–75, 228
Development, adequate:
in classifying, 228–29
of paragraph, 13–14
Diction. *See* Word(s)
Dictionary(ies), 246–47, 286–91
as guide to meaning, 288–89
labeling and, 291
Differences between fact and
judgment, 328–29
Direct quotation, 320
Documentation of sources:
informal, 321–22
works cited lists, 323–25
"Do's and Don'ts":
for classifying, 231
for comparing or contrasting,
195
for defining, 276–77
for describing, 78
for essay, 303–4
for explaining a process,
115–16
for explaining with examples,
152
for narrating, 39
for persuading, 344–45
Double negative, 168–69

Economy, in writing, 53
Empathy, 33, 34

Emphasis, in persuading,
347–48
Enumeration, organization aid,
233–34, 300
Errors in logic, 336–40, 345
Essays, 292–308. *See also* Persuading
body of essay, 293–94
conclusion, 298, 299
"Do's and Don'ts," 303–4
form of, 295–96
logical sequence, 301
outlining, 298–99
subtopic sentences in, 296,
298
thesis statement, 292, 294,
297, 299
titles, 302
transitional devices, 300–302
writing examination, 307–8
Etymology, 271–72, 288–89
Euphemisms, 350
Examination, essay type, 307–8
Examples. *See also* Explaining
with examples
defined, 133
in defining, 271
Exclamation mark, 41
Explaining a process, 100–131
body of paragraph, 105–7
conclusion of paragraph,
114–15
"Do's and Don'ts," 115–16
knowledge needed, 105
logical order needed, 105–6,
115
precise language in, 112–14
secondary details, 107–9, 116
technical process, 109–14
topic sentence in, 103–4
uses of, 100–101
visual aids for, 111–12, 115
Explaining with examples,
132–76
body of paragraph, 138–43
choice of examples, 138–39
choice of topic, 134–35
conclusion of paragraph, 151
controlling idea, 151
"Do's and Don'ts," 152
extended examples, 150, 152
number of examples, 139, 152
organizing examples, 144–49
primary and secondary support, 133, 144–49
relevant examples, 142–43,
152
specific examples, 141–42,
152
subtopic sentences in, 147–48
topic sentence in, 135–37
typical examples, 139–41
Exposition, defined, 2, 26, 132
Expressions, overworked,
212–13
Extended definition, 260,
267–71, 275
Extended examples, 150, 152

Extended metaphors, 210
Facts, use in persuading,
326–31, 334–36, 345
Fallacies, 336–40, 345
False analogy (illogical conclu-
sions), 339–40
False compounds, 199
False conclusion fallacy, 337–38
Faulty coordination, 82
Faulty subordination, 85–87
Fiction, defined, 25
Formal definition, 260–65
Fragments, 16–20
Fused sentences, 40, 42–43

General words, 93–94
Giving credit to sources. *See*
Documentation of sources
Glaring errors in usage, 165–66

Hasty generalization, 336
Honesty in writing, 29

Illogical comparisons, 207
Importance, order of, 12
Incompetent or biased authority
fallacy, 339
Incomplete comparisons, 206–7
Incomplete verbs, 17
Indefinite antecedent, 203–4
Indefinite pronouns, 88,
200–201
Independent clauses, 41, 43–45,
79–81, 84, 301
Informal documentation of
sources, 321–22
Intensifiers, meaningless, 127
Intensive pronouns, 88
Interrogative pronouns, 88
Interrupters, 160–63
Interviews, use in persuading,
333
Introduction of essay, 316, 326
Inverted sentences, 201

Journal, as aid to finding topic,
1
Judgments, 193
distinguished from fact,
328–29

Labeling, 291
Libraries, research in, 318–19
Limited (essential) definition,
257, 260–65
Logical order. *See* Order
Look-alike words, 246–52

Meaningless intensifiers, 127
Memories, as aid to finding
topic, 1–2
Metaphor, 209–11
Methods of definition, combin-
ing, 275
"Ministerial three," 2–3
Misplaced modifiers, 281–82
Missing antecedent, 204–5
Misused words, 169–73

Mixed metaphors, 210
Modifier(s):
  adjectives and adverbs, 95–96
  clear and specific, 94–95
  dangling, 279–80
  defined, 95, 278
  misplaced, 281–82
  restrictive and nonrestrictive,
    157–59

Narrating, 25–60
  action, 30
  body of paragraph, 28, 36–37
  central purpose, 28–29
  chronological order, 36, 39
  conclusion, 28, 37–38
  controlling idea, 27, 39
  defined, 25
  "Do's and Don'ts," 39
  organization of paragraphs,
    27–28
  tips, 28–34
  topic sentence, 27–28,
    35–36
Negation, as method in defining,
  273–74
Negatives, wordy, 127
Nonrestrictive modifiers,
  157–59, 162
Non sequitur, 337–38
Nonstandard words, 166–69
Nouns:
  collective, 199–200
  singular and plural verbs, 201
Number:
  agreement and, 197–201
  shifts in, 284

Objective vs. subjective description, 62–65
Order:
  chronological, 36, 39, 75–76
  in classifying, 228, 231
  climatic, 147, 148
  of details, 74–75
  in explaining a process,
    105–6, 115
  of importance, 75–76
  spatial, 75–76
Outlining, 222, 298–99

Padding, 308
Paragraph(s). *See also* Sentences;
  Word(s)
  adequate development of,
    13–14
  body of. *See* Body of para-
    graph
  classifying. *See* Classifying
  coherence in, 12
  comparing or contrasting. *See*
    Comparing or contrasting
  conclusion of. *See* Conclusion
    of paragraph
  continuity in, 232–33
  defined, 2
  defining. *See* Defining

descriptive. *See* Describing
expansion into essay. *See* Essays
explaining. *See* Explaining a
  process; Explaining with
  examples
functions of, 2
length of, 15
narrative. *See* Narrating
structure of, 2–3
topic sentence. *See* Topic sentence
transitional devices, 233–40
underdeveloped, 155
unity of, 11–12
Parallel wording, 233, 238–40,
  300
Paraphrasing, 320
Parenthetical expressions,
  160–61
Passive voice, 54
Period, 41
Person, shifts in, 284
Personal pronouns, 88
Persuading, 309–53
  body of essay, 326–29
  body of paragraph, 316
  conclusion of essay, 341–42
  conclusion of paragraph,
    316–17
  "Do's and Don'ts," 344–45
  emphasis, 347–48
  facts, use of, 326–31, 334–36,
    345
  fallacies, 336–40, 345
  interviews, use of, 333
  purpose of, 309
  research, 318–19
  slanting, 347
  statistics, use of, 331–32
  thesis statement and intro-
    duction, 316, 326
  tips for, 311–15
  types of, 309–10
Phrases:
  appositive, 122–23
  reducing clauses to, 119–20
  reducing to single word, 126
  repetition of key, 233, 237,
    301
  transitional, 233, 235–37
  verbal, 120, 124, 128–29
Plagiarism, 318–19
Plural forms, 197–99, 235
Point-by-point method of comparison, 184–85, 187–91,
  195
Point of view, shifts in, 283–85
Polarization, 337
Possession, apostrophe to show,
  252–54
Post hoc, ergo propter hoc fallacy, 338
Precise language, in technical
  writing, 112–14
Precision, in writing, 53, 278
Prepositions, 85

Prewriting, 1
Primary details. *See* Secondary
  and primary details or support
Primary supporting details:
  in classifying, 227–28
Process writing. *See* Explaining
  a process
Pronouns, 168
  antecedent agreement, 203–6
  defined, 88
  demonstrative, 88
  indefinite, 88, 200–201
  intensive, 88
  interrogative, 88
  personal, 88
  reference, 233–35, 300
  reflexive, 88
  relative, 87–88, 117
Pronunciation, dictionary and,
  286, 287
Punctuation:
  apostrophe, 169, 252–54
  basic rule of, 162–64
  between clauses, 44–47, 164
  comma, 44, 162–64
  comma splices, 40, 41, 45,
    163
  coordinating conjunctions,
    42–47
  dash, 163
  exclamation mark, 41
  parenthetical expressions,
    160–61
  period, 41
  question mark, 41
  restrictive and nonrestrictive
    modifiers, 157–59
  semicolon, 42, 43, 45, 46, 162

Question mark, 41
Quotation, direct, 320
Quotations, worn-out, 211

Rationalization, 340
Reasoning:
  circular, 337
  fallacies, 336–40, 345
  logical classifying, 228, 231
Reducing:
  clauses reducing to phrases,
    119–20
  phrases to single word, 126
  sentences and clauses to ver-
    bal phrases, 128–29
Redundancies, 126
Reflexive pronouns, 88
Relative pronouns, 87–88, 117
Relevant examples, 142–43, 152
Repetition of key words and
  phrases, 233, 237, 301
Replacing weak verbs, 58–59
Research, use in persuading,
  318–19
Restrictive modifiers, 157–59,
  163
Run-on sentences, 40, 43–44

Secondary and primary details or support:
  in classifying, 227–28
  in comparing or contrasting, 192
  in explaining a process, 107–9, 116
  in explaining with examples, 133, 144–49
Self-delusion fallacy, 340
Semicolon, 42, 43, 45, 46, 162
Sentences:
  combining, 117, 120, 122–25
  comma splices, 40, 41
  continuity in, 232–33
  defined, 16
  eliminating choppy, 124–25
  fragments, 16–20
  fused, 40, 42–43
  independent and dependent clauses, 79–81
  interrupters, 160–63
  modifiers. *See* Modifier(s)
  parenthetical expressions, 160–61
  punctuation between clauses, 44–47
  reducing to verbal phrases, 128–29
  run-on, 40, 43–44
  subject-verb agreement, 197–201
  subtopic, 147–48, 154, 296, 298
  topic. *See* Topic sentence
Shifts in point of view, 283–85
Simile, 209–10
  worn-out, 211–12
Sincerity in writing, 29
Singular forms, 197–99, 235
Slanting, 347
Slippery slope fallacy, 340
Sound-alike words, 246–52
Sources, 179, 320
  documentation of. *See* Documentation of sources
Spatial arrangement, 75–76
Spatial order, 12
Specific, being:
  in controlling idea, 5–6, 22–23
  in examples, 141–42, 152
  verbs, 24
  words, 5, 24, 94
Spelling, dictionary and, 286
Standard and nonstandard usage, 166–69
Statistics, use in persuading, 331–32

Subjective vs. objective vs. descriptive, 62–65
Subject(s), grammatical, 17
  attitude toward, 4–5
  compound, 199
  identifying true, 198–99
  labels, 291
  subject-verb agreement, 197–201
Subordination:
  clauses, 301
  conjunctions, 43, 46, 81, 82, 84–87
  faulty, 85–87
Substitutes the individual for the issue fallacy, 337
Subtopic sentences, 147–48, 154, 296, 298
Synonyms, 196, 260, 270, 289

Technical process. *See* Explaining a process
Tense, shifts in, 284
Thesaurus, 260, 262
Thesis statement of essay, 292, 294, 297, 299, 316, 326
Time order. *See* Chronological order
Titles of essays, 302
Topic of paragraph, aids to finding, 1–2
Topic sentence, 3–7
  attitude in, 4
  in classifying, 223–26
  in comparing or contrasting, 181–83
  in defining, 269–70
  in describing, 63–64, 67–70
  in essay, 292, 294, 297, 299, 301
  in explaining a process, 103–4
  in explaining with examples, 135–37
  in narrating, 27
Transition, defined, 233
Transitional devices, 233–40, 300–301
Transitional (linking) words, 106–7, 189, 195
Two complete thoughts. *See* Comma splices
Typical examples, 139–41

Unclear metaphors, 210
Underdeveloped paragraph, 155
Unity of paragraph and unifying devices, 11–12

Usage, standard and nonstandard, 166–69. *See also* Word(s)

Vague antecedent, 205
Vague phrases, 127
Verbal phrases, 120, 124, 128–29
Verbals, 17–18
Verbs:
  active voice, 53–54
  clear and specific, 24
  connotative, 349
  fragments, 17–18
  incomplete, 17
  passive voice, 54
  subject-verb agreement, 197–201
  weak, replacing, 58–59
Visual aids, in explaining a process, 111–12
Voice:
  active, 53–54
  finding your own, 30–33
  passive, 54
  shifts in, 284

Weak verbs, replacing, 58–59
Wordiness, 125–27
Word(s), 20
  abstract, 94, 258–59, 275–77
  appositive, 122–23
  choice, 21–22, 346–50
  clichés, 211–13
  concrete, 94, 258
  denotation and connotation, 348–49
  euphemisms, 350
  general, 93–94
  glaring errors, 165–66
  labeling, 291
  look-alike and sound-alike, 246–52
  metaphor and simile, 209–11
  misused, 169–73
  modifiers. *See* Modifier(s)
  nonstandard, 166–69
  origin, 271–72, 288–89
  overused combinations, 211
  parallel wording, 233, 238–40
  precision in technical process, 112–14
  repetition of key, 233, 237, 300
  specific, 5, 24, 94
  transitional, 233, 235–37
  transitional (linking), 106–7
Works cited lists, 323–25